Praise for *The Work Cure: critical essays* *lness*

'The idea that work, including the enthusiastic search for work, is integral to mental health has become a key ideological tenet of post-industrial capitalism. "Wellness" and "positive thinking" are goals that divert attention from social and political questions and towards managerial ones. By re-introducing critical and political perspectives to this agenda from those who have witnessed this new psychological government at first hand, *The Work Cure* demonstrates that resistance is possible, and in doing so offers hope of a more emancipatory psychology.'

William Davies, author of *The Happiness Industry: how the government and big business sold us wellbeing*

'Most of us have to sell our labour to survive. What's worse, we also have to listen as a growing army of (well-paid) professionals explain that work is essential to health and wellbeing. This much-needed collection of critical voices (provocative, political, surreal, despairing) provides a forensic interrogation of the imposition of work and exposes the creeping tyranny of wellbeing. With contributions from academics, psy-professionals and activists, this book unsettles tired platitudes about meaningful work and instead focuses on the real consequences of the organisation of labour: work's colonisation of time and energy, to the extent that employers are not so much bosses as owners – a trend enabled by the marriage of work discipline and therapy culture analysed in chapters by David Frayne and Recovery in the Bin. Introna and Casagrande's compelling account of the anti-productivist force of disability also describes the power and possibilities of resistance: "It's up to us to recognise our misfitting as a source of restored dignity and connect our struggles through the refusal of work." This essential book makes a powerful, interdisciplinary contribution to the politics, practice and potential of work refusal.'

Lynne Friedli, researcher and activist

'Some books are useful, and some, like this one, which shows the misery that is caused by the use of psychological and welfare apparatuses instrumentally in the service of an austerity agenda, are indispensable. The contributors together provide a vital resource for understanding how neoliberalism gets inside all of us and, crucially, into the lives of those who should be offered solidarity, rather than subjected to coercion.'

Ian Parker, Emeritus Professor of Management, University of Leicester, UK

THE
WORK CURE

CRITICAL ESSAYS ON WORK AND WELLNESS

EDITED BY
DAVID FRAYNE

First published 2019

PCCS Books Ltd
Wyastone Business Park
Wyastone Leys
Monmouth
NP25 3SR
United Kingdom
contact@pccs-books.co.uk
www.pccs-books.co.uk

The Work Cure: critical essays on work and wellness

British Library Cataloguing in Publication data: a catalogue record for this book is
available from the British Library.

ISBN 978 1 910919 43 9

Cover design by Jason Anscomb
Typeset in-house by PCCS Books using Minion Pro and Myriad Pro
Printed in the UK by Short Run Press, Exeter

CONTENTS

Acknowledgements

I would like to thank Lynne Friedli for inviting me to the 'Reclaiming Our Lives' public debate at Mile End in London, which helped me see why a book like this was needed. I would also like to offer a sincere thank you to Catherine Jackson from PCCS Books, who sparked the idea for this book and gave excellent suggestions throughout the process.

This book's contributors deserve the biggest thank you. The process has been slow, and we have all had to fit writing around other responsibilities, whether jobs, activism, parenting or the ongoing and important work of self-care. Thanks for sticking with it.

Thanks as well to Jen and Louis – for everything.

For the weirdos
@theworkdogma

Introduction – Putting therapy to work

David Frayne

An article for Open Democracy by Izzy Koksal (2012) has an image at the top depicting a bright-red sheet of paper. On the paper, in large bold type, is a quote from Oprah Winfrey:

> The greatest discovery of all time is that a person can change his future by merely changing his attitude.

One might normally expect to find a quote like this taped on the walls of a high-powered business seminar – perhaps one of Tony Robbins' legendary gatherings on 'Unleashing the Power Within' or 'Life and Wealth Mastery'. These are the kinds of words an entrepreneur might pay a lot of money to hear on the way to the top, as an affirmation of their power to exert influence on the world. It's not the kind of quote you would be pleased to hear if you were unemployed – as Izzy Koksal was – and attending a mandatory, two-day training session on 'Finding and Getting a Job'.

Koksal's article explains that she saw this quote in a class run by A4e – one of several for-profit 'welfare providers' hired by the state to deliver work preparation courses to unemployed people. Koksal's attendance was a condition of her unemployment benefit: 'I was coerced into attending by my job centre advisor,' she explains. She goes on to describe the session:

> For two days I sat with 10 other unemployed people being told that we needed to 'talk, breathe, eat, shit belief in yourself' and being compared

to iPhones.[1] The experience was like being in some sort of strange comedy sketch that just went on and on and at times bordered on feeling like a cult... The main point, which was hammered home time and again, was that, if we believed we could get a job, then it would happen. It was simply our mindset that was the barrier and [the trainer] seemed intent on us all having mini epiphanies there and then.

Izzy reacts to the situation as many undoubtedly do, with annoyance about the trainer's emphasis on personal responsibility. Her article discusses the economic fact of unemployment and the variance in rates of unemployment across demographic lines. She recalls with dismay the trainer's interaction with a 60-year-old man called James:

James had found himself unemployed for the first time in his life at the age of 60. He had worked in retail but, despite his experience, he could not find work now because of his age... His agent had confirmed to him that it was his age that meant he wasn't getting past an interview and had suggested to him that he start lying about his age. But our trainer did not accept that age discrimination and a saturated job market were the issues here; rather, it was the barrier that James had created in his mind about his age. 'We are a product. If we're not talking and bigging up that product, then we can't expect anyone to buy that product... Age is not a barrier, the only barrier is *here* [pointing to his head]. We create it.'

Indignant, Izzy decides to jump to James' defence, explaining the need for broader social and economic understandings of unemployment: 'We need to look at the bigger picture and not focus on the individual.' And it is here that Izzy's article delivers its punchline. The A4e trainer suggests that Izzy's reluctance to accept his brand of personal transformation is simply a sign of her *own* obstructive negativity:

He turned it all back onto me – 'You've got all these hooks on you... it's your way of being... you need to shift the way you look at it. You've got all this anger and frustration and that's stopping you from getting a job. It comes across in your CV.'

---

1. Unemployed people are presumably like iPhones that lack the best apps and the latest upgrades. The purpose of the session is to help install these upgrades.

Becoming a productivity ninja

In 2015, when this book was still just an idea, I decided to attend a number of employee 'wellness' programmes. These were organised by human resources representatives in the university where I was employed on a short-term contract, to fill gaps in the department's teaching schedule. The most memorable session I attended was called 'How to be a Productivity Ninja'. A quick web search showed that the two-hour session had cost the university more than £2,000. The company's website promised that the session would teach me techniques to de-clutter my mind, identify my main productivity and wellbeing challenges and develop a 'second brain' to manage projects and actions. Sitting in the back row of the lecture hall, I looked down on a neatly-organised display of 'Ninja'-branded books, pamphlets, stickers and business cards, and waited for the session to begin. A well-dressed and pleasant orator introduced himself and the session began.

First, we were psyched up with images of inspirational public figures: a picture of Malala Yousafzai (the young Pakistani activist who was shot in the face for defending women's right to education) and another of the visionary business mogul Elon Musk (who was, ironically, under media scrutiny at the time over alleged inhumane working conditions in his car factory). There seemed to me to be a harmless absurdity to all of this, not particularly worthy of comment – but stay with me. Things took a more troubling twist when the audience were invited to give their own suggestions about how to feel well and succeed in the workplace. What struck me the most was how effectively the language that our coach used served to regulate, almost by sleight of hand, the parameters of the discussion. The idea was quickly established, for example, that increasing worker wellbeing and increasing productivity are always twin objectives and a win-win for workers and businesses. This was presented as basic common sense, taking off the table any notion that the health of the worker and the goals of the organisation might be in conflict.

Also off the table was any notion that the organisation was responsible for change. Our coach's many references to the importance of 'resilience' placed the responsibility for change on each of us, as individuals. Resilience means adjusting to the existing conditions rather than trying to change them, and there were several more linguistic tricks like this one. References to 'work' and 'the workplace', for example, were always kept at the most general level, avoiding the more fraught territory of addressing *our* work in *our* workplace. Indeed, I am regularly struck by the remarkable way wellbeing experts claim to be able to enter a workplace and tackle its stress problem without any contextual knowledge of who the staff are, the nature of their jobs, their contractual conditions or what their organisational culture is like. The task put before us was to immediately set about resolving our stress issues without any prior reflection on the nature or origin of our troubles. Even the word 'stress' – used to signify 'the problem', as opposed to a symptom of some other problem – seemed to foreclose any opportunity to speak about the organisation.

With this narrow universe of discourse delineated, both the coach and audience members proceeded to talk about the only thing left to us: those advertised tips, tricks and life hacks, to be implemented by the individual worker. We could use self-affirmations and relaxation techniques in order to find our calm. We could install the Bhuddify mindfulness app. We could wear headphones to prevent talkative colleagues from approaching and distracting us. Tips were grouped into categories such as 'Weapon-savviness', 'Zen-like calm' and 'Stealth and camouflage'. In the latter category were suggestions such as finding places to hide from colleagues in order to get work done, or simply switching off your email. A fellow participant whispered to their neighbour that she would probably be sacked if she did these things. And there, I thought, was a point that needed to be heard. All of these tips and suggestions seemed to presume a high level of autonomy among workers who really had very little control over their workloads and daily routines. The empowerment for sale here was a superficial one, with no foot in reality. From my seat in the back row, I fantasised about shouting this out at the top of my voice, but in a room charged with positivity, jokes and the excitement of free pens, who wants to be the misery guts dragging reality back into the room?

Healing the unemployed

How is it that Izzy Koksal, like thousands of others, found herself forced to sit in a room and receive behavioural advice from a self-styled psychologist? To understand, it is necessary to think back over the history of an approach to welfare provision known broadly as 'workfare'. This approach, now adopted by almost every mature welfare state across the globe, combines an ethical emphasis on the importance of participating in paid employment with efforts to 'make work pay', often by making benefits less generous and increasingly conditional on an ever-expanding list of requirements. In the UK, workfare can be traced back to New Labour's 'New Deal', which marked a point where encouraging or coercing people into employment would be adopted as a key function of the state (Lødemel & Trickey, 2000). The aim was to increase labour market participation among a variety of groups, including young and long-term unemployed people, disabled people and lone parents (Department of Social Security, 1998).

Iterations on this approach would continue in the UK following the election of the Conservative-Liberal Democrat Coalition government in 2010. David Cameron's branding of his Conservatives as a party 'for the hardworking people' dovetailed with the government's commitment to reducing public sector spending, resulting in a brutal series of welfare cuts. Welfare reforms would, from this point onwards, take on a more punitive character. People's entitlement to support would be conditional on a tougher and more developed set of requirements, with a wider use of sanctions (financial punishments in the form of benefit freezes) for claimants who failed to comply with the rules (Etherington & Daguerre, 2015). There would also be much tighter restrictions on access to disability benefits. The government would hire the private company Atos to withdraw disability benefits from thousands of people, via its Work Capability Assessment (Butler, 2015). Claimants of unemployment benefits (or Jobseeker's Allowance) would also now be required to sign a 'claimant commitment', forcing them to agree that their right to benefits would be conditional on participation in an expanding range of job search, training and work preparation activities, including mandatory unpaid labour and job-focused training. Unemployment would become a job in itself.

As we will see throughout this book, these shifts have been justified at the official level by the idea that *employment is good for people's health and wellbeing* – an idea that has been echoed by a number of major psychology organisations, mental health charities and influential academics. It is also an idea that is now having very real consequences for social policy. In two key documents – a Green Paper and a White Paper, both entitled *Improving Lives* (Department for Work & Pensions/Department of Health, 2016; 2017) – the Conservative government has set out its goal to promote employment as a 'health outcome', and 'join up work and health' through an integration of health and employment services. At the time of writing (in late 2018), this process is still underway, but many initiatives have already been established. There are courses like the one Izzy Koksal attended, aiming to adjust the psychology of unemployed people. There is the major, state-funded psychotherapy programme known as Improving Access to Psychological Therapies (IAPT), which offers an amalgam of cognitive behavioural therapy and job coaching, the primary aim of which is to set its patients on the path back to employment. There are also proposals to put 'work and health champions' into hospitals and surgeries in order to encourage doctors to refer patients to job centre advisors, and a policy of forcing disabled people to take part in mandatory conversations about their employment ambitions as a condition of their benefits.

Attempting to grasp this legacy of policy reform, a landmark article by Lynne Friedli and Robert Stearn (2015) suggests that, although these reforms slot into a well-established tradition of workfare, they are worthy of fresh critical attention because of their explicit attempt to modify people's attitudes and personalities. There are a number of things that Friedli and Stearn find troubling about this development. The first is the lack of consent involved. Given that submission to workfare interventions is often a mandatory condition of benefit claims, people are being required to submit to psychological reform under the threat of poverty and destitution. What is also troubling is the narrowness of the 'ideal human' being promoted. The entitlement of a person to set their own health and recovery goals and to work autonomously towards them is being abandoned. In its place is the dogma that *employment* represents the highest sign of good health and character. The right kind of person is a person who accepts this proposition and seeks to embody the characteristics of a good worker: the ideals of confidence, optimism, positivity, gratitude and aspiration, borrowed from positive psychology. Izzy Koksal's earlier reference to the jobseeker as being like an iPhone is pertinent, given the similarities between jobseeking and the commercial world of sales and product development. Becoming employable means coming up with new ways to brand and sell yourself, and there is no room here to ask critical questions about what happens to people who cannot work, how work should be defined, or whether there might be other, competing ideas of health, virtue and the good life. There is also no space to ask how we should value people whose efforts and contributions take place outside the market economy.

Friedli and Stearn have helpfully articulated these problems in the concept of 'psycho-compulsion', a term that is now regularly used by activists and one that will appear regularly throughout this book. As a concept, psycho-compulsion describes moves to modify the attitudes and personalities of people who deviate from the ideal of the hard-working citizen. But it also captures a broader side effect of such interventions: the erasure of political and economic explanations for prevalent social problems. This is especially true for unemployment, which is being recast in the public imagination in terms of a moral and mental deficit in individuals.

Unemployment can be properly understood in terms of what the political theorists Nick Srnicek and Alex Williams refer to as the rising and falling of capitalism's 'surplus population' (2016) – a group of people who are without employment because their labour has not been deemed useful for generating private profits. When economies grow, workers are drawn from the surplus population into employment, and if the demand for labour stalls for any reason, or wages begin to cut too much into profits, people are 'let go' from their jobs and the surplus population once again swells. Overlaid onto these cycles of boom and bust are other trends. Innovations in productivity, including the introduction of automated technologies, have complex effects on the labour market, creating new kinds of work for some people but also radically reducing the need for human labour in industries where it is feasible and cheaper to replace workers with machines. Those labourers who are displaced by automated technologies are sometimes known as the victims of 'technological unemployment'. What is euphemistically known as today's 'flexible' labour market, characterised by more temporary and precarious forms of work, has also served to make periods of unemployment a normal part of life for a growing number of people.

We can also observe Marx's suggestion that capitalism *requires* a section of the population to be unemployed. What he famously referred to as the 'reserve army of labour' is required to stand in the wings of the labour market, ready to be activated in times of economic growth and fluctuating demand. Capitalism's surplus population also benefits private interests by helping to keep job competition high, and hence wages low, and workers under control. The point to take from all of this is that unemployment is a *structural feature of capitalist societies*. It is part of our political-economic world. How frustrating, then, that unemployment is so often presented to us as a behavioural or psychological issue.

The Welfare Conditionality Project (2018) – a major study conducted between 2013 and 2018 – drew a degree of public attention to the problems with workfare reforms. It found that the reforms were not only largely ineffectual in terms of boosting employment, but that they had indeed been actively harmful and were linked to a sense of social disengagement, a rise in poverty and destitution, a take-up of survival crimes and an exacerbation of ill health and impairments.[2] News stories abound of people with severe conditions like brain damage, lost limbs, blindness and terminal cancer being

---

2. Findings about the ineffectual nature of welfare reforms should be no cause for surprise. Given the importance of a reserve army of labour for the smooth functioning of capitalism, the purpose of welfare reform is perhaps more accurately understood as an effort to discipline unemployed people, rather than maximise employment. As Srnicek and Williams argue (2016: 101), the goal is to turn as many people as possible into eligible workers and – through a combination of imposed austerity and ideological drills about the importance of employment – to stop unemployed people from developing alternative priorities or turning away from the market.

found 'fit for work' by the government; the website Calum's List[3] began to document deaths believed to be the result of welfare reforms. It is no longer a secret that many disabled people live in perpetual terror of being found 'fit for work' and losing their benefits. Indeed, in November 2018, the United Nations rapporteur Philip Alston released a report in which he roundly condemned UK welfare reforms:

> In the area of poverty-related policy, the evidence points to the conclusion that the driving force has not been economic but rather a commitment to achieving radical social re-engineering... The government has made no secret of its determination to change the value system to focus more on individual responsibility, to place major limits on government support, and to pursue a single-minded, and some have claimed simple-minded, focus on getting people into employment at all costs. (Alston, 2018)

Alston's enquiry concluded that welfare cuts and conditionality had caused widespread and unnecessary harm. In a spoken statement, he added that the 'state does not have your back any longer'. It was refreshing to hear this official confirmation of what anti-workfare groups like the Mental Health Resistance Network and Disabled People Against Cuts had been saying all along: that welfare reforms have done a much better job at punishing people than improving their lives.

Healing the worker

If one of the key goals of this book is to critique a legacy of policy reforms treating worklessness as a psychological deficit, another goal is to trace a link between this problem and certain current trends in workplaces. Here we can point to another structural or endemic issue: not unemployment but the *distress* experienced by workers due to the way labour is organised in capitalist societies. As I write this, statistics published by the UK Health and Safety Executive reveal that, for the first time, more than half the work days lost in the UK are due to work-related stress, anxiety or depression (HSE, 2018) – a fact that has prompted the general secretary of the Trades Union Congress, Frances O'Grady, to officially name the problem an epidemic (Wilson, 2018).[4]

---

3. See http://calumslist.org

4. Some 15.4 million working days were lost in 2017/18 as a result of work-related stress, anxiety or depression, with findings suggesting that workers in education and social work are the most at risk (Wilson, 2018).

Although this book does not claim to provide anything like a comprehensive theory of distress, or even work-related distress, there are many toxic trends we can think about. We might reflect on the armies of Amazon warehouse workers, reduced to machines as they respond to orders from hand-held devices, under strict time constraints and surveillance. We might consider those legions of cheap domestic labourers forced to work long hours, mistreated by unscrupulous employers (Chamberlain, 2013). Or we could consider the masses of workers who staff today's call centres, forced to present with a happy persona, even when the work itself is often repetitive and deadening (Woodcock, 2017).

In his book, *Bullshit Jobs: a theory,* David Graeber (2018) describes in detail the misery that people endure when forced to perform jobs that – by the worker's own admission – have no discernible benefit to society (or perhaps even harm society in some small way). Graeber shines a light on workers hired simply to make superiors look good, manipulate the public's needs, correct errors that could easily be avoided, collect data that nobody uses or supervise workers who could just as well be left alone. He explores the emotional scars of people who are faced with the prospect of wasting their lives on meaningless activities and the pretence of busyness, finding that even workers in relatively cushy circumstances, with good pay and a low level of supervision, feel tortured by the useless nature of their work.

We can also think about the misery of insecurity, as the assault on basic worker protections like a living wage, guaranteed hours, sick leave and secure contracts leaves many people in a perpetual state of anxiety about making plans and meeting needs. An analysis of the Labour Force Survey from the last quarter of 2017 found that one in nine workers (or 3.8 million people) in the UK are employed in insecure jobs – a category that includes temporary workers (like agency workers, casual workers, seasonal workers and so on), workers whose main job is on a zero-hours contract, and self-employed workers earning less than the National Living Wage (Trades Union Congress, 2018). The Conservative government's popular catchphrase that 'work is the best route out of poverty' has completely ignored the vast problem of in-work poverty.[5] For many people, this material insecurity manifests as a kind of ambient dread, constantly playing on the nerves. Anxiety becomes an ordinary part of daily life and thinking about the future becomes difficult. Indeed, the list of work-related troubles

---

5. The Joseph Rowntree Foundation reports that two in three children in poverty in the UK are actually from a household where at least one person is in employment (2018).

goes on, and chapters in this book will revisit these themes, and others, in more detail.

The drive for 'workplace wellness' has no doubt partly come about due to a growing awareness of the economic costs of problems like stress and low morale. Misery costs money, whether in the form of worker disinvestment, rising absences, slowing productivity or soured customer interactions. Estimates from Gallup suggest that employee disengagement costs the US economy $550 billion a year (cited in Davies, 2015: 106). Startling figures like these have put pressure on managers to square up to the challenge of how to deal with employees who experience disengagement, a lack of motivation or low-level mental health problems. In his eye-opening book *The Happiness Industry* (2015), Will Davies describes the work of mental health fixers who now earn their living by intervening in the day-to-day miseries of employment. There is clearly a significant market demand for services like the 'Productivity Ninjas' session described above, which promise to fix a workplace's wellbeing problem and boost productivity in the process. Initiatives range from call-centre 'buzz sessions', designed to gee up workers at the start of the day, to motivational talks and calming lunchtime meditations (all discussed in this book), and also a great many things not discussed here, from team-building away days to fitness initiatives and puppy therapies. Will Davies has described the sometimes odd mishmash of ideas involved in workplace wellness initiatives:

> The psychology of motivation blends into the physiology of
> health, drawing occasionally on insights from sports coaches and
> nutritionists, to which is added a cocktail of neuroscientific rumours
> and Bhuddist meditation practices. Various notions of 'fitness',
> 'happiness', 'productivity' and 'success' bleed into one another, with little
> explanation of how or why. (Davies, 2015: 112)

The main problem with these initiatives, of course, is that they are a poor substitute for real organisational change. Like those workfare initiatives targeted at unemployed people, workplace wellness initiatives are also taking a structural problem and suggesting it can and should be solved through individual self-work. As we will see, they may also contain an element of psycho-compulsion, imposing the same normalising ideas of the model person found in work-preparation programmes: a person who is hardworking, happy, healthy and, above all else, productive.

Although the idea that happy and more psychologically invested workers are good for profit is now widely accepted in management circles (Davies,

2015: 120–123), the first chapter in this book will warn against exaggerating the link between happiness and productivity. As Ivor Southwood notes (Chapter 1), it is also important to recognise the way in which productivity thrives on neglect – a disregard for the human threshold for things like repetition, meaninglessness, heteronomy and toil. From Southwood's perspective, workplace wellness initiatives are not simply implemented to boost happiness and hence productivity; they are perhaps better thought of as one element in a broader set of management technologies (including more traditional disciplinary measures like surveillance, punishments, strict targets and micromanagement) designed to keep the worker at a 'biting point', where productivity can be wrung at the expense of health but without the situation spilling over into outright sickness or work refusal. The value of Southwood's contribution is its insight that it is a manageable, low-level misery, as opposed to happiness *per se*, that keeps the wheels of many organisations turning. And many organisations are not shy about admitting the economic value of neglect. Consider an advert for the company Fiverr (an online platform for freelancers), which celebrates those 'doers' who 'eat a coffee for lunch' and choose sleep deprivation as their 'drug of choice' (Tolentino, 2017). Or Lyft (an on-demand transport company), which publicly applauded a pregnant employee who kept taxiing customers even after her waters broke and she went into labour (Menegus, 2016). It is barely a secret that neglect is what often keeps the wheels of work turning, and some even wear the ability to withstand such neglect as a badge of honour.

To draw these themes together, the essays in this book cover a range of social domains, from the job centre to the therapy room and, indeed, the workplace itself. No matter what the focus is, however, each chapter deals in its own way with what we might think of as the marriage of work discipline and therapeutic practice. Its instances will be elaborated and criticised and forms of resistance and social alternatives will be considered. We will see how the work ethic has spilled over into therapeutic practice, as is evident in the UK's IAPT programme, and we will also see examples where the flow has gone the other way, as therapeutic practice spills into matters of work, whether it is deployed to rehabilitate unemployed people or to heal unhappy employees. In the remainder of this introduction, I will set the context for the discussions ahead by looking broadly at the role and symptoms of therapeutic culture in capitalist societies. My aim is to provide something of a roadmap of themes and ideas that are explored in more detail in the chapters that follow.

Faulty diagnoses, bad prescriptions and toxic side effects

The clinical psychologist David Smail defines mainstream therapy as 'a technical procedure for the cure or adjustment of emotional or psychological "disorder" in individual people' (1998: 3). His thesis is that its efficacy has been highly exaggerated. Smail argues that, while therapy in its most conventional forms has offered people a valuable emotional outlet, an opportunity to clarify predicaments and the indispensable comfort of an empathic listener, what it has not generally been able to provide is lasting liberation from the experience of distress. His conclusion, based on years of clinical experience, is that the curative power of psychological therapy has not only been overstated but that this overstatement has itself become a major problem for society, as more and more people are persuaded that therapy is a solution to everyday problems.

Given the widespread assumption that psychology is a benevolent practice, regulated by the state and offered on the NHS, it is close to sacrilege to think of it as something that can cause trouble. In his book *Medical Nemesis* (1975), Ivan Illich shocked readers with his theory of *iatrogenesis*, arguing that the medical establishment has become a major threat to the health of populations. This is partly through the direct harm caused by surgical injuries, drug side effects and toxicity, but also through the broader way in which the medical profession has colonised our lay cultural knowledge about how to look after ourselves and each other.

Psychology has a similar colonising tendency because of the way it crowds out non-psychological ways of thinking about people's problems. In *The Therapeutic Turn* (2014), Ole Jacob Madsen cites the sociologist C Wright Mills and his axiom that 'neither the life of an individual nor the history of a society can be understood without understanding both' (Madsen, 2014: 11). In Mills' axiom, the individual is imagined as a droplet in a great tide: uniquely themselves, but also swept up in the socio-political currents of history and society. The problem, argues Madsen, is that mainstream forms of psychology overlook an entire side of this duality. Psychology has privileged the inner world of the human psyche, but its interpretations and prescriptions forget that the psyche is always produced and embedded in social structures and norms. This shortcoming is what Madsen refers to as psychology's 'individualisation problem'.

Like Smail, Madsen suggests that the individualisation problem has become a major issue not just for the psychological professions but for society, as therapeutic ideas step outside the doctor's clinic and spread their way into more and more areas of social life. What Madsen refers to as the rise of a 'therapeutic culture' is so commonplace that we may barely even register it. The language and form of therapy has made its way into all corners of daily life, from self-help books, lifestyle columns and reality TV shows to how we run our schools and prisons and, as we have now seen, welfare systems and workplaces. Indeed, it is no longer just the 'psychologist' who gets paid to help people, but a whole range of professionals, from the life coach and the wellness consultant to the mindfulness practitioner and the motivational speaker. While not all of these things pertain to therapy in a traditional sense, what we have perhaps seen is the rise of therapy-like situations: spaces where we go for professional advice on how to improve and manage our lives and selves in order to become healthier, happier and more successful. At their broadest level, the essays in this book cover three problems with the spread of therapeutic culture: its *faulty diagnoses, bad prescriptions* and *toxic side effects.*

'*Faulty diagnoses*' refers to the failure of conventional forms of therapy to properly acknowledge the social context of people's distress. The context we focus on in this book is the organisation of labour under capitalism. As I suggest above, the organisation of labour provides all manner of reasons for a person to feel anxious, stressed, persecuted, exhausted or depressed. These experiences are a normalised part of social life in a labour market characterised by poverty, unemployment, over-exertion, chronic insecurity and a pervading sense of meaninglessness. Within this troubling social context, the problem with conventional therapeutic practices is that they continue to talk about distress as located 'in here', as a result of deficits in attitude and cognitions, as opposed to 'out there', in the toxic effects of social structures and societal norms. Within a toxic social context, the Midlands Psychology Group (2012), in their *Draft Manifesto for a Social Materialist Psychology of Distress*, suggest that distress is often better thought of as a 'state of being' rather than an illness per se, encapsulating how most of us might respond to conditions of adversity. This is an extremely important insight, but equally should not be claimed as particularly original. As several pieces in this book will show, there are survivor movements that have been spotlighting the socio-political causes of distress for quite some time.

There is an added complication here that we should pause on (one that Arianna Introna and Mirella Casagrande will consider further in Chapter 10). While it might be important to spotlight the social and political causes of illness, we must take care not to fall into the trap of simply asserting the opposite proposition: that all illness is 'out there', caused by the stressors of an unjust system or by environments that exclude sick and disabled people from using their capacities. This is because the UK Conservative government has now itself begun to downplay the medical dimension of health conditions, in its efforts to deny people's status as 'disabled' and take away their entitlement to benefits. Whether or not we take a critical view of medical diagnoses, it is undeniable that diagnostic categories perform a social function in allowing people to access what Talcott Parsons (1951) called the 'sick role', where they are socially recognised as ill and deserving of special support. The function of a diagnosis is even more vital in the context of austerity, where people are having their disabilities trivialised by the Work Capability Assessment and their benefits withdrawn. In this context, it is important for people who need support to be able to say, 'I have a medical condition', and this reality has created a tension for activism around issues of health and disability. On the one hand, there is a desire to dispense with biomedical labels and diagnostic categories, so that we may better focus on the social causes and remedies of ill health. Yet, on the other hand, there is a recognition that people in the real world rely on biomedical labels as a way of legitimating illness and maintaining their right to support. There are, in other words, apparently contradictory impulses to both *let go of* and *hold on to* biomedical categories. Quite how this is resolved, I do not know.

Returning to the individualisation problem, a second feature is its *bad prescriptions*. Having persuaded people that the problem lies inside the mind, rather than outside in the social world, conventional therapeutic practice follows up with the idea that it is individual self-work, rather than collective social change, that promises a solution. In the 'Productivity Ninjas' session above, for example, we were told that the solution lies not in an effort to change organisational norms but in our own efforts to cultivate ideals like calmness, resilience and self-discipline.

It would be fair to ask what the solution to the problems with work *really is*, if it is not self-work and psychological reform. The future of work is a quickly-developing field and the diversity of voices in this book do not offer a decisive answer to this question, although many suggestions are offered. These include unionising for better working conditions, suggestions for an alternative political approach to prosperity, experimentation with alternative ways of organising care work and the reversal of welfare conditionality through alternative welfare policies like the Universal Basic Income. Not everybody in this collection agrees: some proposals complement each other and overlap, others contradict.

In my earlier book, *The Refusal of Work* (2015), I drew on a well-established tradition of 'post-work' thinking in order to begin outlining a perspective on what is to be done. For the post-work thinkers, there is no solution other than to deeply interrogate whether the institution of employment is fit to sustain people's need for goods like income, security, meaning and dignity.[6] To quote the activist Roy Bard, it means accepting that 'working isn't working' and, from there, investigating other ways in which people might meet the needs conventionally met (or left unmet, as the case may be) through employment. In real terms, this involves political proposals to redistribute the vital resources of money and free time through alternative welfare policies and a shorter working week. It involves exploring the prospect of new public networks and facilities, so that people are afforded opportunities to exchange goods and co-operate in a more spontaneous and autonomous way outside the world of formal employment. And it also involves addressing the problem of social recognition, so that people are valued even if they cannot work a conventional job or their contributions take alternative forms, outside the market economy.

There is a world of debates to discover and develop on the future of work, and not all of the authors in this book take an explicitly 'post-work' perspective or provide detailed proposals. What all of the authors here agree, however, is that the problems with work are political problems, to be pursued through collective strategies for change. The problems with work must not be tackled with treatment but through social and political alternatives. In this context, our shared purpose has been to spotlight how the marriage of work and therapy has played a part in blocking political solutions by accommodating people, as individuals, to things as they already are.

Consider these comments from André Gorz on the medical industry, which might equally be applied to our more specific examples of therapeutic culture:

> As a social institution, the duty of medicine is to reduce the symptoms
> that make the sick unfit for their social roles. By urging people to take
> illness to the doctor, society keeps them from laying the blame on the
> fundamental and long-term reasons for their ill-health. By treating
> illnesses as accidental and individual anomalies, medicine masks their
> structural reasons, which are social, economic and political. It becomes
> a technique for making us accept the unacceptable. (Gorz, 1980: 150)

---

6. Examples of key works in this area include Kathi Weeks' *The Problem with Work* (2011), André Gorz's *Reclaiming Work* (1999), Nick Srnicek and Alex Williams' *Inventing the Future* (2016) and James Chamberlain's *Undoing Work, Rethinking Community* (2018). Much of the work in this area is also now being promoted and co-ordinated by the UK think-tank, Autonomy.

Gorz's comments here are reminiscent of David Smail's conviction that 'far from curing people's distress, psychology too easily serves to provide us with an excuse for continuing, as a society, to inflict it' (Smail, 1998: 47). The immediate task ahead, then, is to stop accepting the unacceptable. Rather than using psychology in an attempt to optimise the adaptation of individuals to today's economic and social environment, the more progressive task is to scrutinise whether that environment is conducive to health in the first place.

This leads me to the third strand of the individualisation problem, its *toxic side effects*. The most potent of these is self-blame. Diagnosed as psychologically deficient and prescribed a course of self-work, individuals who find that their condition does not improve are left with only themselves to blame. The problem is that, when therapists convince us that people are personally responsible for their fates, they may also be colonising alternative explanatory frameworks with which to interpret problems; they may be crowding out the more political languages of injustice, power, exploitation or inequality. As David Smail writes in relation to the problem of unemployment:

> … for the men and women thrown out of work in the interests of 'flexibility', there are no officially authorised words with which to criticise their condition; if their distress is not simply dumb, it can be given form only in the language of personal responsibility and inadequacy. (Smail, 1998: x)

At this point, individualised explanations for distress are not only inaccurate but also cruel. In a world where problems like unemployment and work-related distress are so common and socially embedded, blaming and shaming the individual is punishment. Describing this tendency, the mental health activist Denise McKenna conveys the sense of worthlessness that can follow:

> Now the causes of all our problems were deemed to be due to something within us as individuals. Not just the biochemistry of our brains but our rotten genes, our stinking thinking, our moral failures, our bad attitudes, our laziness, our choices… Above all it was our choices.[7]

---

7. This quote is taken from a speech by Denise McKenna, representing the Mental Health Resistance Network (MHRN) at the 'Welfare Reforms and Mental Health – resisting sanctions, assessments and psychological coercion' conference, 5 March 2016. The conference was organised by MHRN, Disabled People Against Cuts and the Alliance for Psychotherapy, and a full transcript of the speech is available at https://recoveryinthebin.org/2016/03/10/welfare-reforms-and-mental-health-resisting-sanctions-assessments-and-psychological-coercion-by-denise-mckenna-mental-health-resistance-network-mhrn (accessed 19 January 2019).

The extent to which people are able to stave off these feelings of self-blame will of course depend on whether there are other explanatory frameworks to hand – alternative linguistic resources that allow people to observe and report their problems in different ways. Part of the value of activist and survivor collectives (such as Recovery in the Bin, who have a chapter in this book) is that they help people come together to discuss, in more autonomous and authentic ways, the nature of their problems. Indeed, in my own study of non-workers in *The Refusal of Work* (Frayne, 2015), I spoke to people who had managed to reduce (if not eliminate) their shame about unemployment by discussing their experiences with other non-workers and reading critical literature on the topic of work. Through these activities, people were able to discover a sense of kinship and perceive their situations in terms of broader social and political forces. Yet clearly not everybody manages or has the opportunity to reflect in this way. In a study of white-collar unemployment, for example, Ofer Sharone (2013) suggested that unemployed people are more vulnerable to distress and self-blame if they live in countries like the US, where there is a powerful belief that employment hinges on an effective presentation of self. Sharone writes that the ideal of the self-made man prompts a 'double crisis' for unemployed people:

> In addition to the financial crisis of wondering how one will keep paying the bills and not lose one's home, there is the personal crisis of wondering, 'What's wrong with me?' (Sharone, 2013: 2)

Without the discursive resources to make sense of their problems in other ways, people end up experiencing a flawed system in terms of a flawed self.

Another toxic side effect of the individualisation problem – the flip side of self-blame – is what we might call *phony empowerment*. The outcome of therapeutic culture is often to persuade people that they have a power they simply do not have, whether they are unemployed and being told they can get a job through the simple application of self-belief, or distressed workers informed that their predicaments can be solved by individual effort. The worst extremes of phony empowerment can be found in aphorisms from the self-help industry (remember the Oprah Winfrey quote at the start of this introduction?), in which popular psychologists attribute to individuals an almost magical ability to alter their circumstances and achieve success simply through an application of will. In Rhonda Byrne's best-selling self-help book *The Secret* (2006), readers are let in on the stunning secret that 'thoughts become things'; that merely by visualising goods like money and success, a cosmic Law of Attraction will make them appear. Byrne's book, and others like it, demonstrate an overwhelming failure to engage with reality, seeming to represent a worldview totally emptied of inconvenient realities like inequality and power. It is no wonder that David Smail felt moved to compare popular psychology to magic, since both would seem to privilege the way we see things over how things really are (1998).

In *Smile or Die,* Barbara Ehrenreich (2010) also gives a particularly striking example of phony empowerment in the form of advice (derived from dubious beliefs about the positive effect of happiness on the immune system) that an upbeat attitude can help people 'defeat' cancer. If the situation of people with cancer were not bad enough already, now they are also encouraged to experience guilt about feeling unhappy. As Ehrenreich writes in relation to her own experience of cancer: 'I didn't mind dying, but the idea that I should do it while clutching a teddy with a sweet little smile on my face – well, no amount of philosophy had prepared me for that' (2010: 17).

None of this is to say that people are powerless, of course. But what is often lacking in therapeutic culture is a sober understanding of who really has power and the difficult and collective efforts that are usually required to bring about meaningful change. Overcoming problems relies on having a measure of real power over the environment: on people having the material means, social connections and cultural influence necessary to alter their circumstances. This idea is captured in David Smail's critique of the concept of willpower. Where therapeutic culture has often decreed that individual willpower can bring about change, Smail reminds us that this concept is actually made up of two ideas: *will* – which refers to the idea of an agency located inside individuals – and *power* – which is an external, social phenomenon, possessed by some and not others:

> Whether or not we are able to realise our desires, put our plans into
> effect, do what we know to be right, will depend on our access to
> powers and resources which we need to acquire, or to have acquired.
> (Smail, 2001: 412)

It is a simple but important point that, without resources, the exercise of will is impossible. When issues of power are ignored, the kind of empowerment sold in employability classes or workplace wellness courses can only ever be a phony, superficial variety.

While it is important to recognise the harms of individualised ideas of recovery like self-blame and phony empowerment, something else that will be stressed in this book is that we should resist overstating the effectiveness of attempts to change the mentalities of workers and citizens. Bosses and job centre staff can force people to undergo therapy-style interventions through audits and disciplinary action, and such threats are effective at getting bodies into rooms, yet they can never guarantee a person's full mental co-operation. For every person turned towards blaming themselves for problems like unemployment or work stress, I strongly suspect there is another person who sees through the ruse, and another still who becomes so frustrated by the con that they link up with others and take action.

We will see this refusal to capitulate many times in the chapters that follow. The disability activists Arianna Introna and Mirella Casagrande, for example, will suggest (Chapter 10) that the humiliation endured by people forced to undertake workfare interventions is often what finally triggers them to become activists. Steven Stanley's chapter on mindfulness (Chapter 5) will tell a similar story about how his university's wellness initiatives were met with disdain, having been promoted in a context of a bitter pension dispute. The sheer, infantile silliness of the idea that chronically unhappy staff can be appeased with activities like bake-offs, biking to work and white-water rafting often just seems to so annoy people that it galvanises their appetite for collective action. We will also hear from Recovery in the Bin (Chapter 11), the survivors collective, who have resisted ideas of phony empowerment by encouraging patients and therapists to map out the socio-political barriers to recovery, whether this is discrimination, poverty, inequality, the disappearance of basic social rights and protections or, indeed, the distress caused by therapeutic interventions that fail to take such things into account.

The problem of interests

If the individualisation problem is causing so much harm, and this harm is not necessarily a secret, then there is one final question we must ask: why is therapeutic culture so prolific? This book builds on a tradition of critical thought that explores how psychological knowledge has been used throughout history to reproduce power and maintain discipline (for example, Foucault, 1977; Rose, 1999). In *Taking Care* (1998), David Smail suggests that the best way to understand the proliferation of therapeutic culture is simply to ask whose *interests* are being served. The interests of therapists themselves may be one answer to this question. Something we will be reminded of several times throughout this book is that therapists are themselves workers, dependent on their activities to make a living. This might limit the scope to acknowledge that the causes of people's problems are often beyond the psychologist's traditional remit:

> Professional therapy tends to presume that both the causes and the experience of distress are interior, since this affords the therapist a legitimate ground of intervention: individuals can be worked on in ways that social and material circumstances cannot. (Midlands Psychology Group, 2012)

As the positive energy of many wellness seminars attests, there is also undeniably a comforting feel-good factor to celebrations of empowerment, even if they do turn out to be phony. It is hard, for example, to imagine a lucrative enterprise in coaching people to understand that their influence as individuals is limited and that powerful obstacles stand in their way. Outside the more melancholy world of left-wing publishing, the comforts to be found in trying to perceive the realism and complexity of the world's problems do not sell so well. In an undemocratic world that is characterised by a lack of freedom, therapeutic interventions promise to put us in control of our destinies, and this is a message many people feel glad to hear.

As I have already hinted at, another obvious set of interests are those of the companies that invest in therapeutic interventions for their staff. In Chapter 1, Ivor Southwood will suggest that such interventions give companies a valuable 'reputational alibi': that is, they allow companies to present themselves as compassionate and concerned about employee wellbeing while actually doing very little to improve contractual and working conditions. In this sense, therapeutic interventions are a sensible investment in what we might think of as a controlled detonation: a place where employees can vent stress and receive tips on self-management without disrupting the broader structures and conditions that define their work.

Last but not least, several of the authors in this book will consider the ways in which therapeutic culture helps to consolidate the interests of neoliberal politics. By 'neoliberal', I refer to a bundle of political ideas that have been commonplace since the Thatcher and Reagan governments of the 1980s. This includes the idea that individual responsibility should be emphasised over redistribution; that everyone must work; that there is 'not enough money' to properly fund welfare and public institutions, and that governments are inefficient. The rise of this neoliberal political philosophy can be charted through shifts in language, corresponding with the rise of ideas like entrepreneurship, employability and choice (all of which emphasise individual responsibility and agency) over older ideas like solidarity, justice and freedom (which imply a much stronger role for the state and collective institutions).

The work of Nikolas Rose has suggested that political power can operate more smoothly and effectively if it can coincide with individuals' own ambitions, practices and worldviews (Rose, 1999). The descriptor 'neoliberal' has therefore been used to describe not only a particular political philosophy but also a type of subjectivity, shaped around ideas like responsibility, entrepreneurialism, competitive edge and work-focused ambitions. It is easy to see how the kinds of therapeutic culture described in this book dovetail with neoliberalism, given that they also emphasise individual responsibility and self-work, as opposed to structural change for the greater collective good. Both therapeutic culture and neoliberalism are marked by a one-sided focus on individuals taking responsibility and creating their own reality.

This book

Having considered the possible interests involved in the mis-application of therapeutic culture to the problems with work, I will say a few final words on the chapters that follow. They are written by people with different backgrounds, and each piece has its own style and motivations. My hope is that, by drawing together these diverse pieces, this book will encourage readers to tease out the common ideas and concerns between groups who might not usually move in the same circles or speak on the same platforms. I hope that this juxtaposition of perspectives, although sometimes bumpy, may play a part in provoking new coalitions and communication between groups with a stake in scrutinising the marriage of work discipline and therapeutic culture. Contributors include mental health and disability activists, health practitioners and psychotherapists, critical psychologists, sociologists of work, and at least one person who just really hates his job. My strong suspicion, however, is that none of the writers in this book are particularly attached to labels. What seems to unite everybody is a certain blurriness – a desire to challenge the boundaries between academia and activism, psychological and social concerns, personal experience and politics. The main message I have taken from these essays is that such barriers are maintained to our detriment.

There are a couple more points to clarify here. First of all, this book contains an unanswered but important question about whether the purveyors of therapeutic solutions to the problems with work should be vilified. Indeed, part of what seems to motivate critics of psycho-coercion to speak out is a sense of disgust at its financially lucrative nature. As Friedli and Stearn point out in relation to workfare, the goal to model unemployed people according to the ideals of the market has also been carried out by *means* of the market, as private contractors are paid vast sums of money to orchestrate and deliver psycho-coercive services (2015: 42). There is indeed something profoundly distasteful about profiting from interventions as ineffectual and harmful as the ones criticised here. Within this context, it is important not to shy away from pointing fingers and naming names. Companies like Atos, Igneus and A4e, who delivered the Conservative government's workfare policies, as well as the Secretaries of State for Work and Pensions Iain Duncan Smith and Esther McVey, who orchestrated them, all deserve a special call out.

Yet we must also acknowledge that the spread of therapeutic culture is not always a conspiracy. In the 1980s, David Smail suggested that the alliance between therapy and power is not necessarily conscious and calculated but may correspond to 'a general lowering of moral and political awareness' (1998, 56). In such a context, it is unproductive always to point the finger. It may be that the manager who organises a wellness seminar and the paid guru who runs it both embody a well-meaning intention to provide help. In Chapter 8, we will also read Paul Atkinson's reflections on the experiences of therapists who carry out the government's employment-focused IAPT programme. In the cases Atkinson describes, the burden of standardised procedures, pre-set targets and performance audits effectively prevent therapists from breaking out of the mould of individualised diagnosis and treatment. Many have themselves been driven to illness or have quit the profession due to the ethical and emotional conflicts this has caused. In these complicated circumstances, it seems unwise and unkind to apportion blame to therapists themselves. What such examples do show, however, is that 'helping people' is rarely an innocent act. There are always background assumptions in play about who needs help, what 'the problem' is, who gets to say, and what form that help should take. While this book will not always point the finger, it will highlight the importance of recognising that certain answers to these questions benefit certain interests.

A final proviso I wish to add is that, although this book is an attempt to highlight some of the ideological and disciplinary uses of the ethic of self-work, it is not an attack on self-care itself (this would be a stupid proposition, in my view) and is certainly not an attempt to belittle anyone who has sought and found solace from their work-related troubles in the world of therapeutic culture. In addition, this book will also take pains to avoid any suggestion that self-care and political action are always at odds. The idea that self-care always represents a turn 'inwards', away from the world of politics, is simply too straightforward to be convincing, especially since so many psychotherapists –

some of whom have contributed to this book – are incorporating an awareness of social injustice into their practice. We will hear from people like Jay Watts (Chapter 7) and Psychologists for Social Change (Chapter 9) – psychologists who are all involved in an ongoing effort to keep abreast of policy reforms and skewer government ideologies. Their hope is that more psychologists will pledge to understand the political situation and team up with activists to change it.

There are also examples in this book to demonstrate that turning inwards, paying attention to how we feel, and turning outwards to assess the socio-political climate might act as complementary impulses. Dave Berrie and Emily McDonagh (Chapter 4), representing Mental Health Under Capitalism, see the establishment of collective networks of care and emotional support as vital for nurturing and energising people for political struggles. In a similar vein, Steven Stanley (Chapter 5) sketches an alternative idea of 'social mindfulness', against the conservativism of 'corporate mindfulness', that would attune people to how organisational structures can cause pain. Stanley's conviction is that a form of mindfulness conceived by workers, rather than employers, might help draw attention to the emotional hunger in our workplaces, foster an ethic of care towards struggling colleagues, and perhaps fuel collective efforts to transform organisational structures.

Overall, then, this book is a critique of the ideological and disciplinary *applications* of therapy (what we might call 'neoliberal self-care') to the problems with work, rather than an attack on the ideas of therapy and self-care *per se*. I hope that readers will be prompted not only to think about the insidious side of therapeutic culture but also to consider how self-care and political action can complement each other in networks of care that help subvert and speak truth to power, rather than serving to consolidate it.

References

Alston P (2018). *Statement on visit to the United Kingdom by Professor Philip Alston, United Nations special rapporteur on extreme poverty and human rights*. [Online.] United Nations Office of the High Commissioner; 16 November. www.ohchr.org/EN/NewsEvents/Pages/DisplayNews.aspx?NewsID=23881&LangID=E (accessed 19 January 2019).

Byrne R (2006). *The Secret*. London: Simon & Schuster UK.

Butler P (2015). Thousands have died after being found fit for work, DWP figures show. [Online.] *The Guardian*; 27 August. www.theguardian.com/society/2015/aug/27/thousands-died-after-fit-for-work-assessment-dwp-figures (accessed 7 January 2019).

Chamberlain J (2018). *Undoing Work, Rethinking Community: a critique of the social function of work.* New York, NY: Cornell University Press.

Chamberlain J (2013). Recognition and social justice: what critical theory can learn from paid domestic labourers in the United States. *New Political Science 3*(2): 182–202.

Davies W (2015). *The Happiness Industry: how government and big business sold us well-being.* London: Verso Books.

Department of Social Security (1998). *New Ambitions for our Country: a new contract for welfare.* Norwich: the Stationery Office.

Department for Work and Pensions/Department of Health (2017). *Improving Lives: the future of work, health and disability.* London: The Stationery Office.

Department for Work and Pensions/ Department of Health (2016). *Improving Lives: the work, health and disability green paper.* London: The Stationery Office.

Ehrenreich B (2010). *Smile or Die: how positive thinking fooled America and the world.* London: Granta Publications.

Etherington D, Daguerre E (2015). *Welfare Reform, Work First Policies and Benefit Conditionality: reinforcing poverty and social exclusion?* [Online.] Centre for Enterprise and Economic Development Research. www.mdx.ac.uk/__data/assets/pdf_file/0031/149827/Welfare-and-benefit-conditionality-report-January-2015.pdf (accessed 7 January 2019).

Foucault M (1977). *Discipline and Punish: the birth of the prison* (2nd ed). New York, NY: Knopf Doubleday Publishing Group.

Frayne D (2015). *The Refusal of Work: the theory and practice of resistance to work.* London: Zed Books.

Friedli L, Stearn R (2015). Positive affect as coercive strategy: conditionality, activation and the role of psychology in UK government workfare programs. *Medical Humanities 41*(1): 40–47.

Gorz A (1999). *Reclaiming Work.* Cambridge: Polity Press.

Gorz A (1980). *Ecology as Politics.* London: Pluto Press.

Graeber D (2018). *Bullshit Jobs: a theory.* London: Simon & Schuster.

Health and Safety Executive (2018). *Health and Safety at Work: summary statistics for Great Britain 2018.* [Online.] www.hse.gov.uk/statistics/overall/hssh1718.pdf (accessed 7 January 2019).

Illich I (1975). *Medical Nemesis: the expropriation of health.* London: Calder & Boyars.

Joseph Rowntree Foundation (2018). *Budget 2018: tackling the rising tide of in-work poverty.* [Online.] Joseph Rowntree Foundation. www.jrf.org.uk/report/budget-2018-tackling-rising-tide-work-poverty (accessed 7 January 2019).

Koksal I (2012). *'Positive thinking' for the unemployed – my adventures at A4e.* [Online.] Open Democracy; 15 April. www.opendemocracy.net/ourkingdom/izzy-koksal/positive-thinking-for-unemployed-my-adventures-at-a4e (accessed 21 February 2019).

Lødemel I, Trickey H (2000). *'An Offer You Can't Refuse': workfare in international perspective.* Bristol: Policy Press.

Madsen OJ (2014). *The Therapeutic Turn: how psychology altered Western culture.* London: Routledge.

Menegus B (2016). *Lyft thinks it's 'exciting' that a driver was working while giving birth.* [Online.] Gizmodo. 22 September. https://gizmodo.com/lyft-thinks-its-exciting-that-a-driver-was-working-whil-1786970298 (accessed 7 January 2019).

Midlands Psychology Group (2012). Draft Manifesto for a Social Materialist Psychology of Distress. *Journal of Critical Psychology, Counselling and Psychotherapy 12*(2): 93–107.

Parsons T (1951). *The Social System.* London: Routledge.

Rose N (1999). *Governing the Soul: the shaping of the private self* (2nd revised ed). London & New York: Routledge.

Sharone O (2013). *Flawed System, Flawed Self: job searching and unemployment experiences.* Chicago: University of Chicago Press.

Smail D (2001). *The Nature of Unhappiness.* London: Constable & Robinson.

Smail D (1998). *Taking Care: an alternative to therapy.* London: Constable & Robinson.

Srnicek N, Williams A (2016). *Inventing the Future: post-capitalism and a world without work.* London: Verso Books.

Tolentino J (2017). The gig economy celebrates working yourself to death. [Online.] *The New Yorker;* 22 March. www.newyorker.com/culture/jia-tolentino/the-gig-economy-celebrates-working-yourself-to-death (accessed 7 January 2019).

Trades Union Congress (2018). *1 in 9 workers are in insecure jobs, says TUC.* [Online.] Trade Union Congress; 10 May. www.tuc.org.uk/news/1-9-workers-are-insecure-jobs-says-tuc (accessed 7 January 2019).

Weeks K (2011). *The Problem with Work.* London: Duke University Press.

Welfare Conditionality Project (2018). *Welfare Conditionality Project: final findings.* [Online.] www.welfareconditionality.ac.uk/wp-content/uploads/2018/06/40475_Welfare-Conditionality_Report_complete-v3.pdf (accessed 7 January 2019).

Wilson J (2018). Work-related distress and mental illness now account for over half of work absences. [Online.] *Daily Telegraph;* 1 November. www.telegraph.co.uk/news/2018/11/01/work-related-stress-mental-illness-now-accounts-half-work-absences/ (accessed 7 January 2019).

Woodcock J (2017). *Working the Phones: control and resistance in call centres.* London: Pluto Press.

PART 1
MENTAL MANAGEMENT

1

The black dog

Ivor Southwood

Ivor Southwood is a full-time parent, part-time wage labourer and occasional writer. He is the author of Non-Stop Inertia *(Zero, 2011) and the blog* Screened Out *(http://screened-out.blogspot.co.uk). He is currently working on a new book, to be titled* Against Employability.

A statue of a black dog has been installed at the entrance of the building where I work. Ostensibly there to raise awareness of depression, and sponsored by the employer as part of a charity campaign, the Churchillian hound stands guard, watching the office staff as they enter and leave every morning and evening. Inside, advertisements for awareness-raising campaigns and support groups are everywhere: a banner proclaims that talking about mental health is 'not a red card offence' (what level of offence is it, then? Yellow? A quiet word from the referee?). An organisation called Action for Happiness visits the site regularly, filling the staff restaurant with badges and self-help books and offering employees mindfulness pictures to colour in. The internal computer network advertises wellness webinars, including one entitled 'Maximising Your Happiness Potential' that 'looks at the principles of positive psychology and how we can use them in our daily work and life'. On the walls, posters promoting an 'Understanding Depression' group and an 'Anxiety Workshop' sit alongside the staff performance league tables. As an official notice endorsing the various wellbeing programmes explains: 'We want you to be well enough to perform to your best at work.'

What if this statement is taken literally, not as a touchy-feely we-care-for-you maxim but as a coldly calculated equation aimed at extracting optimum efficiency from the 'well-enough' worker? If the worker is not well enough, she might be unable to perform the tasks assigned to her, to deliver the script convincingly to customers or contribute authentic warmth and applause in team huddles. But if she is too well, her economic performance might suffer also. Too much job security might make her feel unduly comfortable. A lack of inter-team rivalry might fail to keep her and her colleagues sufficiently on their toes; they might cease competing with each other and instead put their efforts into minimising the workload. Having realised their strength as a collective unit, they might stop viewing their team leader as a plausible authority. Is the happy worker one who stays unpaid to finish a task, or one who feels confident enough to leave early with the task unfinished? Which form of happiness would the employer prefer?

Obvious ways of alleviating workplace misery – improvements in material conditions, higher pay, longer breaks, more job security, more space and time, less pressure from management – are conspicuously absent from the chatter of 'wellbeing'. Work-related mental illness is seen as emanating from within the unfortunate individual who is not sufficiently 'resilient'. For those with pre-existing mental health problems, the awareness-raising campaigns enable the employer to suggest it is generously facilitating 'inclusion', with work sold almost as a therapeutic intervention in itself. Nowhere is it mentioned that the workplace itself might create or exacerbate mental health problems; that stress is piped into the environment as efficiently as the air conditioning and keeps the organisation functioning as a productive enterprise.

The daily functioning of such organisations, and indeed of society as a whole, now demands that stresses are continuously reproduced, distributed and intensified. Workers are kept at biting points of anxiety and in states of depressive passivity. We are led to believe that the cause of that distress is located in the individual and not in the institution, and the individual is encouraged to adapt to the pressures of their environment, in preparation for more stresses to be introduced and personalised. This arrangement, which serves to suppress industrial conflicts and disguise – and thereby maintain – relations of power and wealth, is one of the key defence mechanisms of neoliberal society. To paraphrase Mark Fisher, it is easier to prescribe a wellness course for individuals than change how a workplace is organised (Fisher, 2018: 467).[1] Apparently self-

---

1. 'It is clearly easier to prescribe a drug than a wholesale change in the way society is organised' (Fisher, 2018: 467).

created problems require self-help solutions, and this is where the language of wellbeing segues into that of productivity, articulating the managerial aim of a frictionless human assembly line.

The corporate need to translate socio-economic dissatisfaction into a language of self-improvement has given rise to a whole industry of positive psychology and mindfulness. Action for Happiness, for instance, was founded in 2010 by a group including the economist Professor Lord Richard Layard, a Labour peer and welfare-to-work pioneer, and Anthony Seldon, a university vice-chancellor specialising in positive thinking. The organisation cashes in on the era of financial collapse and austerity by pushing the message that happiness is largely decided, not by money or social circumstances, but by 'the conscious choices we make' (Action for Happiness, undated): that is, people are responsible for their own (un)happiness, even as their standard of living is eroding before their eyes.

As well as suppressing demands for better pay and conditions, the backdrop of awareness-raising and self-help serves as a reputational alibi, part of the same narrative of corporate social responsibility that leads a company to justify routine environmental destruction by planting some trees, or to hide its ruthless financial motives behind sponsorship of a community project. As an internal mirror of this marketing exercise, by imbuing its management, human resources and training departments with a warm, pseudo-therapeutic glow, the employer can re-package factory discipline to its employees as personalised 'support'. A recent anonymous letter published in the union newsletter at my workplace appears to confirm this:

> The intranet recently ran a campaign that focused on mental health
> and talking about it not being a red card offence. This is a worthwhile
> campaign which to the external world looks good for [company],
> but internally what is the real story? As someone who has worked at
> [company] for a number of years and seen a number of work mates go
> off sick with stress, anxiety or depression, I had assumed [company] was
> a supportive employer. How wrong was I?
>
> Having the misfortune to recently suffer a number of absences due
> to work-related stress, I personally availed of the support provided. I
> was upon my last return to work invited to a meeting with my manager
> to discuss how they could support me with my condition. I anticipated
> we would be looking at the issues that caused my work-related stress,
> for example over-worked, micro-management, productivity measuring
> systems with unrealistic timing that leave you unable to take breaks

and a performance management system designed to punish rather than reward, and what could be done to help with these. Wrong again.

The opening statement of support was that the business cannot sustain this level of absence and the additional support was attendance targets with the comforting reassurance that, if I did not meet said targets, a more formal action (which I later learned would be a disciplinary) would be taken against me. So I am now back in the same melting pot that caused my mental health condition, with no adjustments made other than an additional threat of punishment.

So, in reality, within [company], talking about mental health issues might not be a red card offence, but having a mental health issue certainly is.

Snarl of the black dog. This account illustrates with chilling clarity how the focus of workplace support is not on the causes of ill health but, rather, on the performance of the affected worker.

The blurb for one of the support sessions states that 'attendees will learn how to manage their own wellbeing'. The discovery of the employee quoted above, that talking about mental health is OK but having a mental health problem is a punishable offence, reflects this duty imposed on workers to 'manage their own wellbeing', regardless of external conditions. While the language of mental health is used as a motivational and reputational currency, real problems are not allowed to impinge on this discourse, which portrays health and profit, and workers and managers, as perfectly compatible partners.

Being an outsourced manual worker, I am excluded from the employee wellness programmes, just as I am from the pay and benefits of the directly employed staff. Such intra-institutional boundaries are as essential for communicating the low status of outsourced workers as the support groups and chillout rooms are to pacifying the directly employed. To use Imogen Tyler's critique of neoliberal power relations, we are to some extent 'abjectified' (Tyler, 2013): designated as an ephemeral and disposable 'other' in relation to the lean, sanitised core-poration. It is not coincidental that in this and many other organisations outsourced status applies to the sort of manual labour – catering, cleaning, deliveries, maintenance – with which the host company literally prefers not to dirty its hands. On several occasions, co-workers have described to me the sense of being looked down upon as we move through the office space in our distinctive uniforms – of office workers averting their eyes from us and the tasks we are required to perform. Similarly, our own managers never cease to remind us of our servitude. The facilities company maintains its own paradisciplinary culture of coercion.[2]

Outsourcing has much in common with the policing of 'citizenship' by governments, as described by Tyler (2013: 48–74), with employers mirroring state regulation of populations through legal and ideological narratives of inclusion and exclusion: us and them, belonging and not-belonging. Outsourced workers are assigned the status of an 'internalised other' within the organisation, inhabiting the same space as the directly employed staff but still excluded from any in-house financial benefits or union representation. The high proportion of ethnic minority and migrant workers among the outsourced workforce gives this arrangement an almost colonial dimension, and it is not surprising that, for workers on the receiving end of outsourcing arrangements in large wealthy organisations, this arrangement can often resemble a form of apartheid (Bakhsh, 2017).

While we are below the wellbeing radar, we are nevertheless expected to facilitate the delivery of these services in the same way that we are needed to serve up food or empty the bins, by pinning up the various awareness-raising posters and shifting furniture to accommodate the happiness sessions. I helped to wheel the black dog into its current position. It is the duty of the cleaners to wash the dog every few weeks with a watering can. Suitably gleaming, the fibreglass animal continues to deflect negativity and protect the organisation against psychic contamination.

The economic case for mental illness

It is somehow symptomatic of the situation outlined above that, rather than a government commissioning an investigation into the psychological and social effects of a particular economic model, mental health itself has to be framed *in* those economic terms. In October 2017, the government published a report entitled *Thriving at Work*, co-authored by the chief executive of Mind, the mental health charity, and a former chairman of HBOS (Farmer & Stevenson, 2017). While the report continually links mental health to productivity, to the point where one begins to wonder which of these is the real focus (in neoliberal terms, of course, they are inseparable), nowhere does it address the possibility of any conflict between work and mental health. Beyond the vague

---

2. I explore this in more detail in my essay *The Uncomplaining Body* (Southwood, 2015), which examines this particular workplace in the form of an organisational case study. The essay also identifies specific factors pertaining to this workplace, such as type of industry, size of workforce, job titles and duties, which are not discussed here.

observation that 'the nature of work is changing', there is no discussion of the impact on mental health of the epidemic of precarious work – outsourcing, temporary contracts and agency work with unpredictable hours and no sick pay – that over the last two decades has turned the traditional labour market on its head and correspondingly shaken up its labourers. In a genuine inquiry into the relation of work to mental health, the effects of precarity and austerity would surely feature prominently, but here the emphasis is on how institutions can better support individuals with mental health problems, regardless of whether the problems are caused or exacerbated by those institutions. Poverty and job insecurity are regarded as fixtures to be manoeuvred around, rather than obstacles to be got rid of.

One of the most widely publicised aspects of the report was its estimate that poor mental health costs employers between £33 and £42 billion a year – a figure largely derived from the surprising claim that presenteeism costs employers between £17 and £26 billion annually (compared with £8 billion due to absenteeism) (Farmer & Stevenson, 2017: 24). If presenteeism was really a loss-maker, then surely the report would urge all employers to provide full occupational sick pay – rather than sick pay being removed from jobs like mine – and call for the scourge of workers staying unpaid beyond their appointed hours to be eradicated. But such measures are curiously absent. It transpires that the headline figure, calculated by multinational accountancy firm Deloitte, relies on an absurdly narrow and misleading definition of presenteeism as 'showing up to work when one is ill, resulting in a loss of productivity'(Farmer & Stevenson, 2017: 20). Hence there is no analysis of the comparable cost of that ill worker not showing up, or of jobs where such a productivity gap is negligible, or of presenteeism provoked by excessive workloads or job insecurity, by which the employer receives a gift of free labour.

Indeed, the overall 'cost' to employers of mental illness relies upon the accountants studiously ignoring the whole other side of the balance sheet: the gains made by businesses as a result of poverty wages, insecurity and overwork – those carefully regulated factors that help to maintain a vast reservoir of distress among workers and upon which the employer routinely draws. Any worker in a warehouse, restaurant or call centre could, if asked, easily list the ways that their stresses are artificially heightened: from low pay, boredom and irregular hours to performance targets, enforced competition with co-workers and lack of autonomy. These stresses have a clear purpose: to maximise revenue and minimise labour costs.

Under these conditions, anxiety and depression are not economic problems: quite the reverse, in fact. Put bluntly, while workers suffer materially and psychologically under such conditions, businesses profit from them. It is only when the employee can no longer function at the required level or risks impairing other employees' performance or imperilling the company's reputation that her mental state becomes problematic in economic terms. An earlier study commissioned by the government's chief medical officer was entitled 'The Economic Case for Better Mental Health' (Knapp & Lemmi, 2014: 146–157), but the contemporary workplace would be more accurately depicted by addressing the economic case for mental *illness*.

It is unsurprising but nonetheless alarming that *Thriving at Work*'s recommendations raise the prospect of a tightening rather than loosening of workplace pressure. Beyond toothless generalities such as 'good working conditions' and 'healthy work-life balance' (Farmer & Stevenson, 2017: 6; see also Murray, 2017), the proposed 'core standards' that employers can implement 'at little or no cost' (Farmer & Stevenson, 2017: 34) involve an intensification of managerial monitoring, more awareness-raising schemes and increased provision of one-to-one support, formalising a culture of psychological surveillance and legitimising the kind of performance-assessment-disguised-as-counselling outlined by the worker above. The report's authors envisage 'a culture of measurement' enacted through 'surveys and mood trackers' and recommend that senior managers have these measurements of their employees' wellbeing built into their own performance reviews (Farmer & Stevenson, 2017: 6, 37, 55), presumably meaning that workers documenting their stress will risk incurring the wrath of figure-conscious executives further up in the hierarchy. Another recommendation – which, as before, demonstrates either spectacular naïvety or complicity with the prevailing economic powers – is that 'self-employed' workers whose work relies on mobile technology are offered a dedicated smartphone app that might offer 'GP consultations, online cognitive behavioural therapy [and] mental health self-care toolkits' (Farmer & Stevenson, 2017: 56). This exemplifies the narrative of self-help and hyper-individualisation: the virtualised stress-inducing structure remains unchanged, but those struggling in isolation within it must reprogram themselves in order to continue to function.

The interest of the ruling class in the inner lives of their subjects is of course far from philanthropic: cultivating the right 'mindset' can make the worker more compliant, and the consequent behavioural changes are measurable in monetary terms (the real 'culture of measurement'). Signs of a happy workforce, even if not straightforwardly faked to please managers/customers, might still be read as euphemisms for pacification, enhanced by narrow aspirational goals (to escape the quagmire by becoming a supervisor or manager, imposing misery on others) and the terror of unemployment. Workplace happiness initiatives should be regarded with scepticism, as ways of nudging employees towards normative behaviours (a facade of enthusiasm, passable scripts of personal growth, aspiration and so on) and imposing duties of flexibility, and what Arlie Russell Hochschild has termed 'emotional labour' (2003: 7),[3] all of which contribute to the illusion of consent for further screw-tightening innovations. Corporate stress manuals also teach managers to address the problem of unhappy labourers by encourging them to adjust their beliefs to fit the work environment.

The debilitating effects of industrial labour are, of course, as old as the work ethic itself; the injuries merely evolve with the technology. In his mid-19th century study, *The Condition of the Working Class in England*, Friedrich Engels observed the various diseases and disabilities wrought by factory work, and noted that the constant uncertainty created by having to compete with advances in machinery exerted 'a dispiriting, unnerving influence... upon the worker, whose lot is precarious enough without it' (Engels, 1993: 149). What is new in today's ideology of work is the partial shift from physical to mental injury and the conversion of those pressures that, in the past, would have sparked industrial unrest and class struggle into matters of individual wellbeing and aspiration that can only be resolved through *more work*. Mark Fisher has written about how, under neoliberalism, the traumas inflicted by precarious work and welfare cuts have been medicalised and depoliticised (Fisher, 2012), and in *Capitalist Realism* he describes how the same process has been applied to discussions of mental illness:

> The current ruling ontology denies any possibility of a social causation of mental illness. The chemico-biologization of mental illness is of course strictly commensurate with its depoliticisation. Considering mental illness as an individual chemico-biological problem has enormous benefits for capitalism. First, it reinforces Capital's drive towards atomistic individualisation (you are sick because of your brain chemistry). Second, it provides an enormously lucrative market in which multinational pharmaceutical companies can peddle their pharmaceuticals (we can cure you with our SSRIs). (Fisher, 2009: 37)

When the social element does appear in relation to mental health, it is on the side

---

3. Hochschild uses 'emotional labour' to refer to the importing of feelings and actions from personal life, such as care, friendship or flirtation, into wage labour – for instance, in the form of customer service.

of capital, either as retail therapy and mind-numbing leisure consumption or in the promotion of work as cure, rather than cause, of disease (and poverty). This is most obviously illustrated by the Department for Work and Pensions' new Work and Heath Programme, which threatens to medicalise unemployment by installing mental health professionals in job centres and pushes 'the value of work as a health outcome' (as further explained in Chapters 7 and 8). Fisher points to 'parallels between the rising incidence of mental distress and new patterns of assessing workers' performance' (2009: 37–38). This can refer to the endless trials by appraisal and micro-management that Fisher discusses in relation to teaching, but it also applies to the regulation of 'performance' more generally. *We want you to be well enough to perform to your best at work.*

An insecure base

The economic system designed to keep workers in a state of material and existential insecurity has been refined over recent years by a new emphasis on short-term flexibility and temporary contracts, 'lean' and 'agile' production, outsourcing and the use of employment agencies. To these can now be added zero-hours contracts and the bogus 'self-employment' of the gig economy, where the worker, despite being subjected to the hours and conditions of wage labour, is nevertheless assigned the status of a freelance contractor, allowing employers to bypass legal obligations relating to, for instance, the minimum wage or holiday pay. Such changes have been made possible by the erosion of employment rights, declining union membership and the paring down of welfare benefits through real-term decreases and increased conditionality, all of which occur alongside high rents, cuts to social housing and soaring levels of personal debt. Capitalism has thrived since Engels' day by maintaining the 'precariousness' of its labourers, and, after a brief post-war interval of relative stability, precarity has now once again become institutionalised and normalised. Its current incarnation is fuelled by a digital culture of 24/7 availability and connectivity and is inscribed in a subservient body language familiar to all those toiling in the depths of a low-pay/no-pay economy: workers and 'jobseekers' are required not just to accept whatever is thrown at them, but to express enthusiasm and gratitude for the most demeaning scraps of labour.

Although specific cases of exploitation are periodically highlighted by visible media campaigns,[4] the structural trend towards full precarity remains

---

4. See, for instance, the campaigns for Uber drivers and Deliveroo couriers to be legally recognised as employees rather than self-employed, and to end the outsourcing of support staff at the University of London.

unchecked. This becomes a vicious cycle: being kept in such a state of flux and lacking any cohesive group identity means precarious workers cannot focus outwards on social or political concerns. Their attention is instead constantly being forced inwards, onto their own survival and prospects of escape. The chances of resistance are therefore further diminished, while feelings of isolation, anxiety and powerlessness become ever more entrenched, whether or not they are formally classified as mental health problems. This is the climate in which entrepreneurial therapists and wellbeing trackers have emerged and flourished.

While the material and psychological effects of precarity are all too clear, its structural causes have been repressed, pushed into the social unconscious, hence the depoliticisation described by Fisher. Workplace mental health awareness-raising campaigns are in this sense aimed at *lowering* awareness of socio-economic factors by focusing on individual coping strategies.

The concept of the 'secure base' (developed by anthropologist Mary Ainsworth and popularised by psychoanalyst John Bowlby in the 1970s as part of so-called attachment theory) might – after some serious modifications – be usefully appropriated to interpret the social dynamics of precarity (see Berrie and McDonagh's Chapter 4). The secure base refers to the parental zone of protection that in early life enables the child to explore the world and form an identity in the knowledge that she is being looked after and will be supported when necessary (Bowlby, 1988: 12). As the child grows older and periods of time away from home become longer, the parental base becomes correspondingly sophisticated and internalised, or transferred to other figures, but some form of attachment and need for security remains into adulthood, even if its influence is unconscious (1988: 137, 146). For Bowlby, 'this concept of the secure personal base, from which a child, an adolescent, or an adult goes out to explore and to which he returns from time to time, is... crucial for an understanding of how an emotionally stable person develops and functions *all through his life*' (1988: 51, italics in original).

Limited empirical evidence, the assumption that the mother will be the primary attachment figure/caregiver/homemaker and the idea of a future identity being fixed by this inner process, regardless of historical and social conditions, constitute significant and well-documented problems with attachment theory (see, for instance, Cleary, 1999: 132–142). However, if the theory is turned around to concentrate on those very social and historical conditions, rather than the individual, then the idea of the secure base (or its opposite) might be applied more broadly to the analysis of society and organisations. Rather than feeding forward and looking inward – the infant's experience determining patterns of behaviour in later life – the term should feed back and out: particular social and institutional mechanisms of attachment or detachment, security or insecurity channel and amplify near-universal latent fears and desires, and this has a large, if mostly unacknowledged, influence on how organisations are structured and power is exercised upon groups and individuals.

This concept of the secure social base echoes a comment made in 1952 by Labour politician and architect of the NHS, Aneurin Bevan: 'You can make your home the base for your adventures, but it is absurd to make the home itself an adventure' (Bevan, 1976: 58). The post-war creation of the welfare state, the NHS and public housing might be seen in this way as the literal and metaphorical construction of a secure base, from which the working class could safely explore life's possibilities.

Bevan was pointing out that, contrary to the promises of private enterprise, subjecting every facet of life to a climate of unpredictability and speculation does not bring social benefits. In recent times, however, governments and corporations have sought to bring this 'adventure' back into the home and the mind of every citizen. Housing, health and welfare have succumbed to the demands of the marketplace, and those reserves of time and energy that could previously be kept free from the clutches of capital (or for which capital found no use) have been increasingly colonised or eliminated. A key objective under Thatcherism, and then throughout New Labour and the current regime of austerity, has been the deliberate engineering of an *insecure base*.

Precarity is not an unintended consequence of neoliberal policies of marketisation, privatisation and outsourcing; it is, rather, a central aim of those policies. This structural insecurity, which prevents attachment to any workplace or occupation and pulls away the safety nets of welfare or housing, exerts its power by invoking and, in some cases, realising the most primal fears: of falling/failing, of being lost or abandoned, of floating in an endless void, of starving, of being left to die. This is the constellation of anguish that ensures an obedient and unhindered flow of labour, from just-in-time temp work to institutional performance targets, from casualised drudgery to service with a smile. A particularly acute example of this state-endorsed precarity is Universal Credit, the new welfare benefit being introduced by the current government. Universal Credit is *designed* to be impractical and convoluted and to put its low-paid and unemployed claimants at risk of debt and homelessness through routine payment delays and arbitrary sanctions. Factors often characterised by politicians and commentators as glitches in the Universal Credit system are, in fact, deliberate features. To be effective in neoliberal terms, the new welfare regime must undermine its own stated purpose: it must reinforce and intensify, rather than provide shelter from, the miseries and insecurities of the work environment.

Considering such circumstances, it might be argued that, contrary to the caricatures drawn by politicians, attachment to a secure social base would not not foster 'dependency' but rather independence through the freedom to challenge, develop and think. Conversely the insecure social base, beyond its flimsy rhetoric of empowerment and aspiration, in fact inculcates an atrophying dependence on capital.

Predictably, the original therapeutic form of the secure base has already been adopted by management gurus looking to re-stage a healthy mother–infant bond as a productive manager–employee relationship (see, for instance, Crawshaw & Game, 2015: 1182–1203). The infantilisation is obvious enough from the teambuilding games and gold stars, but what if the relationship being nurtured and reproduced between worker and employer, between individual and state, in the era of post-Fordist capitalism, is one not of security but insecurity? As the cultural base has disintegrated into precarity, the so-called social contract has been nullified and replaced by what Angela Mitropoulos calls a 'neocontractual' relation (Mitropoulos, 2012: 27) – an abstract, all-encompassing but ungraspable tie between the individual and global capital, of which the boss, the recruitment agent, the work coach, the landlord, the utility provider, the credit card company are all mere avatars.

As class conflict has given way to myths of individual aspiration, work has ceased to be understood as wage labour and has become a personal journey. This shift can be tracked by the rise of the discourse of 'employability', which visualises life as an entrepreneurial talent show in which the winning formula is the ability to market oneself as a competitive and infinitely flexible human product. Here, insecurity is an integral part of the game and success cannot be achieved without it, just as it cannot be achieved without hard (often unpaid) work and relentless positivity. The employability coaches in universities and job centres preach a supine acceptance of precarious employment and promise future riches through continuous self-improvement: are you selling yourself effectively? What gives you the edge over your co-workers? How can you impress your boss? Or, conversely, self-blame: if you can't find a job, then what is wrong with you? The employable individual is always haunted by the figure of the unemployable other. All gaps in the CV must be filled: order, cleanliness and enthusiasm must cover over any unproductive episodes or conflicts that might devalue the product of yourself.

The unemployable other is created from the same ideological template as the sick worker. Both are viewed as damaged goods, insufficiently resilient, a drain on the company/state, and both need intensive 'support' in order to be returned to the status of citizen and team member. This process of subjugation, enacted through a superficial language of inclusivity and diversity, is a manifestation of what Imogen Tyler calls 'the abjectifying logics of neoliberal governmentality' (Tyler, 2013: 2).

Inclusion and abjection

Tyler's concept of social abjection might in fact be the key to understanding the real impetus behind workplace wellbeing schemes and mental health awareness-raising campaigns. 'Social abjection' borrows elements from psychoanalytic discussions of horror and disgust, but crucially adds to this an understanding of how power is exerted and how identities are projected onto individuals and groups in a particular socio-economic context. Here, abjection functions as a 'regulatory norm' and an instrument of power wielded by states, corporations and media that decides who is visible and who is (or should be) invisible, who is deemed to be part of society and who is 'other' to it, who is valuable and who is disposable (Tyler, 2013: 19-47). As discussed, the outsourced worker is already on the way to abjection, being of lower economic status and associated with the waste products of capital – excluded from the institution while working within it. This abjectifying process also operates on the unproductive worker, the sick worker, the disharmonious worker, by patrolling the borders of citizenship and identifying scapegoats, sending messages about what is acceptable in a state where one's passport is one's valuation as human capital.

In his article 'The Political Economy of Unhappiness', Will Davies suggests that, while capitalism must not satisfy its workers/customers, it also must not make people so dissatisfied that they reject or resist it (Davies, 2011: 71). In terms of work, however, where a proportion of an employer's capital might once have been invested in providing staff with a pacifying dose of satisfaction (a social life, career progression, a reasonable standard of living), as the social contract has given way to neocontractual precarity, these same resources (space, time, human interaction, technology) are now increasingly directed towards making rejection or resistance impossible, regardless of levels of dissatisfaction.

Resistance is now almost always a purely self-destructive act, rendered incomprehensible by the fake language of freedom permeating the hostage situation of work: attempts at sabotage simply bounce back onto the individual. If one worker walks out, another is hired, the ex-worker starves and the business carries on exactly as before. While passive compliance has been rebranded as a heroic journey, any expression of dissent is viewed as a personal tragedy. This casting of the individual who questions the state of things as a case for treatment can be illustrated by specific experiences: for instance, when leaving a previous job on ethical grounds, I was subjected to conversations with managers who, rather than engaging with the issue itself, insisted on saying how 'difficult' it must be for me, as if I were in need of counselling. After raising concerns as an agency temp about a practice at my current workplace, I was briefly fired for not being 'happy'. In both these instances, the personalising of the conflict closed down any argument: I was regarded as eccentric, pitiable. It is easy to see how these characterisations can take hold, especially if one has a known mental health history. Capital ventriloquises its crushing of such counter-conduct through the usual chorus of common sense: 'If you don't like it, get another job'; 'If you know so much, then why aren't you running the business?'; 'It is what it is.'

This is the paradox: abjection signifies a state outside the dominant order but, by definition, the totalising worldview of neoliberalism cannot countenance an 'outside'. It must include everything and everyone, from alternative culture to political revolution, from unemployment to mental illness, in its personalised and privatised vision. In neoliberal-speak, no one must be left behind, even those hardest-to-reach customers. Tyler describes the abjectified population being 'included through their exclusion' (Tyler, 2013: 20): that is, their presence as an other is necessary to shore up the identity of the dominant group. But the marginalised groups of neoliberalism (the outsourced, the unemployed, the sick, the unresilient) are also excluded through their inclusion. Institutions cannot explicitly exclude the people they want rid of, as this would be an admission of prejudice or systemic failure. Instead, people are *forcibly included*: medicated, 'supported' in the workplace or made to attend work-focused interviews. Everyone, regardless of their level of mental distress, is deemed 'fit for work', in the words of the government's rigged disability benefit test. Those who cannot be incorporated are then made out to be excluding themselves. From the office worker who cannot stomach another dose of mindfulness to the precariously employed courier whose financial worries are not solved by a CBT app to the Universal Credit claimant who is sanctioned 'as a last resort', these are viewed, not as instances of institutional expulsion but, rather, as the happiness gurus would say, matters of personal choice.

The workplace discourse of mental health (with its negative connotations, 'illness' is rarely used) is self-congratulatory and moralising in tone, boasting about how stigma is being overcome, how diversity and tolerance are celebrated. It is intended to boost the esteem of the institution's bosses and shareholders, not its workers. Negativity is banished, exclusion itself is excluded, replaced by forcible inclusion and mandatory positivity. Pressure is exerted – in the same empowering, supportive language – on the individual to own the problems of the institution and the wider culture. This is the new stigma, the institutional scapegoating behind the inspirational slogans, all the more powerful for its disavowal – disgust at the individual who cannot (or will not) 'manage' her distress, whose negativity threatens to spill out into the team and jeopardise the organisational ethos.

These various initiatives aim not to eliminate mental illness, which roams the call centres and warehouses of capital more freely than ever, but rather to quell healthy dissent. In this sense, the black dog at the threshold of my workplace represents the spectre of the individual who *does not belong*. It serves as a ritualistic reminder of the abject other languishing outside the gate, or even hiding inside, passing as a regular colleague, smiling, chatting, but not believing, not performing to their best, holding something back, for whatever deviant reason.

I am aware of this warning as I pass through the revolving door on my way into work. I know that I too am secretly disharmonious, matter out of place. The black dog is a signal to those of us who might consider challenging the demands of our masters that if we do, one way or another, the guardians of wellbeing will seek us out and cure us.

References

Action for Happiness (undated). *About us.* [Online.] Action for Happiness. www.actionfor happiness.org/about-us (accessed 7 January 2019).

Bakhsh A (2017). I love my security guard job, but there's a subtle apartheid dividing the staff. [Online.] *The Guardian*; 25 April. www.theguardian.com/commentisfree/2017/apr/25/ love-job-security-guard-but-subtle-apartheid-strike (accessed 7 January 2019).

Bevan A (1976). *In Place of Fear.* Wakefield: EP Publishing Ltd.

Bowlby J (1988). *A Secure Base.* Abingdon: Routledge.

Cleary RJ (1999). Bowlby's Theory of Attachment and Loss: a feminist reconsideration. *Feminism & Psychology* 9(1): 32–42.

Crawshaw J, Game A (2015). The role of line managers in employee career management: an attachment theory perspective. *International Journal of Human Resource Management* 26(9): 1182–1203.

Davies W (2011). The Political Economy of Unhappiness. *New Left Review 71*: 65–80.

Engels F (1845/1993). *The Condition of the Working Class in England*. Oxford: Oxford University Press.

Farmer P, Stevenson D (2017). *Thriving at Work: the Stevenson/Farmer review of mental health and employers*. [Online.] www.gov.uk/government/uploads/system/uploads/attachment_data/file/658145/thriving-at-work-stevenson-farmer-review.pdf (accessed 7 January 2019).

Fisher M (2018). *K-Punk: the collected and unpublished writings of Mark Fisher (2004–2016)*. London: Repeater.

Fisher M (2012). Why mental health is a political issue. [Online.] *The Guardian;* 16 July. www.theguardian.com/commentisfree/2012/jul/16/mental-health-political-issue (accessed 7 January 2019).

Fisher M (2009). *Capitalist Realism: is there no alternative?* Ropley: Zero Books.

Hochschild AR (2003). *The Managed Heart: commercialization of human feeling*. Berkeley, CA: University of California.

Knapp M, Lemmi V (2014). The economic case for mental health. In: Davies S. *Public Mental Health Priorities: investing in the evidence. Annual Report of the Chief Medical Officer*. London: Department of Health (pp147–156).

Mitropoulos A (2012). *Contract and Contagion: from biopolitics to oikonomia*. [Online.] New York, NY: Minor Compositions.

Murray N (2017). *The Flaws of the 'Thriving at Work' Report*. [Online.] The Autonomy Institute http://autonomy.work/portfolio/nic-murray-comments-thriving-work-repoty/ (accessed 10 June 2018).

Southwood I (2015). *The Uncomplaining Body: an organisational case study*. [Online.] Manual Labours. www.manuallabours.co.uk/wp-content/uploads/2014/11/Ivor-Uncomplaining-body-report-final.pdf (accessed 7 January 2019).

Tyler I (2013). *Revolting Subjects: social abjection and resistance in neoliberal Britain*. London: Zed Books.

2

No crying in the breakroom

Nic Murray

Nic Murray is a mental health researcher and activist based in London. His trade union has done more to support his mental health during the writing of this chapter than any workplace wellbeing initiative.

This is why I don't allow crying in the break room. It erodes morale. There's a place to do that, like your apartment.

Joan Southwood, Mad Men

In a normal state of things, wages at any given time and place should not fall below... whatever the contemporary local civilisation recognises as indispensable for physical and mental health.

Trades Union Congress Annual Report, 1880

We have always sought to some degree to resist the ills of work, but this resistance is no longer emerging through an organised voice. Instead, it emerges through the experience of distress – fleeting moments of mental and physical pain that may give rise to more sustained illnesses, acting as a form of embodied resistance to the current nature of work. Yet, without any form of political or collective expression, such resistance will only be felt as individual pain. If we are to have any hope of building collective resistance to toxic work, we urgently need to talk about what it is – at the core of the modern organisation of work – that is causing such levels of distress.

This chapter suggests that the potentially radical impact of talking about distress has been thwarted. Either our employers have sought to minimise and manage our distress, or our ways of talking about suffering have been captured within organisational channels and rhetoric. If the desire for change does surface, it is usually softened and filtered through the more benign language of 'anti-stigma', where it does less to upset prevailing interests and social structures. Whatever the scenario, it seems we have been steered away from talking about the pressing issues of injustice, lack of meaning and powerlessness at work. The challenge before us is to forge a collective discussion about how these problems connect to our distress. What are the social and structural causes of these elevated heart beats, shortened breaths and racing thoughts, and how might we begin to change things for the better?

The curious thing about this need to develop a collective discussion is that it arises in a climate where, perhaps more than ever, we are already being constantly encouraged to talk about mental health. The idea I want to explore, however, is that the settings and framings in which we are most readily invited to discuss our problems are not conducive to real change. People are continually faced with the assertion that mental illness is 'an illness like any other', yet I struggle to imagine any other form of illness, disease or even basic ailment where we only ever discuss the symptoms. We need to recognise how the current prompts to talk about our mental health can actually work to dehumanise, degrade and foreclose the radical potential of our words. If our words, our stories and our experiences are the tools we have to speak out about mental distress, we must work to ensure they are as powerful as possible. Above all, this might involve resisting and reconfiguring the existing prompts and exhortations from employers to talk about mental health and starting a discussion on the terms of the worker. We might have to find ways to speak about our distress that are less palatable to those in power.

Our minds are a battleground

The earliest battles for mental health at work were fought to gain the material conditions necessary for workers' wellbeing. The main tools were strikes, wage struggles, political organisation and mutual aid. By taking as a starting point the discussion of the workplace as a site of collective misery, it was possible for workers and organisers to demand a social minimum that would enable them to live well outside the factory gates. From this position, every bargain negotiated by trade unions provided a benefit to workers' collective mental health, but it could also have a more sustained impact on feelings of solidarity. The recognition of the misery inherent in the workplace and the norm of speaking openly about it could produce a clarity of purpose, and even moments of exhilarating joy, in resistance. Fairer pay, reduced working hours and better working conditions were all necessary victories won by many workplaces in these early struggles and, along the way, the efforts to produce change allowed workers to cultivate and reaffirm their ties to each other and to the wider world (Segal, 2017). People started new conversations and paused to imagine what a richer life would look like.

When the 1880 TUC annual report cited at the start of this chapter was being written, our current conception and discussion of 'mental health' were aeons away. Mental health in this earlier time can be read as a shorthand for a more folk-like understanding of flourishing, imbued with political demands such as a life rich in autonomy, safety and security. It comes as a stark realisation then, that growing knowledge about the causes and antecedents of poor mental health in the last century has brought with it the loss of the political demands required to realise human flourishing. Collectively, across the UK, 322,000 working days were lost due to industrial disputes in 2016, and 12.5 million were lost due to work-related stress, anxiety or depression (Health & Safety Executive, 2017). And yet discussion about mental health at work has never been louder. The theme for the 2017 World Mental Health Day was 'Workplaces', which saw widespread declarations from employers that it was 'time to talk about mental health'.

While this could be seen as progress, it is hard to see it as anything other than the latest effort by employers to delineate the nature and terms under which emotions and distress may be expressed at work. Such efforts have a history. From the 1960s onwards, with the emergence of occupational health as a field of study, the workplace was seen as a rational environment, where emotions would get in the way of sound judgement. Human resources departments sought to optimise the health of workers via greater micromanagement (Davies, 2015). As the number of service-based jobs proliferated in the economy, so too did the level of managerial control over workers' emotions (see Jamie Woodcock's Chapter 3 in this book). Arlie Hochschild's seminal 1983 study of flight attendants and 'emotional labour' (Hochschild, 2012) highlighted the attempts of managers to standardise workers' emotional conduct, as employees were intensively coached to display warm personalities or manage their anger in the presence of frustrating customers. These approaches to the management of emotions and distress at work have mushroomed in the decades since, filtered through many different iterations of how we conceptualise or understand mental health – whether this is the heavy management speak of the 1990s or the more empathic language of the 'time to talk' campaigns beginning in the mid 2000s.

The anti-authoritarian collective Plan C (WEAREPLANC, 2014) has noted that: 'One aspect of every phase [of capitalism]'s dominant affect is that it is a public secret, something that everyone knows, but nobody admits, or talks about.' They argue that the dominant mood of our age is *anxiety,* and that it remains a public secret, due to widespread social isolation. Without the opportunity to collectively interpret the link between working conditions and collective misery, anxiety is instead channelled inwards, as workers seek to make it through their day by hunkering down and trying not to draw attention to themselves. Communication is more pervasive than ever, but only happens through certain mediated channels – channels in which workers are unable to fully express themselves and may continue to self-censor. This means that the public secret of distress and burnout tends to remain hidden in plain sight, between the lines of thousands of messages on work intranet systems and email channels. Even in workers' personal communication channels, there remains a lingering sense of caution about saying what one truly feels. Bolder statements must always feature the caveat, 'Views my own'. When it comes to mental health at work, while we are talking more, it seems that we may be saying less.

Achieving success

Whereas in the past, the prompt to start discussions about mental distress may have come from a union meeting or conversation with a union rep, current encouragement to broach these topics in offices across the UK will most likely come from Time to Change, the mental health campaign founded in 2007, aimed at reducing mental health-related stigma and discrimination. The 'About Us' section of their website proclaims: 'Still too many people are made to feel ashamed or isolated because they have a mental health problem but we're here to change that' (Time to Change, 2018). 'Time to change', and indeed to end stigma and discrimination, does sound like a clear and powerful rallying cry. But what is made less clear is how this proclamation came about, and why sights were so firmly set on the workplace.

In March 2006, a statue appeared in Norwich depicting Winston Churchill constrained by a straitjacket. It later turned out that the nine-foot figure was commissioned by mental health charity Rethink (who currently run the Time to Change campaign, together with Mind) as part of their campaign to tackle mental health stigma. This served as something of a harbinger for the years to come, for both mental health policy and discourse. Churchill was undoubtedly chosen as a mental health icon due to his writings on the 'black dog' that visited him during periods of poor mental health. The choice was justified by a statement put out by Rethink explaining: 'The message we want to portray is that it is possible to recover from mental illness and overcome it and be successful – because Churchill is an example of someone who was able to do that' (BBC News, 2006). The role that recovery plays in this statement is significant, as is the expectation that it involves overcoming mental illness and being 'successful'. A later report, published to mark the official launch of Time to Change and co-written by former Labour Party communications director Alastair Campbell (Campbell & Jones, 2009), would suggest that one of the main discriminations that people with mental health difficulties face is being kept out of top jobs.

This emphasis on recovery as 'success' – particularly in the parameters of employment – stands in stark contrast to the conception of the recovery model, which was rooted in the civil rights movements of the 1960s and 1970s. The recovery model sought to question power and emphasised the importance of autonomy and self-determination, while attempting to shine a light on the harm emerging from coercion and medical models of psychiatry. Recovery, in this sense, meant taking back the power that was held by a select few, and ensuring that mental health treatment upheld the rights of patients. This is a long way from the idea of recovery inherent in the statement from Rethink, which presents a guise of offering something empowering, while doing little to upset the status quo.

Another significant strand here pertains to the Equality Act, which in 2010, after the consolidation of hundreds of pieces of legislation, officially declared mental illness as an equality issue for employers. Although mental illness had been included under the previous discrimination legislation, the breadth of mental health problems covered was more limited and, in some cases, the onus was on workers to prove that their condition was 'clinically well recognised' (HM Government, 1995). By contrast, there is now an official responsibility on employers to understand the impacts of particular mental health problems, and for workers to explain the adverse effects of their condition on their 'day-to-day activities'. In turn, employers are obliged to make reasonable adjustments if they know, or could be reasonably be expected to know, about the illness in question.

A report published in the same year as the Equality Act found that only 23% of managers were able to name a single mental health condition (The Shaw Trust, 2010). This strengthened the assertion of campaigns like Time to Change that the main problem we face is mental health stigma, or a lack of awareness around mental health problems. It was suggested that mental health could be improved if people could be helped to conquer their fear of speaking up. It was another academic finding, however, that really gave weight to these emerging campaigns. The 2007 British Adult Psychiatric Morbidity Survey (McManus et al, 2009) had found that, at any given time, one in four British adults would be experiencing a diagnosable mental health problem. The 'one in four' figure was leapt on by mental health charities, who began to exclaim that these one in four people were likely to be our friends, family members and colleagues. The inherent belief seemed to be that, once the public realised this truth, the problems of mentally distressed people would begin to melt away.

Much like the inconvenient political truths in the occupational health reports of the 1960s, these efforts ignored many of the additional findings emerging from these data (The Shaw Trust, 2010). For example, later analysis found that job insecurity, being in debt and working at the bottom of the occupational hierarchy were all strongly and independently associated with depression (Meltzer et al, 2010). However, these subsequent findings seemed to matter little once the terms of the Time to Change campaign had been set. It adopted the narrative that 'success' for people living with mental health conditions meant being able to find employment, and a key barrier to success was the presence of mental health stigma. In order to break this barrier down and change the hearts and minds of employers, what was needed was for those with mental health problems to share their personal stories and experiences. It was 'time to talk'.

Changing hearts and minds

While they persistently encourage us to talk about mental health, campaigns like Time to Change fail to address the structures of power and interest that shape what workers can say and when. The prevailing idea seems to be that, simply by gathering management and colleagues around for a coffee morning and sharing a personal narrative of mental distress, a person will be protected from any future prejudice and discrimination. I would suggest not only that this is naïve about how change occurs, but also that such practices may even be actively harmful for some workers. The employer's concern for mental health, couched though it may be in this positive language of encouraging open discussion, might never truly be authentic. At the forefront of the organisational mindset will always be the crude economic calculus wherein the main problem with mental distress is its impediment to productivity. This reality leaves workers at a cruel impasse, since those in low paid, insecure work, who have little autonomy – ie. those workers most at risk of mental distress at work (Thorley & Cook, 2017) – are the very same workers who might stand to lose the most by being candid about their unhappiness. If the only resources they have to support them are some flyers and bunting for their annual coffee morning – rather than, say, the long-term support of their union and an awareness of their employment rights – sharing personal experiences of mental distress can be actively harmful for workers. As Ivor Southwood demonstrates in Chapter 1 of this book, all they may be doing is drawing attention to themselves as a threat to productivity. A survey of the English public's attitudes to mental health indeed found that the percentage saying they would not feel comfortable talking to their employer about their mental health actually rose by a quarter from 2010 to 2012 (Time to Change, 2015). Is it any coincidence that, at the same time, the use of zero-hour contracts began its dramatic rise, with the number of workers on zero-hour contracts doubling from 2010 to 2012 (Pennycook, Cory & Alakeson, 2013)?

Nestled in the middle of Mind's 2016 annual report is the surprising fact that, while more than 700 employers to date had signed the Time to Change 'employer pledge', demonstrating their 'commitment to change how we think and act about mental health in the workplace and make sure that employees who are facing these problems feel supported', only slightly more than half had actually changed HR policies and practices as a result. Figures like these highlight the toothless nature of workplace wellbeing campaigns like Time to Change. What matters from the perspective of the employers backing such campaigns is that workers 'feel supported', not that workplace practices and balances of power are genuinely tipped in favour of the worker. As a result, anti-stigma campaigns and talk sessions might merely be just another way in which employers manage their workers' emotions.

Another issue we might consider here is the extent to which telling stories about mental distress might *itself* constitute a kind of labour. Although many workers may now feel that they are being encouraged to speak up about mental distress, it is often employers that take and run with these stories, releasing them into the public domain in order to project an image of themselves as supportive and benevolent. That many people who choose to speak up about their distress at work no longer get to harness the power of personal testimony only shows how far we have drifted from the radical aims of talking about our mental health. In the context of encouragement from employers to speak about mental health, it would be wise to ask ourselves what ends our personal testimonies serve. The Reclaiming our Stories Collective, a loose group of Canadian scholars and activists, has argued that, rather than promoting any form of structural change, personal testimonies often function to strengthen an organisation's professional reputation and brand (Costa et al, 2012). The group produced a series of information cards highlighting some points to think about for anyone considering sharing their story. They should ask themselves:

- Who profits from you telling your story?
- What purpose does personal story sharing serve?
- How do large organisations use stories to make material change?
- Story-telling is an exercise of labour/work. Do you get paid for telling yours?

Such questions seem particularly pertinent in the context of initiatives such as Time to Change's 'champions' scheme, which encourages workers to become champions of mental health in the workplace. Although Time to Change states that this is a voluntary and flexible commitment, suggested activities for champions include running workshops and events on the theme of mental health. There is no mention, however, of the significant unpaid labour that might be involved in such a role. In encouraging employers to sign the Time to Change employer pledge, the point is made that 'mental health is an issue your organisation can't afford to ignore… [as it costs] an average of £1,035 per employee per year' (Time to Change, 2018). If Time to Change champions are sharing difficult personal stories, chairing workshops to improve mental health literacy and spreading awareness of mental health issues, then it would seem only fair that they receive some of the dividends from any emerging financial savings. Sadly, it is unlikely that employers would fully agree to such a proposal, and, in any case, personal stories about the experiences of mental distress should be harnessed to fulfil greater potential than merely cutting employers' costs and improving productivity. Instead, there is a need for workers to consider how they can harness the value of their stories in order to fulfil more radical ends. We must collectively consider what it is worth to speak up and how we can organise to protect each other when we do choose to speak. Most importantly, however, if we begin to share our stories with more radical aims in mind, how do we make sure that we will continue to be listened to?

Ticking all the wrong boxes

If talking about mental health at work has often served the employer more than the worker, another way in which our personal testimonies can lose their radical potential is when they are simply distilled down to quantitative data. The Mind Workplace Wellbeing Index, launched in 2016, sought to survey workers and produce metrics that would 'celebrate the good work employers are doing to promote and support positive mental health, and to provide key recommendations on the specific areas where there is room to improve' (Mind, 2017). Mind has stated that the index explicitly draws inspiration from the work done by the Stonewall Equality Index, which seeks to encourage LGBTQ+-inclusive workplaces. Before launching the index, Mind commissioned Deloitte to carry out a series of interviews with organisations across the UK, in order to better understand their workplace wellbeing needs. Conveniently for Mind's ongoing work, this research found that measuring baseline performance via tools like their index was central to improving processes and measuring change within workplaces. As a result, this means that the path employers will take to try to improve workplace mental wellbeing is already laid out before them, with the experience of their workers simply abstracted to data points that indicate how great an effort should be made to change current processes. In this system, workers merely answer questions provided to them, with no opportunity to ask questions of their own. The meaning of the stories they tell has been decided in advance.

A recurrent theme in all the informational materials for the index is that participation will involve celebrating the good practice that is already present in the organisation. This means that the key 'buy-in' for employers is to gain the positive reputational benefits that come from participating in the index and emerge with the argument that what they are already doing is, if worth celebrating, then probably already sufficient. Participation grants all employers a gold, silver or bronze medal (compared with the Stonewall Index, where only the top 100 (about 20% of all annual participants) are rewarded), meaning it may be several years before workers are ever even questioned again about improving mental health at work.

A similar survey-based approach to measuring and trying to improve practices for disabled staff was previously established in the NHS and further demonstrates how such schemes can be used by employers to simply rest on their laurels as champions of a certain equality cause. The 'Two-Tick' scheme grants participants the opportunity to use and display the 'Two-Tick' logo once they have agreed to take action to meet five commitments relating to the employment, retention, training and career development of disabled employees. However, research by academics from Middlesex University, who had been commissioned to appraise the scheme, found that, unless it shed its neoliberal underpinnings, it was unlikely to help those it claimed to in any real way. They suggested that, with no clear business case for fulfilling the five commitments of the index, employers may well simply display the Two-Tick symbol for impression-management purposes (Ryan et al, 2016).

The inaugural *Impact Report* for the Mind Workplace Wellbeing Index (Mind, 2017) makes clear that the index aims to carry on the ineffectual approach to mental health and disability adopted by the Two-Tick scheme, while also placing the business case front and centre. The foreword to the report suggests that 'FTSE 100 companies that prioritise employee engagement and wellbeing outperform the rest of the FTSE 100 by 10 percent. By supporting staff wellbeing, they reap the benefits through enhanced... productivity and profitability' (Mind, 2017). It is worth considering this emphasis on FTSE 100 companies. The hundred firms listed on the FTSE 100 are there not because they are the largest companies in the UK or because they employ the most workers, but because they have the highest market capitalisation. Implicitly, Mind is drawing a link between participation in their index and the financial prosperity of the firm and the UK economy. Top professional organisations may continue to engage with the index for its reputational benefits, but it seems unlikely that any benefits will trickle down to the most overworked, underpaid and mentally distressed employees.

The main problem is that the terms of reference for the discussion on workplace practices and processes that can impact on workers' mental health are set and owned by Mind, rather than the workers themselves. The issue here is perhaps not with the survey method *per se*, but with the fact that the parameters of the discussion have been set out in advance, and from above. For example, the worker's inquiry, a proposal made by Marx in 1880, involved the preparation of a comprehensive questionnaire aimed at uncovering the conditions of life and work among the labouring classes. The difference here, however, is that the survey was by and for workers. It sought to change the world from the worker's point of view, combining knowledge production with collective organising from the bottom up. The socialist journal *Notes from Below* has recently sought to revive these methods and has undertaken workers' inquiries with hospitality workers, couriers and university staff. It argues that a contemporary questioning and understanding of how workers are managed and organised grants workers the confidence and ability to change these structures from below.

Mental health charity campaigners, policy researchers and business leads envisage a workplace in which a coffee morning can easily be held, a poster encouraging us to speak up can be tacked to the wall or an employer can buy into an expensive index. But, in the process, they have colonised ground from worker-led movements, setting the parameters and goals of the discussion about mental health at work. What is more, the offices in which the coffee mornings are held and the posters tacked up may represent only a partial slice of the labour market, at best. Current forecasts suggest that some of the most rapidly growing areas of employment are in roles such as personal care assistants, home health nurses and cleaners (UKCES, 2014). We have also seen the rapid rise of workers in the so-called 'gig economy' – those drivers and couriers who ferry food and people around our cities, without standard workplace protections like guaranteed hours or holiday pay. These roles are increasingly being filled by a hyper-exploited class of workers, who complete this work in fragmented chunks, often for very low wages and with almost no protections. The workplace wellbeing initiatives discussed so far will clearly never reach these workers.

Great dream

I have discussed the way in which our stories about distress at work have been blunted and exploited, filtered through the more ineffectual rhetoric of 'anti-stigma' or used to generate data that, in the last instance, belong to and serve the organisation. One final way in which our stories are divested of their radical potential is through initiatives that seem designed to convince us that the problem was with us all along. We are told that our situation does not require concerted organisational and structural change and can actually be improved with a greater commitment to self-maintenance and personal wellbeing.

A poster from the organisation Action for Happiness adorns my old workplace kitchen. It is there to remind me about the acronym GREAT DREAM, to prompt me to look after my mental health. One by one, the letters instruct all workers to take proactive steps for their happiness by, among other things, 'Giving', 'Exercising' and finding 'Meaning'. Each of the bullet points in the acronym is laid out in bold primary colours, against a backdrop not unlike a child's drawing: a blue sky adorned with clouds, a horizon adorned with green shrubbery. However, the idyllic nature of this background could not be further from the reality of the many cramped and dingy office kitchens across the UK on whose walls the poster may be taped. The instruction to find 'meaning' seems particularly cruel in the context of a 2015 YouGov survey finding that 37% of people in the UK thought that their job made no meaningful contribution to the world (Dahlgreen, 2015). 'Giving' presents a similar irony. While it emphasises the happiness benefits of 'doing things for others', it neglects to consider the context in which people are making these gestures of goodwill. Amid substantial cuts to public services in the UK, it is estimated that unpaid carers are providing £57 billion worth of free social care annually (ONS, 2017). Welfare claimants have also been compelled to 'Give' by the instruction that they perform unpaid labour (or 'volunteer') as a condition of their benefits. This can culminate in a Kafkaesque situation where someone can be both a food-bank user and a volunteer, and end up preparing a food parcel for themselves.

Although perhaps unremarkable in itself, the GREAT DREAM poster is just one example of the infantilising nature of many workplace wellbeing initiatives that, rather than inviting a concerted discussion around the causes of distress, present workers with a series of personal choices or 'life hacks' to improve their happiness and wellbeing. This approach chimes with what the critical psychologist David Smail describes as the ethos of 'magical voluntarism': the idea that, through sheer will, a person can change their own world – a world for which they are, in the last analysis, responsible – so it no longer causes them distress (2005). Magical voluntarism is the purest distillation of the aspirational viewpoint that frames individuals as strivers within a fully meritocratic system. It serves to elide the realities of power, class and inequality, suggesting that individuals can be anything that they want to be, so long as they adopt the right attitudes and have the will.

The presence of magical voluntarism in a therapeutic context inverts the relationship between the individual and their social environment, so that the person becomes, in effect, the creator of their own world. Smail argues that this inversion suits the interests of those who assert it and those who assent to it (2005). It benefits the therapists and counsellors who assert it because maintaining the notion that the patient is in charge of their world allows professionals to justify their practice and sustain their ongoing careers. It benefits the patient because it makes them feel empowered – however false or compromised their agency might really be.

It is also easy to see the interests served by magical voluntarism outside the therapy room and in the workplace. Workplace wellbeing is a multi-million-pound business and a social issue that many employers want to be seen publicly to care about, but not at the expense of ultimate economic goals such as productivity and profit. The appeal of magical voluntarism is that it takes the onus off the employer to make any substantial changes to organisational structures and norms. It is easier, and less threatening to the organisation, to task workers with the childlike duty of imagining and willing into being the world they want to inhabit. We are told that creating this world then just comes down to a series of 'choices' that will magically bring happiness into being. We are treated like children whose imaginations need to be set loose, rather than intelligent adults who aspire to a better world of work, achieved through strategic and collective action. To paraphrase Freud (as Smail himself does), there are significant vested interests in portraying 'neurotic misery' as simply the mask of 'common happiness'. Infantilising workers with wellbeing tips is a far safer approach than allowing them to collectively unmask the commonality of their misery at work and take action.

Overall, then, it seems that organisations like Action for Happiness end up producing a lot of bright and positive materials that, on closer inspection, are rather ineffectual and incoherent, not to mention infantilising. 'Consciously choosing to find ways to increase happiness at work can make a difference to how we, and others, feel and how well we do' (Action for Happiness, 2018a); 'People who tried using their strengths in new ways each day for a week were happier and less depressed'; 'Do something supportive and friendly for your colleagues'; 'Say friendly things to people who work in your local shop or café'; 'Gaze up at the stars and realise we are part of something bigger' (Action for Happiness, 2018b). At best, such suggestions might offer only a temporary respite from distress.

The power of silence

What is left to say when the way in which we talk about our distress at work has either been managed and minimised, used to generate data for the benefit of employers or filtered through the language of anti-stigma? Perhaps having a concerted discussion about the relationship between work and mental distress first involves grappling with the realisation of just how far we have drifted from collective action to applying individualised sticking plasters to our distress. Inherent in the conception of the trade union movement was the realisation that wage labour should provide sufficient rights and material resources to maintain the mental health of all those engaged in work. But the increased micromanagement of our working lives has drawn the focus away from such demands.

In the face of the constant assertions that we need to speak up about our mental health, particularly at work, perhaps the strongest immediate stance we can take is that of silence. Although this may sound like a retreat, there is still much that we can do collectively in the silence before speaking up. Implicit in that silence is a withdrawal of the unpaid labour that comes from sharing our stories – stories that employers can then use to gain their reputation as champions of mental health. Not speaking up means rejecting the coercion that may be a part of having to tell our stories, and recognising that, if we do share our stories, we deserve to retain ownership of what we say. Refusing to describe the nature of our distress at work could also mean disavowing the quantification of our wellbeing as merely an input into a calculation to maximise productivity. Withdrawing our inputs into these processes could bring into focus the inauthenticity of our employers' expressed concerns for our mental health.

The calls to speak up have been so loud and so frequent that we must now press pause, seek to regain control over the discourse and steer the conversation towards more radical ends. With the urgency of the demand to talk about mental health ringing so loudly in our ears, we often overlook the fact that speaking up without first pausing to think often serves to keep the discussion contained within the existing frames of reference. New and different conversations will need to focus on how we can protect one another in the process of talking about our distress. They will involve calling out the inequalities, imbalances of power and lack of rights that impact on mental health at work and resisting invocations to simply accommodate ourselves to the realities of our lives. They will involve channelling our anger, frustration and anxiety, while still defending the joy of our collective pursuits. The picket line of the past was a much more reliable space where these discussions could flourish. We need to consider how we can revive such spaces, and create new ones, in order to speak out. If Action for Happiness is telling us to connect with others, then we should demand more free time to do so. We must contest the notion that recovery is achieved when we get a job and allow for the creation of stories that emphasise different ideas about what constitutes success. Most importantly, we must begin to reclaim our stories as a radical and political form of knowledge that highlights social injustice and the ills of work. Through sharing these and collaborating together, we may begin to consider the more radical aims that lie on the other side of silence.

References

Action for Happiness (2018a). *Action 49. Find happiness at work.* [Online.] Action for Happiness. www.actionforhappiness.org/take-action/find-happiness-at-work (accessed 7 January 2019).

Action for Happiness (2018b). *Monthly action calendars.* [Online.] Action for Happiness. www.actionforhappiness.org/calendars (accessed 7 January 2019).

BBC News (2006). *Churchill sculpture sparks uproar.* [Online.] BBC News; 11 March. http://news.bbc.co.uk/1/hi/uk/4795832.stm (accessed 7 January 2019).

Campbell A, Jones M (2009). *A World Without: the fantastic five.* [Online.] Time to Change. www.time-to-change.org.uk/sites/default/files/World%20Without%20report.pdf (accessed 7 January 2019).

Costa L, Voronka J, Landry D, Reid J, Mcfarlane B, Reville D, Church K (2012). Recovering our stories: a small act of resistance. *Studies in Social Justice* 6(1): 85–101.

Dahlgreen W (2015). *37% of British workers think their jobs are meaningless.* [Online.] YouGov. https://yougov.co.uk/news/2015/08/12/british-jobs-meaningless/ (accessed 7 January 2019).

Davies W (2015). *The Happiness Industry: how the government and big business sold us well-being.* London: Verso Books.

Health and Safety Executive (2017). *Work Related Stress Depression or Anxiety Statistics in Great Britain, 2017.* [Online.] National Statistics. www.hse.gov.uk/statistics/causdis/stress.pdf (accessed 7 January 2019).

HM Government (1995). *Disability Discrimination Act 1995.* [Online.] London: HM Government. www.legislation.gov.uk/ukpga/1995/50/introduction (accessed 7 January 2019).

Hochschild AR (2012). *The Managed Heart: commercialization of human feeling* (3rd ed). Berkeley, CA: University of California Press.

McManus S, Meltzer H, Brugha TS, Bebbington PE, Jenkins R (2009). *Adult Psychiatric Morbidity in England, 2007: results of a household survey.* Leeds: NHS Information Centre for Health and Social Care.

Meltzer H, Bebbington P, Brugha T, Jenkins R, McManus S, Stansfeld S (2010). Job insecurity, socio-economic circumstances and depression. *Psychological Medicine* 40(8): 1401–1407.

Mind (2017). *Mind's Workplace Wellbeing Index 2016/17: key insights.* London: Mind.

Mind (2016). *Report of the Council of Management Year Ended 31 March 2016.* London: Mind.

Office for National Statistics (2017). *Unpaid Carers Provide Social Care Worth £57 Billion.* [Online.] Newport: ONS. www.ons.gov.uk/peoplepopulationandcommunity/healthandsocialcare/healthandlifeexpectancies/articles/unpaidcarersprovidesocialcareworth57billion/2017-07-10 (accessed 7 January 2019).

Pennycook M, Cory G, Alakeson G (2013). *A Matter of Time: the rise of zero-hours contracts.* London: Resolution Foundation.

Ryan P, Edwards M, Hafford-Letchfield T, Bell L, Carr S, Puniskis M, Hanna S, Jeewa S (2016). *Research on the Experience of Staff with Disabilities within the NHS Workforce: project report.* London: Middlesex University.

Segal L (2017). *Radical Happiness: moments of collective joy.* London: Verso Books.

Smail D (2005). *Power, Interest and Psychology: elements of a social materialist understanding of distress.* Ross-on-Wye: PCCS Books.

The Shaw Trust (2010). *Mental Health: still the last workplace taboo? Independent research into what British business thinks now, compared to 2006. [Online.]* Bristol: Shaw Trust. https://trajectorypartnership.com/wp-content/uploads/2013/09/Mental-Health-Report.pdf (accessed 7 January 2019).

Thorley C, Cook W (2017). *Flexibility for Who? Millennials and mental health in the modern labour market.* [Online.] London: IPPR. www.ippr.org/publications/flexibility-for-who (accessed 4 January 2019).

Time to Change (2018). *Employer pledge.* [Online.] Time to Change. www.time-to-change.org.uk/get-involved/get-your-workplace-involved/employer-pledge (accessed 7 January 2019).

Time to Change (2015). *Attitudes to Mental Illness: 2014 research report.* [Online.] Time to Change. www.time-to-change.org.uk/sites/default/files/Attitudes_to_mental_illness_2014_report_final_0.pdf (accessed 4 January 2019).

TUC (1880). *Trades Union Congress Annual Report.* [Online.] London: TUC. www.unionhistory.info/reports/ContactSheet.php (accessed 7 January 2019).

UK Commission for Employment and Skills (2014). *Careers of the Future.* [Online.] London: UKCES. https://assets.publishing.service.gov.uk/government/uploads/system/uploads/attachment_data/file/391911/15.01.05._UKCES_Career_Brochure_V13_reduced.pdf (accessed 7 January 2019).

WEAREPLANC (2014). *We are all very anxious: six theses on anxiety and why it is effectively preventing militancy, and one possible strategy for overcoming it.* [Blog.] Plan C; 4 April. www.weareplanc.org/blog/we-are-all-very-anxious/#f1 (accessed 19 January 2019).

3

Understanding affective labour: the demand for workers to really care

Jamie Woodcock

Jamie Woodcock is a researcher at the Oxford Internet Institute, University of Oxford. He is the author of Working the Phones, *a study of a call centre in the UK, inspired by the concept of the workers' inquiry. He is currently researching with workers in the so-called gig economy.*

The role of emotions at work has intensified with the rise of new kinds of service work. The importance of this 'emotional labour' was demonstrated by Arlie Hochschild in her book *The Managed Heart* (2012), where she documented her famous study on the emotional labour of flight attendants. Here she defined emotional labour as 'the management of feeling to create a publicly observable facial and bodily display'. This form of labour is central to customer service roles, from hospitality to call centres, and is integral to how products and services are marketed, sold and consumed. Emotional labour has also historically been divided along gendered lines, de-valued, and often classified as unskilled, if it is acknowledged at all.

Subsequent to Hochschild's book, 'emotional labour' has been developed into the broader concept of 'affective labour'. The key difference here is that, if feelings are *personal* and emotions are *social*, affects are *prepersonal*. Affect is a 'non-conscious experience of intensity; it is a moment of unformed and unstructured potential' (Shouse, 2005). This broader conceptualisation – to which I will return – serves to help us understand what is at stake in new forms of work, and particularly how capital can tap into this potential. The affective definition therefore 'refers equally to body and mind' and the labour involved 'produces or manipulates affects' (Hardt & Negri, 2004: 108) – something more complex than only emotions.

The use of affective labour at work is increasing across sectors and becoming an important new area in which capital seeks to extract value. In the workplace itself, this is expressed as a new demand for qualities like positivity, authenticity and spontaneity. The pressures documented by Hochschild can also be clearly seen in today's call centres (Woodcock, 2017). Affective labour, like all kinds of labour at work, has at its core an indeterminacy. When an employer buys someone's time, they only purchase a potential. This is a key problem for management: how to extract the most from the labour power they have purchased, complicated by the fact that it is embodied in people whose interests differ from the interests of the organisation. This challenge is further complicated with affective labour, which is even more indeterminate and nuanced. This often leads to ridiculous management strategies such as call-centre 'buzz sessions', designed to prepare workers before a shift.

> [Buzz sessions are] an opportunity for the company to remind workers of the different rules, stress the importance of quality, and then attempt to encourage some kind of enthusiasm for the upcoming shift. The content of these sessions varied, but most involved playing some sort of game. These range from competitions testing product knowledge (perhaps not the most exciting) to word games – for example, each person in turn shouting out the name of a country, following alphabetical order with no repetition, eliminating those who fail to do so until only the winner remains. Although being made to play children's games was somewhat demeaning, it did offer the benefit of stretching out the time before we had to be on the call-centre floor. (Woodcock, 2017: 40)

This chapter will explore why these sorts of 'buzz sessions' take place, along with how the workplace is changing, both in customer service roles and more broadly. It begins with an example from my own work experience of using affect by text to set up the discussion of what constitutes emotional and affective labour. The chapter then moves on to discuss how affective labour is organised at work, before considering the negative personal effects of this kind of work, particularly in relation to mental health. While the implications for workers are considered, the chapter also discusses the possibilities for resistance and the subversion of affective labour.

Affect by text

In 2009, I worked for a very unusual company in what was – technically – my first research job. The role involved responding to questions submitted by the public via SMS text message. The service was used by people without immediate access to the internet or a smartphone (these were less widespread at the time), or often by people who were simply too inebriated to find the answer for themselves. Although, several years later, this service sounds quite anachronistic, even at the time I was surprised that people would use SMS services to get answers to questions – especially given the steep cost per message.

Over the course of my job, I never met anyone from the company: not during the recruitment process, and not while I worked for them. In an arrangement that has become far more commonplace with the rise of Uber and Deliveroo (Waters & Woodcock, 2017), I was falsely categorised as 'self-employed'. In this way, the company operated like an online platform. There was a forum for workers to communicate, but this was administrated by managers and mainly provided advice on how to deal with the problem of registering for self-employment, tax and national insurance.

I had only one client, the company, which had developed a piece of software that distributed the incoming text messages to the workers who were logged in. I did not respond from my own phone; instead, the system operated like a call centre, distributing incoming and outgoing messages. I could choose to log in whenever I wanted and was paid a small fee per answer. The organisation of the work was therefore closely mapped to the demand for the service. Although I could log in whenever I chose, I found I could only make money at particular times. The peak times to work were easy to gauge, particularly as the programme provided a numerical indication of the current incoming texts. Visually, the programme itself was fairly basic and lacked any aesthetic appeal. It was much closer to Ceefax than modern websites, with lots of grey space and clashing RGB colours. There were options similar to the call centre, allowing the worker to log in, enter a waiting/idle mode or log out.

As soon as I logged in, the flow of questions would begin streaming in. The text of the question would be displayed, a second-by-second timer would start ticking and I would be given the option to accept the question or skip. Skipped questions would be sent to other active users before re-entering the queue. Skipping a question also counted negatively towards my performance metrics, which were displayed at the side of the screen. They included things like length of time active, questions successfully answered, and so on.

Once a question was accepted, the option to reply became activated. This created something analogous to the 'assembly line in the head' that Taylor and Bain (1999: 109) have discussed in the context of call centres. This is the feeling of pressure that takes hold when the automated system sets the pace of the work. The difference between my job and a call centre is that my shift did not have a set length, and nor did it involve the direct intervention of a supervisor. Instead, the logic of reaching targets was effectively internalised. If you wanted to take a break or slow down the pace of work, you could – so long as you were prepared to receive less money. The positive side is that, with no direction from management, the labour process could be performed in different ways. I could ignore the often-arbitrary rules from the call centre, such as scheduled and timed toilet breaks, uniform requirements and so on (Woodcock, 2017). I would sometimes watch TV in the background or listen to my own choice of music while working. These changes make the labour process more bearable, but the online nature of the work also isolates the worker.

After I had responded to a question, the online system would send my response to the customer in the form of a text. The response itself was limited to a character length of 160, and therefore involved a counter (similar to the one on Twitter). The demand for brevity was therefore a significant part of the labour process – I needed not only to find a suitable answer but also to be able to express that answer in a suitable format. There was a specific rule-set for acceptable abbreviations and these rules had to be learned in advance (or looked up when answering, which increased the time it took to complete responses). The computer system also provided a list of answers that had been provided to similar questions. This search function meant that if someone, say, had asked which takeaways were open at 4am in Northampton, recent answers would appear on my screen. These could have been provided to customers automatically, but the worker was expected to double check for validity (considering things like whether the answer previously provided was recent, whether the takeaways had different opening hours on weekdays, and so on). Clicking the answer copied it over into the reply, where it could then be modified before sending.

This meant that there were two broad categories of questions: those that could be replied to rapidly with a stock answer (perhaps even risking the information being incorrect) and those that required some research. Broadly, there were four kinds of typical questions: first, obvious questions that could be answered very quickly; second, challenging questions that required research beyond using Google; third, questions from people who were high or drunk and did not necessarily make sense, and fourth, stupid questions that did not really have an answer. The worker was expected to go beyond just providing an answer – by, as the company explained, 'being accurate and by adding value in terms of relevant content, style, humour, personality'. What was unusual about this requirement was that workers were expected to take on the persona of the company, presenting themselves as some sort of omniscient artificial intelligence. Unlike in a call centre, in which workers draw on their own personalities (or at least the performance of a personality), this meant drawing on emotional or affective dimensions while performing as a non-human. Customers would regularly follow up with questions about the company – was it an artificial intelligence? How was it automated? Was it 'real'? – and these became another option to display 'humour' or 'personality'. Just like in many other forms of work, this affective labour had to be performed according to strict requirements and under significant pressure. The difficulty of doing this was neither recognised nor remunerated by the company.

Emotional and affective labour

Emotions, like communication, have always played a part in collective work. Even when Marx was writing, there were huge numbers of domestic servants (even more than there were industrial workers) – a form of labour that very clearly involves emotional engagement. As Dalla Costa and James have remarked in relation to the role of the housewife: 'Where women are concerned, their labour appears to be a personal service outside of capital' (1972: 10). Despite technological innovations and new consumer goods, the housewife 'is always on duty, for the machine doesn't exist that makes and minds children' (p11). The gendering of work (and what is considered to be work) has involved devaluing the work and skills historically associated with women. Care and domestic work are neither remunerated nor, often, considered to be *real* forms of work.

Yet the emotional labour associated with domestic work has now become part of the capitalist labour process, where it is managed and regulated. My experiences of sending 'humorous' text-message replies involved this kind of emotional labour, and so too does the way that call-centre workers are routinely expected to bring more to a call encounter than just verbally reproducing the script. They must do it with feeling, reminding us once again of Hochschild's study of flight attendants, who were told by their trainers and managers to 'smile like you really mean it' (2012).

The growth of the service sector has seen increasing numbers of workers subjected to these requirements, in sectors including care work, office work, shopping and hospitality, to name a few. What is important to note is that, across many of these organisations, what is being sold is not a finished commodity but a service. Hochschild argued that the emotional style of offering the service has become part of the service itself. In other words, the worker's feelings and emotional conduct have become a key part of how money is made and profit extracted. This means that emotions are no longer personal; instead, 'emotional labour is sold for a wage and therefore has exchange value' (Hochschild, 2012: 7).

The historical division of emotional labour along gendered lines has rendered it invisible in a number of ways. For example, Adkins and Lury (1999: 605) argue that:

> ... women do not gain and retain jobs because of the particular
> occupational resources they possess... but rather they are employed as
> 'women' with an assumed responsiveness.

This contrasts, they argue, with men, who are more likely to be hired on the basis of their skills – and often these are not skills that have a recognised emotional component. In this sense, emotional labour has become a normative expectation of women, and is perceived to be a 'natural' component of femininity rather than a distinctive skill.

Pan (2014) illustrates a number of these dynamics in a discussion about public relations (PR) – a profession composed mostly of women. Pan argues that 'in PR, a certain overlap of professional and personal relationships is not only likely, but ideal' (2014). The labour process involves the 'expression of enthusiasm for a product because of pay rather than passion' (Pan, 2014), which has resulted in workers being criticised for their 'phoniness'. When journalists launch an attack on bad PR, 'the unspoken heart of their criticism is the failure on the part of the publicist to adequately conceal that she is performing emotional work for money' (Pan, 2014). Whereas the artist or cultural producer follows their passions seemingly regardless of money, those who perform passions or emotions for money are often degraded and undervalued in this way.

We find a good example of this policing of affective labour in the case of the coffee shop chain Pret à Manger, where workers are subjected to a complex set of management tactics to maximise affect while they are selling coffee. All new staff are given a book of 'Pret Behaviours', divided into 'Don't want to see',

'Want to see' and 'Pret Perfect!'. If this does not sound dystopian enough, these behaviours are policed by mystery shoppers – assessors posing as customers, who buy their coffees and then write up detailed reports on the performances of the workers. The outcome of these undercover operations, which take place every week, determines whether all the staff at that outlet receive a bonus (Preston, 2012). This functions to make workers feel responsible for one another's bonuses and leads to them effectively policing each other, as well as being policed by the mystery shopper (Kinniburgh, 2013).

It seems the demands of affective labour have developed extensively since Hochschild first documented the phenomenon. The 'outward countenance' of the worker – to use Hochschild's term – is now mediated through a complex package of affects. The affective labour process attempts to produce 'intangible feelings of ease, excitement, or passion' (Hardt & Negri, 2000: 293) across more and more contexts. This is not only in the context of selling services, but also in a:

> ... series of activities that are not normally recognized as 'work' – in other words, the kinds of activities involved in defining and fixing cultural and artistic standards, fashions, tastes, consumer norms, and, more strategically, public opinion. (Lazzarato, 1996: 133)

Call centres

In the UK, call-centre work has become almost universally reviled, both by workers and customers. When employment agencies ask prospective recruits whether they are prepared to go to a call centre, it often comes with the warning that 'this job isn't for everyone!' (Woodcock, 2017: 149). Call centres have become a flagship example of emotional labour managed under particularly oppressive technological control. As Enda Brophy explains:

> Working in a call centre tends to include a well-established mix of low wages, high stress, precarious employment, rigid management, draining emotional labour and pervasive electronic surveillance. (2010: 471)

In the call centre, a worker is expected to go significantly beyond simply reading out a script. In high-volume sales call centres, like the one I worked in to research my book, *Working the Phones* (Woodcock, 2017), this brought an additional quality to the labour process that was difficult for managers to measure and regulate. It meant workers had to use their emotions to bring a script alive, and also to manage the customer's emotions – particularly anger (Deery, Iverson & Walsh, 2002). Call-centre work thus becomes a complex process, the 'outward countenance' of Hochschild's emotional labourer now mediated through the demand to 'smile down the phone' (Taylor & Bain, 1999: 103). Since workers in a call centre are never face-to-face with their customers, this performance must be achieved verbally, through the tone and pace of speech and the choice and emphasis of particular words.

The technologies of control in the call centre allow for the collection of precise quantitative data on a whole range of different variables, including the number of sales, length of calls, time between calls, length of breaks and so on. This surveillance technology allows for 'an acceleration of the rhythm of work, achieved by the elimination of the workday's "pores" (that is, of "dead" production time)' (Marazzi 2011: 76). However, the affective dimension is indeterminate by nature, and is hard to capture, measure and compare between different workers and calls. It is here that the electronic surveillance becomes less useful to organisations and, rather than monitoring what workers are doing, the chief concern becomes regulating how they are doing it.

It is here that we find a contemporary variation of 'Taylorism' (named after Frederick Taylor, the inventor of scientific management and the so-called Taylor System). Taylor pioneered the famous time-and-motion studies that were conducted in factories to break down the labour process into discrete tasks that could be precisely timed and measured. Taylorism is thus the use of measurement and control to micro-manage the labour process in order to extract the greatest efficiency possible (Braverman, 1999). Comparing the Taylorist factory with the 'electronic Taylorism' of the call centre, Cederström and Fleming write that the latter demands 'every fiber of your organism to always be switched on' (2012: 7). Today 'the enemy of production is what human resource managers like to call presenteeism: being present only in body with every other part of you being far, far away' (2012: 7). Supervision becomes not only about monitoring whether the worker is doing the correct action, but also about ensuring that they are *feeling* the right way about it. In this way, emotional labour demands a high degree of authenticity: the display of emotion must feel real.

This requirement introduces new challenges for workers. In the call centre, like many workplaces, aspects of 'creativity' and 'self-expression' have become intrinsic to labour, resulting in 'affective, as well as productive demands on workers' (Fisher, 2009: 40). In circumstances where call centres are located in different countries to their customers, the job also involves an additional demand for 'authenticity' with respect to race and geographical location (Mirchandani, 2012). Indian call-centre workers, for example, are now increasingly pressured into using names that are more similar to those common in the countries where their clients are calling from. They may also be required to learn contextual information about topics like the local weather and sports results at the start of their shifts, in order to be able to pretend they are in the same country.

The problem for management is how to measure whether workers are meeting these emotional demands. The obsession for electronic surveillance in the call centre allows the minute monitoring of a whole range of quantitative aspects, but these qualitative aspects remain elusive to managers and are a constant source of conflict. In pursuit of work discipline, managerial techniques are introduced to overcome the intransigence of emotions and affect. The 'buzz session', for example, aims to motivate workers before they start calling, but there is no real consensus on how to do this.

In their study of 'Sunray Customer Service' (a pseudonym), Cederström and Fleming describe such management initiatives as an attempt 'to inject life into the dead-zone of work' (2012: 10). It is at this point that managers implore workers to 'just be yourself!', with the obvious but obscured caveat that self-expression can only take a form that harmonises with the organisational goal of increasing sales. Unlike working on an assembly line, work is by this point no longer about turning up and completing set tasks. The worker must be seen to participate in a particular way. The claim that buzz sessions and other extra-curricular activities are 'fun' also involves a coercive side. Anyone who fails to embody the spirit of fun risks being labelled a party-pooper, 'the most serious crime you could commit' (Cederström & Fleming 2012: 16) – workers are expected not only to commit time and efficiency; they are required to enjoy the process too. The question that remains is what effect these demands have on the workers subjected to them on a daily basis.

Mortification of body and mind

The control and disciplining of emotions and affect at work have serious implications for workers' health. As Marx noted (in the gendered language of the time), alienated labour has a profound effect on the worker: it 'mortifies his body and ruins his mind' (1844/1988). I have previously written this about my own experience of working in a call centre:

> The affective package that workers are required to perform during
> the labour process is demanding. The experience was exhausting and

emotionally draining. From my own experience of working eight-hour afternoon/evening shifts – unfortunately also complemented with a morning of reading and writing about call centres – the labour process was exhausting. In particular it made social phone calls something to avoid, as I became unable to break out of the routinised pattern of sales calls; in-person conversations became difficult too. Arriving home by about 10pm, my food preparation fell into a pattern of baked beans on toast, followed by slouching on the sofa watching television. (Woodcock, 2017: 53–54)

I was aware of the stress of the work – it was hard to miss. However, the depth of the effects only really became clear to me at the launch of my book. An audience member asked about the effects of working in a call centre for my mental health and I quickly gave the deluded reply that it had not really been an issue. A friend in the crowd – who I had lived with at the time – then spoke up for me. He explained that, actually, I had noticeably suffered during the time, with observable effects on both my mental and physical health. Call-centre workers are often left with an echo of the labour process that continues after work: things like a whooshing noise from when the next call connects, which continues when you use the phone for other calls. The emotional toll of the work makes escaping the call centre harder, particularly when trying to relax afterwards. You no longer want to use any phones at all.

One of the reasons that call-centre work is so draining is that the requirement to produce emotions on demand results in a kind of 'emotional dissonance' (Morris & Feldman, 1997). This is the experience of having to express an emotion that is not actually felt – an internal contradiction that results in increased strain and exhaustion. In her study of flight attendants, Hochschild referred to this as the 'pinch' (2012: xi) – a conflict between the feelings of the worker and the company's demand for authenticity. In a call centre, emotional dissonance might lead to the 'feelings of guilt and stress callers experience as they try to convince customers to buy insurance while maintaining a positive and enthusiastic demeanour' (Woodcock, 2017: 53). A study of Australian call-centre workers warns that 'emotional dissonance may ultimately lead to lowered self-esteem, depression, cynicism and alienation from work' (Lewig & Dollard, 2003: 368). Franco Berardi has summarised the problem: 'Communication loses its character of gratuitous, pleasurable and erotic contact, becoming an economic necessity, a joyless fiction' (2003: 87). Instead of constituting an enrichment of experience, the invitation to communicate at work has become an impoverishment. For Berardi, what is represented in modern forms of affective labour is not just the industrial exploitation of bodies, muscles and arms, it is the soul itself that has been put to work (Berardi, 2003: 21).

In the BBC documentary 'The Call Centre' (2013), the owner of the company, Nev Wiltshire, articulates the problem from a manager's perspective: 'Happy people sell, miserable bastards don't. Isn't that right?' A powerful responsibility is placed on workers to perform in a certain way, regardless of any emotional challenges they may face. In a later scene in the documentary, for example, the camera focuses on workers receiving torrents of abuse down the phone from prospective customers. The workers find it difficult to cope but the managerial response reframes the problem, not in terms of substandard products and uninterested customers, but rather as a problem with the attitude of the workers. What is needed is further coaching and training to force workers to admit where they went wrong and commit to improving their conduct. This attempt to get workers to internalise and take responsibility for the problem is deeply pernicious, and is itself a further source of distress, as workers are encouraged to blame themselves for the difficult client calls. This in turn contributes to an individualising environment, where workers are encouraged to make sense of their distress in terms of individual failings rather than the atrocious working conditions.

Towards an alternative

At present, the ability to mobilise emotions in the labour process seems like a particularly human activity – something that could not be adequately replicated by machines. Whether sending 'humorous' text messages or making emotionally persuasive phone calls, it appears that human labour remains essential to the process, especially when sales are involved. However, given that automation continues to become a possibility for a growing range of work tasks, it would perhaps be a mistake to rule out emotional domains as ripe for automation. The use of emotions by low-paid workers is, in any case, rarely a genuinely human experience, as 'even a child... knows that the smile and "have a great day" from a customer-service-worker is fundamentally creepy' (Cederström & Fleming 2012: 7). It isn't easy to fool people into believing that an emotion is real, whether the performance is by a human or a machine. When emotions are put to work, the customer often finds the interaction robotic.

The possibility of a robot engaging in emotional or affective labour would first require us to bridge what, in videogame circles, is often called the 'uncanny valley'. Before the invention of photorealistic game graphics, it mattered less to people that virtual creations could not accurately show emotions. However, as technological sophistication increases, the 'virtual characters approaching full human-likeness will evoke a negative reaction from the viewer, due to aspects of the character's appearance and behaviour differing from the human norm' (Tinwell et al, 2011: 1). The uncanny valley describes the paradoxical way in which it becomes harder for people to relate to virtual characters as they become more life-like, and represents a difficult sticking point in the virtual representation of emotions. Yet there is always the possibility of exiting the valley with new technological developments. The videogame journalist Alec Meer, for example, explains how the facial animations in the latest *Call of Duty* game represent a new leap: 'I'm not saying it's real. But I'm saying it's an awful lot more convincing than anything else I've played in my life' (2017). It seems feasible that virtual and robotic substitutes could replace certain spheres of emotional labour in the future, but it is also important to recognise that this would not necessarily liberate human workers. The tendency of automation is often to displace human labour into other sectors of work. In the case of artificial intelligence, innovations ride on the hidden labour of human workers behind screens across the world, who are labouring in conditions so bad as to induce regular emotional 'meltdowns' (Roberts, 2016: 5).

What is perhaps required is not simply the automation of undesirable emotional labour but greater recognition of emotional labour as a form of personal estrangement, and an attempt to challenge this through action. This action would not have to appeal to some idea of an essential, universal, non-alienated human nature in order to have legitimacy. There is simply a need to counter the previous invisibility of emotional labour by recognising that it is both a skilled and potentially damaging form of work. There is a need to shift the critical focus away from workers' apparent 'failure to perform' and onto the structural demands of affective labour. There is a need to recognise the struggles and refusals of workers as a point of strength and a latent form of resistance. And there is also a need to ask questions about what kind of work is useful and work that we want to do, and whether the emotions might be put to work in more worthy ways.

References

Adkins L, Lury C (1999). The labour of identity: performing identities, performing economies. *Economy and Society 28*(4): 598–614.

BBC (2013). *The Call Centre*. [TV documentary.] London: BBC.

Berardi F (2003). *What is the Meaning of Autonomy Today?* [Blog.] Republicart; September. http://republicart.net/disc/realpublicspaces/berardi01_en.htm (accessed 7 January 2019).

Braverman H (1999). *Labor and Monopoly Capitalism: the degradation of work in the twentieth century*. London: Monthly Review Press.

Brophy E (2010). The subterranean stream: communicative capitalism and call centre labour. *Ephemera 10*(3/4): 470–483.

Cederström C, Fleming P (2012). *Dead Man Working*. Winchester: Zero Books.

Dalla Costa M, James S (1972). *The Power of Women and the Subversion of the Community*. Bristol: Falling Wall Press. https://libcom.org/library/power-women-subversion-community-della-costa-selma-james (accessed 19 January 2019).

Deery S, Iverson R, Walsh J (2002). Work relationships in telephone call centres: understanding emotional exhaustion and employee withdrawal. *Journal of Management Studies 39*: 471–496.

Fisher M (2009). *Capitalist Realism: is there no alternative?* Winchester: Zero Books.

Hardt M, Negri A (2004). *Multitude: war and democracy in the age of empire*. New York, NY: Penguin Putnam.

Hardt M, Negri A (2000). *Empire*. Cambridge, MA: Harvard University Press.

Hochschild AR (2012). *The Managed Heart: commercialization of human feeling*. Berkeley, CA: University of California Press.

Kinniburgh C (2013). Partial readings: the smile economy, Nick Kristof's hugs, tweeting about tipping. [Online.] *Dissent*; 9 February. www.dissentmagazine.org/blog/partial-readings-the-smile-economy-nick-kristofs-hugs-tweeting-about-tipping (accessed 7 January 2019).

Lazzarato M (1996). Immaterial labour. In: Virno P, Hardt M (eds). *Radical Thought in Italy*. Minneapolis, MN: University of Minnesota Press (pp133–150).

Lewig KA, Dollard MF (2003). Emotional dissonance, emotional exhaustion and job satisfaction in call centre workers. *European Journal of Work and Organizational Psychology 12*(4): 366–392.

Marazzi C (2011). *Capital and Affects: the politics of the language economy*. Semiotext(e) foreign agents series. Los Angeles, CA: Semiotext(e).

Marx K (1844/1988). The *Economic and Philosophic Manuscripts of 1844* (Milligan M trans). New York, NY: Prometheus Books.

Meer A (2017). *Call of Duty WW2 has solved face-rendering – and it scares me*. [Blog.] Rock Paper Shotgun. www.rockpapershotgun.com/2017/11/23/call-of-duty-ww2-graphics/ (accessed 7 January 2019).

Mirchandani K (2012). *Phone Clones: authenticity work in the transnational service economy*. London: ILR Press.

Morris JA, Feldman DC (1997). Managing emotions in the workplace. *Journal of Managerial Issues 9*(3): 257–274.

Pan J (2014). Pink collar. [Online.] *Jacobin*; I July. https://www.jacobinmag.com/2014/06/pink-collar (accessed 7 January 2019).

Preston R (2012). Smiley culture: Pret à Manger's secret ingredients. *Daily Telegraph*; 9 March. www.telegraph.co.uk/foodanddrink/9129410/Smiley-culture-Pret-A-Mangers-secret-ingredients.html (accessed 21 February 2019).

Roberts ST (2016). Commercial content moderation: digital laborers' dirty work. In: Noble SU, Tynes B (eds). *The Intersectional Internet: race, sex, class and culture online*. New York, NY: Peter Lang Publishing (pp147–160).

Shouse E (2005). Feeling, emotion, affect. [Online.] *M/C Journal 8*(6). http://journal.media-culture.org.au/0512/03-shouse.php (accessed 4 January 2019).

Taylor P, Bain P (1999). An assembly line in the head: work and employee relations in the call centre. *Industrial Relations Journal 30*(2): 101–117.

Tinwell A, Grimshaw M, Williams A, Abdel Nabi D (2011). Facial expression of emotion and perception of the uncanny valley in virtual characters. *Computers in Human Behaviour 27*(2): 741–749.

Waters F, Woodcock J (2017). Far from seamless: a workers' inquiry at Deliveroo. [Online.] *Viewpoint Magazine*; 20 September. www.viewpointmag.com/2017/09/20/far-seamless-workers-inquiry-deliveroo (accessed 19 January 2019).

Woodcock J (2017). *Working the Phones: control and resistance in call centres*. London: Pluto Press.

4

Reproducing anxiety: social reproduction and communities of care

David Berrie and Emily McDonagh

David Berrie has been an organiser in the group Mental Health Under Capitalism since its beginning and has also been involved in various other autonomous left groups throughout his life. He lives in south-east London and sells his labour as an art psychotherapist.

Emily McDonagh has also been an organiser in Mental Health Under Capitalism since its beginning and has been involved in a number of groups and projects on the autonomous left. She lives in north London and works as an assistant psychologist, with a particular interest in working with survivors of trauma.

Anxiety seems increasingly to colour our experience of relationships, work and life more generally. While anxiety is not a new phenomenon, we believe its ubiquity today is a pressing political issue and presents a useful point of departure when trying to understand contemporary problems of work. As the anti-capitalist group Plan C puts it:

> Today's public secret is that everyone is anxious. Anxiety has spread
> from its previous localised locations (such as sexuality) to the
> whole social field. All forms of intensity, self-expression, emotional
> connection, immediacy, and enjoyment are now laced with anxiety. It
> has become the linchpin of subordination. (Plan C, 2014)

State mental health services reflect the ubiquity of anxiety, with Improving Access to Psychological Therapy (IAPT) services in the UK designed predominantly to treat anxiety and depression. NHS research estimates that 17% of adults experience a 'common mental health disorder' and over half of these cases are anxiety related (McManus et al, 2016). Significantly, women are twice as likely to be diagnosed with anxiety disorders compared with men (Martin-Merino et al, 2009). With this comes a booming industry in pop-psychology and self-help.

The problem with many psychological models, however, is that they approach anxiety as an individual problem. In mental health services, the medical model is still prevalent. Meanwhile, individualist therapy models such as cognitive behavioural therapy (CBT) or dialectical behavioural therapy (DBT) are promoted above alternatives like community psychology or systemic therapy, which place symptoms within relationships and wider social structures. Furthermore, existing research in the field often overlooks the familiar and constant low-level anxiety with which many people live daily, without these feelings reaching the thresholds for access to mental health services. This prevalence of anxiety suggests it cannot be explained purely in individual or medical terms. It instead reveals something about our shared existence in society.

Any chapter-length attempt to address the complexities of anxiety will of course be partial, and here we have chosen to focus on the relationship between anxiety and the organisation and control of labour under capitalism. We define labour in a broad sense, as waged and unwaged, productive and reproductive, physical and immaterial. At the heart of the problem we perceive an absence or unreliability of care and social bonds in people's lives that, coupled with increasing demands on workers, leads to an everyday normalisation of anxiety.

We will start by developing a working description of anxiety. How is it experienced? What processes and dynamics are involved? We begin with ideas from Freud, and move through Donald Winnicott and John Bowlby, thinking about anxiety as a product of severance from care and social bonds. However, the limitations of these approaches will lead us to also introduce the idea of 'social reproduction', as understood by the Wages for Housework movement. By social reproduction we mean the unwaged labour involved in maintaining ourselves and each other: sustained efforts of mutual care, the fostering of supportive relationships, the raising of children and the provision for everyday needs, such as food, clothing and shelter.

We go on to explore how social reproduction is organised, distributed and controlled in the capitalist present, using Marx's concept of 'subsumption'

– a process in which more and more aspects of social life are incorporated into the capitalist production process. We claim that a number of capitalist trends have undermined the care that each of us relies on. With the failure to match the entrance of women into the sphere of paid work with a rebalancing of care responsibilities or a reduction in work-time, care is often carried out in the form of a 'second shift', under the stressful conditions of overwork. Furthermore, as capitalism's market logics of productivity, standardisation and calculability seep their way into the caring professions, the autonomy of care workers and their ability to adequately provide care have also been compromised.

Finally, capitalism has also commandeered our capacity for caring for the sake of profit and enlisted our capacities for emotional or relational work into the production process itself (see Jamie Woodcock's Chapter 3 in this book). We will also think about what this means and argue that the accumulation of these trends has created a crisis of care under capitalism, and a corresponding and pervasive sense of anxiety.

Our response to the problem of anxiety is to explore the possibilities and limitations of a 'care strike', running in parallel with the creation of new communities of care, or what we might call the collectivisation of social reproduction. To these ends, we will finish by telling the story of Mental Health Under Capitalism, a group that attempts to put these ideas into practice.[1]

Anxiety

Anxiety can be experienced in various ways. Some people experience dizziness, tiredness, heart palpitations and muscle ache; others describe dry mouth, sweating, shortness of breath, nausea and difficulty sleeping. The experience is comparable to fear: an anticipation of danger and feelings of being overwhelmed or 'on edge'. For some, anxiety can develop into panic attacks. In Franco 'Bifo' Berardi's words, anxiety creates the feeling of being 'unable to govern your own body' (Berardi, 2010: 36).

In *Inhibitions, Symptoms and Anxiety,* Freud distinguished between 'primary' and 'signal' anxiety (Freud, 1959). His argument is that babies are born totally dependent on carers for survival and exist in a confused, fragmented and helpless state. Anything that threatens to separate the baby from its carers can therefore be experienced as traumatic or unbearable.

---

1. Although we do not claim to represent the group as a whole, the ideas in this chapter draw from our experience of being a part of Mental Health Under Capitalism, so we would like to thank all those involved.

This is what Freud defines as primary anxiety. Unable to do anything about this separation from the carer, the infant represses its primary anxiety. This becomes what Freud calls signal anxiety – an unconscious reference that anxiety-provoking situations in later life warn against. Others, such as John Bowlby and Donald Winnicott, developed these insights further.

Bowlby saw the spatial proximity and emotional availability of carers as crucial to an infant's emotional development. For him, attachment relationships are rooted in a deep-seated biological need for care (Bowlby, 1997), and it is the absence of secure attachment relationships in infancy that forms the foundations of anxiety. At first, babies find distance from their carers intolerable, but gradually, as their attachments become more secure, the infant's tolerance for distance grows. Working with evacuee children in World War 2, Donald Winnicott developed the comparable idea of *holding*. In infancy, the infant's helplessness and state of 'unintegration' means they are unable to live or develop without caring relationships. Holding is the vital form of care needed in this early stage of dependency (Winnicott, 1960). As the term suggests, holding involves the physical act of embracing, but it also involves routines of care like feeding, cleaning and help sleeping. Holding also involves the reliability, sensitivity and attention of the carer and their responsiveness towards the infant's needs, particularly when the infant is unable to communicate these needs verbally. For Winnicott, holding is the combination of these elements – this 'total environmental provision' (Winnicott, 1960: 43).

Holding protects the child's emerging sense of continuity and coherence from complex and confusing sensations and experiences outside its control and understanding (Winnicott, 1956). Without holding, the infant becomes overwhelmed – the earliest experience of anxiety. Particularly intense experiences can surpass the protection holding provides, overwhelming or traumatising the child. Gradually, as the infant becomes able to signal its needs and desires more clearly and the carer learns to respond to its cues and demands, it is able to move from a state of 'unintegration' to one of 'structured integration'; the caring or holding relationships provide a frame for it to venture out to experience, understand and interact with the world, always with the possibility of rapid return, should it encounter anything too strange or hostile.

What is key for our argument is the way in which both Bowlby and Winnicott saw anxiety as related to the potential loss or instability of care and emotional availability. 'It is the child's fear of separation that leads them to display acute anxiety. Having experienced it previously as distressing in the carer's absence, when something suggests separation, anxiety follows' (Bowlby, 1973: 26-27). Seen this way, *anxiety communicates a need for care.*

Winnicott qualified his ideas with the suggestion that childcare only needs to be 'good enough' and recognised the great emotional and physical cost of holding for the carer (Ogden, 2004). However, critics of both Bowlby and Winnicott have suggested that their theories of development place high expectations on the parents, who are expected to completely identify with the child's needs, often at the expense of their own (Slochower, 2014: 11; Dalley, 1988: 95), and, under the capitalist organisation of child rearing, it is women, mothers, who bear the brunt of these expectations (Federici, 2012: 16-17). In fact, it is pertinent to note that carers *themselves* can experience anxiety as a result of the intense demands of child-rearing, which is to say that carers need care too (Winnicott, 1960: 49).

These high demands of caring reveal some of the shortcomings of a purely psychoanalytic understanding of care. In focusing on parent-child relationships, psychoanalysis tends to naturalise care and family relationships along heteronormative and patriarchal lines, or view the relations of care in ahistorical terms (for example, Harris, 1997; Layton, 2004). We also need to take into account the fact that the need for holding never really disappears: as people grow older, they still experience a need for holding, but this care tends to come from more dispersed relationships and structures. Friends, family, partners, comrades, communities and institutions all provide (or fail to provide) holding. Holding depends on the physical and emotional efforts of individuals within particular social structures. To really understand the roots of anxiety in the present day, we therefore need to perceive the provision of holding as a form of labour, embedded in the wider systems and organisation of work under capitalism. There is a need to think about how the labour of holding is distributed, and how it links to exploitation, inequality and control. What are the relations, burdens, failures and inequalities of care under capitalism? It is here that the concept of 'social reproduction' has proven useful.

Social reproduction

Karl Marx understood that our ability to work, our labour power, is not a natural given but must be constantly reproduced (1908: 585). In order to be available for the production process, people (traditionally men) need to be fed, clothed, rested and emotionally prepared for the trials of the day. During the 1970s, feminists involved in the Wages for Housework movement, such as Silvia Federici, stressed the centrality of unpaid domestic labour for this reproduction of labour power (Federici, 2017: 88–89). Vital activities, such as raising children, cleaning, cooking and caring, are performed disproportionately by women, whose labour is absolutely essential in making workers available for employment. For example, a worker in a traditional nuclear family comes home from work, his dinner is on the table, and his wife consoles him as he complains about his day. She provides comfort, warmth and holding, so he can get up and do it all again tomorrow. As Selma James wrote:

> First it must be nine months in the womb, must be fed, clothed and trained: then when it works its bed must be made, its floors swept, its lunchbox prepared, its sexuality not gratified but quietened, its dinner ready when it gets home... This is how labor power is produced and reproduced when it is daily consumed in the factory or the office. To describe its basic production and reproduction is to describe women's work. (James, 1972: 11)

By calling for a refusal of socially reproductive work, feminists like Federici and James helped reveal the gendered division of labour that is fundamental to the capitalist organisation of production. What was previously seen as part of a woman's 'natural' activity and attitude was redefined as exploited labour (Dalla Costa, 1972).

> We are told frequently that women are more intuitive, more empathetic, more innately willing and able to offer succor and advice. How convenient that this cultural construct gives men an excuse to be emotionally lazy. How convenient that it casts feelings-based work as an internal need, an aspiration, supposedly coming from the depths of our female character. (Zimmerman, 2015)

While this realisation has been key in women's labour struggles, it can be argued that, by identifying socially reproductive labour mainly with the family and household, the Wages for Housework movement ended up proposing too narrow a definition of social reproduction (Weeks, 2011: 225). What is clearer today is the extent to which capitalism has gained control of socially reproductive labour, incorporating it, commodifying it and exploiting it for the purposes of private profit. The service industry, for example, which encompasses sectors from hospitality to retail, education, advertising and health and social care, depends extensively on socially reproductive labour. In these sectors, workers are tasked as much with producing relationships and emotions as with producing material goods (Morini, 2007). It is indeed not uncommon to see job adverts use phrases such as 'join our family', or workplaces focusing on 'team spirit' and conviviality. Companies like Pret à Manger even go so far as to enforce 'friendliness' between staff (Myerscough, 2013). Is this simply ideological fluff, or does it tell us something about the attempt to draw social reproduction into the workplace?

We have also witnessed the expansion of the care industry; for-profit care providers are a rapidly growing sector in Western economies. As the privatisation of state services continues and public subsidies are removed, profits are increasingly sought through the control and exploitation of socially reproductive labour (Marie, 2017). From the care industry to cleaning, cooking and childcare, social reproduction is increasingly commodified into services, even when the cost of these services makes them inaccessible to many, including those who work in them.

However, it is clear that capital cannot turn all socially reproductive activity into waged labour. There must remain a sphere of activity 'outside' production, reproducing labour power and thereby making production within the economic sphere possible. What is left is still mostly performed by women, who essentially work an unpaid 'second shift' outside the formal economy (Hochschild, 2003). Since the 1970s there has been a move to maximise women's involvement in waged labour again (Marie, 2017), but this move has not been matched by an equal effort to relieve women of their caring roles or to increase the free time available to men. As a result, social reproduction becomes 'crushed by the general intensification of labour, by the over-extension of the working day amidst cuts to resources' (Dalla Costa, 1995: 13). We know, for example, that the UK saves approximately £60 billion a year thanks to unpaid carers (Office for National Statistics, 2016). We end up with a situation in which many women are working every waking hour, at increasing costs to their physical and mental health. Although unpaid, this activity remains structured by capital through the time constraints imposed by waged work, through financial constraints and through the norms of gendered and racialised divisions of labour.

Subsumption

In the context of our discussion about the rise of anxiety, what we need to ask is why our personal and social needs are not being met by the organisation of socially reproductive labour under capitalism. It is here that we have found Marx's concept of subsumption useful. Marx uses subsumption to describe the process by which work is integrated into capitalism. Tasks that were once performed in networks outside the economic sphere are incorporated into the capitalist labour process, where they are subject to the wage relation. In the process, capitalists also direct and control the process of production, often through a detailed division of labour whereby complex work tasks are divided into simple, repetitive and measurable ones, divesting workers of their knowledge of the production process (Vercellone, 2007). This leads to rapid developments in technology and automation and provides those dramatic increases in productivity associated with industrialisation and large-scale manufacturing.

Subsumption has a transformative impact on the whole of society, including the work of social reproduction. For example, state services in the UK, such as schools, hospitals and universities, are not (yet) profit making. But their goals and aims are subordinated to the capitalist need for workers. Through marketisation and budget restrictions, they are forced to adopt similar management structures and labour processes to production in the economic sphere and are subject to the same techniques of surveillance and accounting.

Socially reproductive labour has been divided, controlled and measured to increase productivity (Hardt, 1999: 97–98). For example, the division of labour within nursing and the care industry is increasingly fragmented and hierarchically organised. Personal care involving bodily functions is valued least and the co-ordinating of care plans valued most (Twigg, 2000). Meanwhile, emotional labour and the forming of relationships – although requirements of the job – are undervalued and made invisible because they cannot be captured by accounting processes (Hunter & Smith, 2007). All activity must be measured and costed and anything escaping measurement is under-recognised and probably unpaid.

We are also seeing a standardisation and micro-management of the work of social reproduction. Marx described how capitalist organisations appropriate the knowledge of workers and codify it. Capitalism 'transforms the workers' operations into more and more mechanical ones, so that at a certain point a mechanism can step into their places' (Marx, 1971: 163). We now see this in the service industry. Consider the shop assistant who is required to follow a standardised script in their interactions with the customer. This script, repeated and repeated, eventually allows the shop assistant to be seamlessly replaced by an automated checkout machine. We see a similar process under way in NHS mental health services, with a move from long-term talking therapy to manualised CBT, as offered in IAPT services, and thence seamlessly to codified support from online and computerised self-help programmes (NHS England, 2017). In the process of subsumption, socially reproductive labour is distorted and dissected beyond recognition and workers' autonomy undermined to the extent that they can no longer provide adequate holding and care.

In another incidence of subsumption, the very complex and personal work of relating emotionally to others has also been commodified and incorporated into the capitalist labour process for the sake of profit. In her book *The Managed Heart,* Arlie Hochschild (1984) calls this style of work 'emotional labour', building her theories around an observational study of the training and daily work of flight attendants (see also Jamie Woodcock's Chapter 3 in this book). We find a situation in which organisations now have a vested financial interest in regulating employees' emotional conduct as part of the work process. Waiting staff, for example, not only serve food and drink; they are expected to ensure customers are enjoying themselves and feel cared for, and to listen to their complaints. In other words, the provision of holding has become a routine part of paid work for an increasing number of people. Emotional conduct has become a key source of economic value, and often a source of exhaustion for the people who have to summon the energy to perform it, day in, day out. Women, especially, are encouraged to instrumentalise their emotions – perhaps to gain extra money on top of wages, for example, in the form of tips. Thus capital denies workers autonomy over their emotions, using them for its own ends, and failure to perform puts workers at risk of being fired. Although it could be argued that increased opportunities to communicate and express emotions at work can bring people closer together, it often contributes to feelings of burnout: emotional exhaustion, depersonalisation and a reduced sense of accomplishment (Hochschild, 1984: 186–198).

The care strike

Marx saw objective limits to the working day, such as time for sleep, food and hygiene. He designated time to satisfy 'intellectual and social wants' as the moral limits of the working day, related to the 'general state of social advancement' (Marx, 1908: 215). What we argue is that 'social wants', such as the need for care and holding, are not simply moral limits to the working day; they are real needs – needs that have been pushed to the point of crisis.

In our view, an absence of care has been formalised within the capitalist organisation of labour. Because the entrance of women into the domain of paid work has not been matched by a re-balancing of care responsibilities, unwaged care is often provided under conditions of strain and overwork. Workers have little time available to them that is outside of capital's control where they can think of others and develop capacities for concern and empathy. There is no space for care.

Capitalism has also enrolled our capacity for emotional work and care to its own ends. It has standardised our relational capacities, intruding into a deeply private aspect of ourselves. This feeling of intrusion overwhelms our holding environment. Workers repeat emotive gestures and linguistic fragments to the point of exhaustion and absurdity. Incorporated into the ambit of waged work, emotional labour fails to reproduce communities, relationships and holding. Instead it spreads anxiety (Winnicott, 1960: 46). On top of this, forms of care or emotional and socially reproductive labour that cannot be enlisted for profit, standardised or measured have remained undervalued, unrewarded and invisible. We are left anxious and frantic in a desert of codified, mechanical exchanges, circulating capital and endless pressure. Given the key role of socially reproductive labour in maintaining the relationships, communities and sense of holding that sustain us, we should not be surprised that anxiety spreads as a result of these trends. This crisis of social reproduction is felt and expressed as the near-omnipresent, gnawing anxiety that seeps into every aspect of life: sleeplessness and strained relationships, fragmented thoughts, pervasive worry and a difficulty imagining a future worth striving for and organising towards.

How can workers respond to the crisis of care under capitalism? Despite worsening standards of living and growing inequality, we live in a period of comparatively low resistance. In the 1980s, on average, 7.2 million working days were lost each year to strikes in the UK. This declined to an average of 647,000 between 2010 and 2015. Meanwhile, work-related stress has exponentially increased. In 2016, 12.5 million work days were lost to stress, anxiety and depression (Adams, 2016). This, of course, only refers to waged work and, without doubt, other areas of life have also been put on hold due to stress and poor mental health. This is what we might think of as an automatic work refusal – the body's unthinking revolt against unbearable conditions.

The inhospitable conditions of work, combined with a crisis of care, manifest unconsciously in exhaustion, panic attacks and sick days. The challenge before us is to give political extension to these unconscious forms of resistance. We need to see how they can fuel the desire and collective effort to resist capitalism and recognise our shared interest in reducing its structural power over all our lives (Fanelli & Noonan, 2017: 142). Our embodied work refusals must be made more conscious and politically organised. We call for a care strike.

The care strike would be a conscious withdrawal of reproductive labour, taking place at various speeds – subtle and gradual, and also rapid and visible. Taking a cue from the Wages for Housework movement, we want to force socially reproductive work back into view in order to reveal its gender inequalities and indispensability for capitalism.

However, with the growing integration of socially reproductive labour within the realm of paid employment, the care strike is also a workplace struggle. Women are concentrated in industries involving large amounts of reproductive labour, such as education and healthcare, where what they do is systematically under-valued, with poorer pay and working conditions (Barrett, 1993). In these domains, a care strike might complement more traditional disruption techniques, such as blockades, workplace walkouts and sabotage.

The withdrawal of 'care' through strike action could be condemned as drastic. It is important to highlight the 'dual character' of social reproduction (Plan C, 2015). On the one hand, it reproduces workers for the production of capital; on the other, our love and care for each other is a genuine source of comfort, safety, joy and meaning. Holding is a condition of life itself, so of course we are not arguing for the abolition of care. The ultimate goal is to wrest social reproduction from the control of capital and remedy its patriarchal division of labour. The care strike encapsulates a demand for the autonomy, de-gendering and collectivisation of social reproduction.

At the same time as we withdraw care, we must also create new systems, environments and networks for caring. In our work with Mental Health Under Capitalism, we refer to this as the need for collectivised care, and point to the fact that the care strike, while necessary, is insufficient on its own. Contained in the refusal of care work is a demand for the creation of new collectives and communities not determined by capital (Dalla Costa, 1995). Luckily, there is a rich history to draw on for inspiration. Nineteenth century feminists, for example, organised communal kitchens and co-operative households and called for workers' control of social reproduction (Hayden, 1981). The East London Federation of Suffragettes established crèches and clinics, providing medicine, clothes, baby care, milk centres, information and cheap cafés for working class women (Dalley, 1988: 5). Collectives during the Spanish Civil War transformed domestic arrangements through collective child care, the sharing of responsibilities and equal incomes in the household (Richard, 1975). The Black Panther Party in the US famously organised free breakfasts for 20,000 children (Collier, 2015). Many traditional strikes would have been impossible without collectivised social reproduction, such as the soup kitchens organised by women in striking communities. The ability to reproduce workers without wages was integral to the success of many historic labour struggles. In the current decade, in Greece, we find solidarity economies and refugee-based mutual aid (Rakopoulos, 2013), and in the US, care co-operatives are forming (Kolokotrinis, 2017).

It is perhaps important to note the contrast between these examples and today's obsession with the self and self-care. We should resist the idea that the collective problem of anxiety can be solved through individual acts alone – acts that often merely boost our tolerance for the injustices of capitalism and distract attention from the need to change social structures (as described in several chapters in this book). We need collective responses to anxiety, not more individualism. We need the creation of what Federici calls 'communities of care' (Federici, 2012: 125).

'Communities' is undoubtedly a contested term. It can bring to mind tightly defined groups with shared interests and identities, or it can be associated with the negatives of nationalism and exclusion. 'Community' for our purposes means the collectivisation of socially reproductive labour and the 'commoning' of systems of care and support – a 'principle of cooperation and responsibility' (Federici, 2012: 145). We want to blur the currently rigid distinctions between political and personal life and to suggest developing solidarity as an everyday practice, through sustainable structures of mutual support – habits such as checking in on each other's wellbeing, sharing food, sharing out childcare responsibilities and forming new groups and friendships. We do not envisage this as an isolated effort; we hope to see communities of care grow into larger structures and become an integral part of organising for change. By redefining our reproduction more co-operatively, we can create self-reproducing movements and infrastructure (Anon, 2008).

This will, of course, involve challenging entrenched assumptions about care and ways of being together. Socially reproductive labour is fundamental to gender constructions (Federici, 2004), so dominant ideas of masculinity immediately present a barrier. Distributing care more equally will challenge these forms of masculinity. The role of the state also deserves considerable thought, but we do not have space to discuss this complex issue here. Let us simply paraphrase Federici, who says: 'Let the state pay for it, but we must control it' (Federici, 2012: 21). Whatever relationship the state has to our communities of care, we must demand control over our socially reproductive labour, in the confident knowledge that we have spent long enough giving it for free.

Our collectively organised care work might counter the spreading anxiety generated by capitalist work, not only by providing more robust and authentic structures for holding but also by the very act of coming together to organise for change. However, it is also important to realise that empathy, care and relationships need *time*, and it is perhaps time, above all, that the capitalist organisation of labour denies us. Significant, then, to our hope to see the emergence of new communities of care are those struggles and proposals currently under way for a reduction and redistribution of work time (eg. Stronge & Harper, 2019). The struggle for new communities of care links to struggles for a shorter working week, a redistribution of income, and other demands that fall under the broad rubric of 'post-work' politics. The less time that capitalism takes from us, the more we will have for collectivised care. And the more there is collectivised care, the more we will have scope to wage further struggles against capital's control over our lives.

Mental Health under Capitalism

Mental Health under Capitalism was formed in London in 2015. Following in the feminist tradition, it is partly a consciousness-raising group where we try to make connections between our personal experiences, capitalism and structural oppression. Yet it is also partly an experiment in collectivising social reproduction through communities of care. After many conversations and meetings on the topic of mental health in various left-wing groups, we recognised a need for spaces to talk about mental health in political yet supportive ways, and set about forming a group for this purpose.

We began meeting monthly at the Common House social centre in Bethnal Green, London. There were aims and objectives to define and difficult questions about how we would achieve them. What were the structure and purpose of meetings? Should we be involved in direct action, such as protests against cuts to mental health services and plans to offer psychological therapies in job centres (as discussed in Chapters 7 and 8)? Some of us hoped for a more theoretical direction and wanted to explore the relationship between capitalism and mental health. We came to a consensus that a group focused on discussion, support and the sharing of experiences of mental health in capitalism would be the most fruitful.

The next debate was about how to structure a 'support section', and how it should be run. Some wanted a closed therapy group, for continuity and safety. However, concerns arose about running a therapy group in case members needed additional support we could not provide. We also felt the support section should be open to anyone. Furthermore, because Mental Health under Capitalism includes members with lived experience of mental health difficulties and mental health workers, we felt it would be difficult to manage inherent imbalances of power within a therapy group.

We eventually decided to structure our meetings as follows. Food is shared before the meeting starts and we begin by introducing ourselves, our names, preferred pronouns and how we are feeling. This creates a more personal atmosphere and shows it is safe to speak. In some left-wing meetings we never learn the names of comrades, nor consider how they are feeling. Next, someone gives a short lead into the discussion topic. Some examples of previous topics are housing and mental health, hearing voices, precarious work, unemployment, police violence, relationships under capitalism, LGBTQIA+ mental health, self-care and emotional labour. We agree three discussion points, in case conversation fails to flow. Some members engage better in smaller groups; others prefer larger ones, so we use combinations of both.

After a 10-minute break, the 'support section' starts. We break into small groups of between three and four people and talk about our personal experiences in relation to the topic or simply describe how our week has been. We emphasise the confidentiality of these groups: what is discussed stays within the group. Groups thus provide a space for people to emotionally support one another, develop ideas about mental health under capitalism and create communities of care. People often comment how refreshing it is to share experiences and feel supported and less isolated.

The collectivisation of care is emphasised throughout meetings and we also try to foster relationships outside them, encouraging a culture of looking out for each other. By collectively organising care labour in this way, we are able to provide a sense of holding and reproduce social bonds relatively autonomously. Although our reach is undoubtedly limited, we hope the ideas and the effects of creating supportive spaces for care and holding in our movement resonate and are replicated.

Conclusion

When seen as a response to separation from the holding, care and community of social reproduction, anxiety is revealed as a condition of capitalist domination. In *Caliban and the Witch*, Federici describes how violence against women and the destruction and control of social reproduction enabled capitalism to expand (2004). Engels' study of the early industrial working class in Manchester also revealed a general condition of anxiety, as workers lived in constant fear of destitution (Engels, 1987). Because capitalism relies on replacing social bonds with economic ones, wherever it expands, anxiety follows.

However, we now feel anxiety even more intensely and pervasively as attacks on social reproduction become a consequence not simply of capitalist expansion but of the very way capital extracts value from labour. Socially reproductive labour is embedded in contemporary work, but is unrecognisable from the holding provided when it is not controlled by capital. With the intensification of work, lack of free time and cuts to state-provided support, anxiety has become a constant feature of people's everyday lives.

As Federici says:

> We cannot mechanize childcare or the care of the ill, or the psychological work necessary to reintegrate our physical and emotional balance... We cannot robotize 'care' except at a terrible cost for the people involved. (Federici, 2012: 146)

Unfortunately, the 'robotization' of reproduction is the direction in which subsumption takes us. Without a healthy, autonomous sphere of reproduction, capital reproduces us in its own image and we all suffer.

The combination of a care strike with new, collective forms of social reproduction would enable us to organise the work of care on our terms. Groups like Mental Health under Capitalism are attempting to achieve this. We call for new structures of care now. This is not because we want isolated, perfect communities away from confrontations with capital and the state (Gilman-Opalsky, 2014: 32); nor is it because we want to 'prefigure' the society we wish to see. We call for them now because they are weapons against capitalism. Our mental health, and sometimes our survival, also depends on them. To Marx's famous call for workers to have control over production and its organisation, we must add the call for autonomous control over social reproduction.

References

Adams T (2016). Is there too much stress on stress? [Online.] *The Guardian*; 14 February. www.theguardian.com/society/2016/feb/14/workplace-stress-hans-selye (accessed 15 January 2019).

Anon (2008). The importance of support: building foundations, sustaining community. *Rolling Thunder: an anarchist journal of dangerous living* 6: 29–39.

Barrett M (1993). *Women's Oppression Today*. London: Verso.

Berardi F (2010). *Precarious Rhapsody: semiocapitalism and the pathologies of the post-alpha generation*. New York, NY: Autonomedia.

Bowlby J (1997). *Attachment and Loss. Volume 1: Attachment* (2nded). *London:* Pimlico Publishing.

Bowlby J (1973). *Attachment and Loss. Volume II: Separation: anxiety and anger*. London: Hogarth Press.

Collier AK (2015). The Black Panthers: revolutionaries, free breakfast pioneers. [Online.] *National Geographic*; 4 November. http://theplate.nationalgeographic.com/2015/11/04/the-black-panthers-revolutionaries-free-breakfast-pioneers (accessed 15 January 2019).

Dalla Costa M (1995). Capitalism and reproduction. In: Bonefield W, Gunn R, Holloway J, Psychopedis K (eds). *Open Marxism Vol 3: emancipating Marx*. London: Pluto Press (pp7–16).

Dalla Costa M (1972). Women and the subversion of the community. In: Dalla Costa M, James S. *The Power of Women and the Subversion of the Community*. Bristol: Falling Wall Press (pp21–56).

Dalley G (1988). *Ideologies of Caring: rethinking community and collectivism*. London: Macmillan.

Engels F (1845/1987). *The Condition of the Working Class in England*. London: Penguin Classics.

Fanelli C, Noonan J (2017). Organised labour. In: Fanelli C, Schmidt I (eds). *Reading 'Capital' Today: Marx after 150 years*. London: Pluto Press (pp138–159).

Federici S (2017). Capital and gender. In: Fanelli C, Schmidt I (eds). *Reading 'Capital' Today: Marx after 150 years*. London: Pluto Press (pp79–96).

Federici S (2012). *Revolution at Point Zero: housework, reproduction and feminist struggle*. Oakland, CA: PM Press.

Federici S (2004). *Caliban and the Witch: women, the body and primitive accumulation*. New York, NY: Autonomedia.

Freud S (1926/1959). *Inhibitions, Symptoms and Anxiety*. London: WW Norton & Company.

Gilman-Opalsky R (2014). *Precarious Communism: manifest mutations, manifesto detourned*. New York, NY: Minor Compositions.

Hardt M (1999). Affective labour. *Boundary 2*: 89–100.

Harris A (1997). Beyond/outside gender dichotomies. *Pyschoanalytic Dialogues* 7: 363–366.

Hayden D (1981). *The Grand Domestic Revolution: a history of feminist designs for American homes, neighborhoods and cities*. Cambridge, MA: MIT Press.

Hochschild A (2003). *The Second Shift*. New York, NY: Penguin.

Hochschild A (1984). *The Managed Heart*. Berkley, CA: University of California Press.

Hunter B, Smith P (2007). Emotional labour: just another buzzword? *International Journal of Nursing Studies 44*(6): 859–861.

James S (1972). Introduction. In: Dalla Costa M, James S. *The Power of Women and the Subversion of the Community*. Bristol: Falling Wall Press (pp5–20).

Kolokotronis A (2017). Municipalist syndicalism: organizing the new working class. [Online.] *ROAR Magazine*; 9 September. https://roarmag.org/essays/municipalist-syndicalism-alex-kolokotronis/ (accessed 15 January 2019).

Layton L (2004). *Who's that Girl? Who's That Boy? Clinical practice meets postmodern gender theory*. New York, NY: Taylor & Francis.

Marie A (2017). Women and children in capitalism. Part 2: women in capitalism. [Online.] *New Socialist*; 18 September. https://newsocialist.org.uk/women-and-childcare-in-capitalism-part-2/ (accessed 15 January 2019).

Martin-Merino E, Ruigomez Wallander M, Johansson S, Garcia Rodriquez L (2009). Prevalence, incidence, morbidity and treatment patterns in a cohort of patients diagnosed with anxiety in UK primary care. *Family Practice 2*(1): 9–16.

Marx K (1857–58/1971). *Marx's Grundrisse* (McLellan D ed). London: Flamingo.

Marx K (1908). *Capital: capitalist production*. London: Swan Sonnenschein & Co.

McManus S, Bebbington P, Jenkins R, Brugha T (eds) (2016). *Mental Health and Wellbeing in England: adult psychiatric morbidity survey 2014*. [Online.] Leeds: NHS Digital. http://content.digital.nhs.uk/catalogue/PUB21748/apms-2014-full-rpt.pdf (accessed 15 January 2019).

Morini C (2007). The feminization of labour in cognitive capitalism. *Feminist Review 87*: 40–59.

Myerscough P (2013). Short cuts. *London Review of Books 35*(1): 25–26.

NHS England (2017). *NHS Apps Library*. [Online.] NHS England. www.nhs.uk/conditions/online-mental-health-services/Pages/introduction.aspx (accessed 15 January 2019).

Office for National Statistics (2016). *Home Produced 'Adult Care' Services*. [Online.] www.ons.gov.uk/economy/nationalaccounts/satelliteaccounts/compendium/householdsatelliteaccounts/2005to2014/chapter3homeproducedadultcareservices#gross-value-added-of-informal-adult-care (accessed 15 January 2019).

Ogden TH (2004). On holding and containing, being and dreaming. *International Journal of Psychoanalysis 85*: 1349–1364.

Plan C (2015). *On social strikes and directional demands*. [Online.] WEAREPLANC; 7 May. www.weareplanc.org/blog/on-social-strikes-and-directional-demands (accessed 20 January 2019).

Plan C (2014). *We are all very anxious*. [Online.] WEAREPLANC; 4 April. www.weareplanc.org/blog/we-are-all-very-anxious (accessed 20 January 2019).

Rakopoulos T (2013). Responding to the crisis: food co-operatives and the solidarity economy in Greece. *Anthropology Southern Africa 36*(3–4): 102–107.

Richard V (1975). Foreword. In: Leval G. *Collectives in the Spanish Revolution* (Richard V trans). London: Freedom Press.

Slochower J (2014). *Holding and Psychoanalysis: a relational perspective*. New York, NY: Routledge.

Stronge W, Harper A (2019). *The Shorter Working Week: a radical and pragmatic proposal*. London: Autonomy.

Twigg J (2000). *Bathing: the body and community care*. New York, NY: Routledge.

Vercellone C (2007). From formal subsumption to general intellect: elements for a Marxist reading of the *Thesis of Cognitive Capitalism*. *Historical Materialism 15*: 13–36.

Weeks K (2011). *The Problem with Work: feminism, Marxism, antiwork politics and postwork imaginaries*. Durham/London: Duke University Press.

Winnicott DW (1960). The theory of the parent-infant relationship. In: Winnicott DW (1965). *The Maturational Processes and the Facilitating Environment: studies in the theory of development*. London: Hogarth Press (pp37–55).

Winnicott DW (1956). Primary maternal preoccupation. In: Winnicott, DW (1992). *Through Paediatrics to Psycho-Analysis*. London: Karnac Books (pp300–305).

Zimmerman J (2015). *'Where's My Cut?' On unpaid emotional labor*. [Blog.] The Toast; 13 July. http://the-toast.net/2015/07/13/emotional-labor (accessed 15 January 2019).

5

Challenging McMindfulness in the corporate university

Steven Stanley

Steven Stanley is a critical psychologist in the School of Social Sciences at Cardiff University and currently leads the Mapping Mindfulness project, a social study of the UK mindfulness movement, funded by the Leverhulme Trust. He is a co-author of Handbook of Ethical Foundations of Mindfulness *(Stanley, Purser & Singh, 2018).*

Living, working or studying now, it is seemingly impossible to avoid encountering 'mindfulness'. Mindfulness has become part of our contemporary 'therapy culture' (Furedi, 2003). It has travelled from monastery and retreat centre into the psychological laboratory and beyond. Researchers have charted the emergence of a mindfulness 'movement' with articles bearing titles such as 'From the Bodhi tree, to the analyst's couch, then into the MRI scanner' (Cohen, 2010), 'From retreat center to clinic to boardroom' (Farb, 2014), and 'Between Buddhism and science, between mind and body' (Samuel, 2014). Inspired by Buddhist practices, and now often integrated with cognitive behavioural therapy (CBT) and positive psychology, mindfulness has become a potentially lucrative strand of the so-called 'happiness industry' (Davies, 2015). Many people are turning to mindfulness as a way of coping with mental and physical ill health, with more than two million adult Americans using mindfulness meditation for health purposes (Morone, Moore & Greco, 2017). More than 3,000 scientific articles have been published since 2010 claiming mindfulness may be a useful therapeutic intervention (American Mindfulness Research Association, 2017).

Whether presented as the latest management fad, popular self-help therapy or revolutionary 'movement', within the last 20 years mindfulness has moved into the mainstream. Travelling rapidly from the offices of counsellors and therapists, mindfulness can now even be found in the UK public sector – parliaments, job centres, and classrooms. Since 2015, the UK Westminster government has hosted a Mindfulness All-Party Parliamentary Group (MAPPG) to lobby parliament to fund the public provision of mindfulness in health, criminal justice, education and workplaces. A key aim of the MAPPG is to turn the UK into a 'mindful nation' (Ryan, 2012; MAPPG, 2015).

In the private and industrial sectors, managers have become enamoured by the potential for mindfulness to enhance worker productivity, performance, and efficiency – or at least to put a limit on their 'presenteeism'. Interest in mindfulness dovetails with broader trends in promoting resilience, happiness and wellbeing. Classes teaching mindfulness as a stress reduction technique are now commonplace in workplace and educational settings.

In this chapter, I review the roots of mindfulness and chart its parallel rise with neoliberal capitalism, specifically in relation to corporate models of higher education. I argue that, when we look at the ways mindfulness is made manifest in different contexts, we find its practice may bring outcomes unanticipated by its proponents and critics. To make this argument, I bring together scholarship on mindfulness with critical commentary on neoliberalism and how it manifests in the ethos, culture and practices of the higher education sector in the UK today. I also reflect on my own personal experience working as a university lecturer working within that milieu.

The roots of mindfulness

The common story told about mindfulness is that it is a therapeutically effective technique for the relief of stress, depression and anxiety. Along with possessing the power to release people from their distress, it is also promoted as a way of enhancing our mental health, 'wellness' and 'flourishing' during times of social, political and economic turmoil. Mindfulness, so it is said, represents ancient perennial wisdom translated for modern times and now proven by neuroscience. Proponents of mindfulness say that, to change the world, we all need to change ourselves – to learn how to be more awake, aware and attentive to the present moment, one mindful individual at a time. To change ourselves, we need to change our brains by regularly paying attention with mindfulness. This is especially the case in our digital worlds, in which our attention is increasingly being captured by internet technology companies – companies that, in turn, sell back to us 'apps' to train us in mindfulness (such as Headspace, Buddhify and Calm). It is said that the techniques and skills of mindfulness that might heal us are applicable to anyone, anywhere, and that the essence of mindfulness is universal.

If mindfulness was originally informed by Buddhism, then its Buddhist roots have been secularised for everyone's benefit, or these roots were never religious in the first place. The Buddha was, after all, the first psychologist. This is, at least, how the popular story of mindfulness tends to be told.

Taken as a whole, the mindfulness 'movement' is an Anglo-American invention with Asian roots and a transnational reach. A turf war has been going on over who 'owns' mindfulness and who has the power and authority to define it and thereby provide expert access to 'the present moment'. In a broad sense, the authority to define mindfulness has shifted away from the Buddhist monastic community and toward lay populations of American and European scientists, clinicians and professionals. The mindfulness of the modern mindfulness movement centrally comprises standardised, clinical evidence-based 'mindfulness-based' applications or interventions of various types, such as mindfulness-based stress reduction (MBSR), mindfulness-based cognitive therapy (MBCT) and mindfulness-based pain management.

Yet, when we turn to historical scholarship, we find that some of the deeper roots of the 'mindfulness-based' therapies that are now popular in the West are around 100 years old and can be found in Southeast Asia. The mindfulness movement emerges out of intercultural encounters with Buddhist cultures, especially the late 19th and early 20th century mass lay meditation movements of Sri Lanka, Myanmar and Vietnam. Buddhist teachers such as the Mahasi Sayadaw, SN Goenka and Thich Nhat Hanh adapted Buddhist practices in response to pressures from Western colonisers – especially Anglo-American missionaries, orientalists and Buddhologists. The later counter-cultural renouncers of the 1960s went in search of wisdom in Hindu and Buddhist societies and came back to Europe and America to help create the humanistic psychologies of the human 'growth' and 'potential' movements of the 1970s. The humanistic emphasis on authenticity and emotional expression was later combined with cognitive behavioural therapy, positive psychology and the measurement of national 'happiness' and 'wellbeing' by economists in the 1990s.

The fundamental role of humanistic, cognitive, and positive psychologists in revisioning and constituting mindfulness as a beneficial way of paying attention is relatively under-appreciated. Indeed, when it comes to the application of mindfulness in workplaces and educational settings, it is not easy to separate it from mid-20th century humanistic psychology and scientific management and the turn-of-the-century interest in wellbeing, happiness and flourishing in health policy and positive psychology (Caring-Lobel, 2016; Cromby, 2011). A notable example of the latter is the UK Government Office for Science's Foresight Mental Capital and Wellbeing Project and subsequent report (2008). Its recommendation to 'take notice' as one of its five 'ways to wellbeing' was inspired by mindfulness research:

> Be curious. Catch sight of the beautiful. Remark on the unusual. Notice the changing seasons. Savour the moment, whether you are walking to work, eating lunch or talking to friends. Be aware of the world around you and what you are feeling. Reflecting on your experiences will help you appreciate what matters to you. (p21)

Positive psychology, or the 'science of happiness', which underpins the Foresight report, aims to shift the focus of psychological research and applied practice away from 'negative' concepts of pathology and deficit, such as depression and anxiety, and towards 'positive' notions of happiness, wellbeing and resilience. Positive psychology has made a notable impact on wider debates in US, UK and European government health policy, as the Foresight report suggests (Pykett, Jones & Whitehead, 2017). Indeed, the Westminster government All-Party Parliamentary Group on Wellbeing Economics (2014) boasts that the UK has become a 'global leader by measuring national wellbeing', but goes on to say that evidence has not often led to policy changes. For the members of this all-party group, mindfulness is a key to unlocking the potential to improve measurements of national wellbeing.

This emerging policy focus on 'wellbeing' was initiated by the New Labour government when they initiated the Improving Access to Psychological Therapies (IAPT) programme in the 1990s to make CBT widely available in England through the NHS (explored further by Jay Watts and Paul Atkinson in Chapters 7 and 8). These trends draw upon, and feed back into, attempts by happiness economists to switch global measures of national 'Gross Domestic Product' to measurements of 'Gross National Happiness' or life satisfaction, famously initiated by the Himalayan Kingdom of Bhutan. To improve the self-reported happiness (or life satisfaction) of the

UK population, the all-party group recommended that the UK government devote funds to training health and education professionals – doctors, nurses, teachers – in mindfulness to strengthen their 'personal resources', 'improve wellbeing' and 'save public money', especially during times of economic austerity and cuts to public expenditure (All-Party Parliamentary Group on Wellbeing Economics, 2014). It is obvious, when considering these recent developments, that mindfulness is not only mainstream 'self-help', but has also become serious political business.

The Foresight report's recommendation that people 'take notice' articulates a common understanding of mindfulness that has been developed since the mid-20th century. Mindfulness itself is understood within the field in diverse ways, depending on its contexts of use. The most common professional definition to emerge is the one offered by Jon Kabat-Zinn, who developed MBSR. Kabat-Zinn is an American mindfulness teacher, trained in molecular biology, who in 1979 started a stress reduction clinic at the University of Massachusetts Medical Centre for outpatients with chronic pain. In his popular self-help book *Wherever You Go, There You Are* (1994), Kabat-Zinn defines mindfulness as an awareness that emerges when we pay attention in a particular way: intentionally, in the present moment, and non-judgementally. This definition was taken up and developed by the cognitive therapists who created MBCT in the 1990s (Segal, Williams & Teasdale, 2013). They describe mindfulness as an awareness that reorients or 'decenters' consciousness, allowing the practitioner to alternate between 'being' and 'doing' modes of mind, thus releasing themselves from the psychological and emotional cycles that lead to depressive relapse.

If you read about mindfulness in the contexts of learning and education, rather than in healthcare, however, you are more likely to come across a definition of mindfulness by the American social psychologist Ellen Langer (1989). She defines it as the creation of novel conceptual distinctions and categories, openness to new information, and an awareness of more than one perspective. She distinguishes mindfulness from 'mindlessness' and has applied her experimental studies to the process of learning (see Langer, 1997, 2000). This definition is commonly used in studies of decision-making. In organisation studies literature, you will find Karl Weick's concept of 'organisational mindfulness' is more commonly used (Weick & Sutcliffe, 2006). Nevertheless, the majority of mindfulness teachers consider Kabat-Zinn to be the founding leader of the mindfulness movement, and most use some variation of his operational definition, rather than Langer's or Weick's, when they teach and practice mindfulness meditation.

Since 2015, the field of mindfulness has continued to expand rapidly, and mindfulness can now be found in Westminster and the devolved UK governments and parliaments, in private, public and third-sector workplaces, and (notably) in schools, colleges and universities. The MAPPG asked the Secretary of State for Education in Westminster to make mindfulness training compulsory for teacher training, current teachers and teaching assistants and argued that funding for mindfulness in schools should be a priority, given concerns about a growing mental health crisis among under-18s and the promising scientific evidence base for the effectiveness of mindfulness in treating mental health conditions among adult populations (Mindfulness All-Party Parliamentary Group, 2015). The Oxford Mindfulness Centre received funding from the Wellcome Trust for a seven-year, £7-million implementation and evaluation of mindfulness in schools called Mindfulness and Resilience in Adolescence (MYRIAD), which is based on MBCT. The education sector has now become a major growth area for mindfulness provision in the UK, following mindfulness initiatives in the health, wellbeing and workplace sectors.

For and against mindfulness

Recent implementations of mindfulness in workplaces and educational settings have prompted much controversy and debate. To date, academic and popular discourse about mindfulness has been characterised by polemics, starkly polarised between proponents and critics of mindfulness. Debates have revolved especially around the ethical, social and political aspects of mindfulness in the modern world (Purser, Forbes & Burke, 2016; Stanley, Purser & Singh, 2018).

On the one hand, of the almost 3,000 psychology and neuroscience articles on mindfulness published since 2010, the overwhelming majority present positive evaluations of mindfulness as being an effective therapeutic tool. Yet, while for many people mindfulness is simply a useful self-help 'technique' to help them cope with modern living and just the latest product of the global self-help industry, for those who promote it most vigorously, it represents much more. For its most vocal advocates, the mindfulness movement symbolically transcends the materialistic and consumer concerns of business and industry. Mindfulness represents a way of living and 'being in this world', and may be our best hope for saving humanity from the worst ravages of capitalism and rescuing the planet from continued war, injustice and imminent environmental collapse. Corporate evangelists promote mindfulness as a universal panacea for world peace (Tan, 2012). And the mindfulness movement as a whole tends to be presented as a bottom-up, 'grass-roots' social movement initiated by workers, citizens and children themselves to campaign for the better provision of mindfulness to improve mental health.

On the other hand, critics argue that mindfulness has been 'over sold' (Brazier, 2013); that it is a neoliberal self-technology that medicalises, psychologises and individualises wellbeing and suffering (Arthington, 2016). The mindfulness movement, or revolution, in America has recently been interpreted as a top-down, elite-led social movement, promoting 'trickle-down' mindfulness for the masses (Kucinskas, 2019). Purser and Loy (2013), for example, expose 'McMindfulness' as a capitalist bandwagon: a 'fast-food' style of training especially adapted to corporations. For them, McMindfulness is the 'shadow' of the mindfulness movement that corporations use as a 'stripped-down', secularised technique, or form of 'banal, therapeutic, self-help', to shift the blame for stress away from the institution and onto individual employees.

According to this argument, managers may use mindfulness to place the responsibility for health and illness squarely on the shoulders of their employees. Indeed, managers may even use the rhetoric of mindfulness to present institutional change and reorganisation – and any resulting job losses – as being 'natural' consequences of unavoidable, changing circumstances (Cederström & Spicer, 2015). This naturalising of change is well illustrated in the discourse of Kabat-Zinn (1994) himself, when he suggests: 'You can't stop the waves, but you can learn to surf.' If we go along with his argument, the routine reorganisation (or 'redisorganization', as Oxman and colleagues (2005) put it) of private businesses and public institutions is the result of natural causes rather than human agency. If one of the functions of ideology is to soften or conceal the workings of power, thereby making inequality and injustice seem natural (Eagleton, 1991), then mindfulness might play an ideological function in our society. Social, political and institutional change might be assumed by corporate leaders and managers to be the result of natural changes, like the changing of the seasons. There is no alternative to permanent change.

Critiques of the mindfulness movement mirror the broader critiques that have been made of 'therapy culture' since the mid-20th century. In *The Culture of Narcissism*, Christopher Lasch (1979) argues that the focus on 'the now' or the 'present moment' in what he describes as the 'awareness movement' – the 1970s human potential movement – is de-politicising and ahistorical. In paying attention solely to the present moment, we risk forgetting the past – a historical amnesia. The teaching of mindfulness, with its emphasis on 'being in the present moment', may, sometimes quite subtly, encourage anti-intellectualism, political quietism and employee pacification (Purser, 2015). Slavoj Žižek makes a similar criticism of the Western Buddhist 'meditative stance' as the 'paradigmatic ideology of late capitalism', which allows the meditator to:

> ... fully participate in the frantic pace of the capitalist game, while sustaining the perception that you are not really in it, that you are well aware how worthless the spectacle is – what really matters to you is the peace of the inner self to which you know you can always withdraw. (Žižek, 2001: 12–13)

Carrette and King (2005) show how Asian mind-body disciplines and training regimes such as mindfulness have been psychologised as 'spiritualities' in order to accommodate people to the society in which we live. They suggest that practices such as mindfulness, when transformed into a therapeutic technique, may encourage 'accommodation' to the status quo. The awareness or mindfulness movement, therefore, represents a continuation of the self-spirituality so central to the New Age, in which therapy may go hand-in-hand with selfish consumption. Mindfulness, along with the broader therapy culture, may encourage a self-absorbed narcissism. The American Buddhist monk Bhikkhu Bodhi similarly argues that 'absent a sharp social critique, Buddhist practices could easily be used to justify and stabilize the status quo, becoming a reinforcement of consumer capitalism' (cited in Eaton, 2013).

The rise of the corporate university

Debates at the intersection of mindfulness, therapy culture and consumerism can be similarly applied to the topic of mindfulness in higher education. As many commentators have pointed out, universities, especially in the UK, are increasingly modelled on corporate business. Critical studies of universities use various terms to capture this trend – the corporate, neoliberal or entrepreneurial university. Deem (2004) describes how 'contemporary business practices and private sector ideas or values have permeated publicly funded institutions and work practices' (p288), which she names as 'New Public Management'. Universities are commonly understood as companies or corporations; vice chancellors as chief executive officers (CEOs); staff and educators as service providers and sales people, selling educational products and offering educational services, and students as customers, consumers and clients who buy their 'student experience' in the same way that they would buy a consumer product.

A key driver influencing this corporate model of higher education was the introduction in 1997, by the New Labour government, of £1,000-per-year tuition fees for undergraduate students in England and Wales. These were increased to £3,000, and then to £9,000 in 2010 by the Coalition government, and are expected to rise further in the future. The idea of the university student as primarily a consumer was officially instituted in UK higher education policy in 2005 with the introduction of the National Student Survey (NSS), and is now part of the shared common sense of university staff and students alike. The NSS is basically a customer satisfaction survey, the results of which feed into national university league tables and are reported in our national newspapers. The newly developed Teaching Excellence Framework (TEF) further extends this spirit of evaluating teaching and learning from a consumerist perspective, awarding institutions gold, silver and bronze medals for 'teaching quality', based largely on student retention rates, NSS scores and graduates' employability and earnings.

The main question about higher education from a consumer point of view is whether you are 'satisfied' with the educational product you have purchased. Is the product value for money? Some commentators compare university attendance to taking out membership of a gym. Just as it is up to the gym member to take advantage of the gym equipment, it is up to the individual student whether they take advantage of the 'learning opportunities' made available to them upon payment of their fees (for a critique of this argument, see Rivers & Webster, 2019).

The introduction of tuition fees, along with the accompanying idea that students are customers seeking the best 'value for money' from their courses, has meant that university staff and students are sometimes pitted against each other within an increasingly hostile and brutalising corporate-style environment. For example, university teaching and administrative staff are pressured by their managers to promote the National Student Survey (NSS) to their final year undergraduate students, in part to improve their institution's status in university league tables. The NSS asks students how 'satisfied' they are with the 'quality' of their course and their 'student experience'. By positioning students as customers and implying that the 'customer is always right', politicians and university leaders challenge the traditional authority of universities and university staff. The University and College Union and

National Union of Students have both urged their members to boycott the NSS for perpetuating the marketisation of higher education, corroding the value of learning and undermining relations between students and staff (University and College Union, 2018).

The rise of the corporate university seems to have gone hand-in-hand with a gradual corrosion of basic human rights and loss of values of dignity and respect between staff and students alike. This erosion can sometimes be subtly felt in our ordinary, everyday working and studying lives. In my 15 years as a lecturer, I have noticed a growing absence of ordinary human practices of gratitude and appreciation in the academy. Education, particularly undergraduate education, which is subject to tuition fees, is increasingly experienced as an economic exchange, rather than as involving a reciprocity of human relations. Unlike the audience of an academic conference, who will clap at the end of each talk, students do not routinely clap at the end of a lecture. In 'delivering' my lecture, I am expected to have provided students with a product that they have paid for with their tuition fees (or will do, when they reach a certain earning threshold, once qualified and employed). Students and staff alike seem to have internalised the corporate ethos of the university as a business and to have lost sight of the simple reciprocity of human relations involved in teaching and learning. I have come to feel eager, sometimes, to be thanked by students at the end of my classes. But, more often I will instead thank them for attending and listening to me.

Yet it is, arguably, the casualised and precarious workers, especially postgraduate research students, graduate teaching assistants (GTAs) and part-time teaching staff, who feel the violence arising from academic capitalism most acutely (Jones & Oakley, 2018). It has been estimated that over 50% of academics teaching or doing research in British universities are on so-called 'atypical' fixed-term contracts, which includes short-term, insecure, non-permanent, hourly-paid and 'zero-hours' contracts (Chakrabortty & Weale, 2016). Around three quarters of junior academics, who are most likely to be doing frontline teaching, are on these kinds of precarious contracts.

The idea that higher education is principally an economic exchange can be traced to the neoliberal political reforms of the US and UK economies from the 1970s onwards. Neoliberal ideology was developed especially during the Thatcher (UK) and Reagan (US) governments of the 1980s. Their emphasis on 'freeing' university institutions, academics and students to pursue their 'enterprise' and engage in unfettered competition within a free market is still present within contemporary political discourse and education policies now.

Researchers argue that, in the last 30 years, higher education has progressed from an 'elite' model to a 'mass' model – what academics call 'massification' – with some suggesting that a 'universal' model of higher education now prevails (Billig, 2013). The historian Anthony Grafton (2010) has criticised the 'disgrace' of UK universities because the old-fashioned 'slow-food' feel of 1970s British scholarship, where academics took their time to develop idiosyncratic ideas, has given way to a 'fast-food' style that serves up the latest fashionable ideas to meet short-term goals. I would suggest that, while the 'mass' higher education of today has enabled many more thousands of students to enter higher education for the first time – a potentially democratising trend that may challenge traditional, elite academic hierarchies – there are intellectual, cultural and ethical costs and unforeseen side effects of this 'massification' and privileging of the power of the student as a consumer.

The corporate culture of university life is perhaps best exemplified in the endemic competition that characterises the sector. Becher and Trowler (2001) call the disciplines 'academic tribes and territories', inhabited by ambitious and career-minded individuals. University managers act like venture capitalists and there is economic competition among institutions, academic disciplines, colleges, schools and individuals. Universities compete with each other for students; academics compete with each other for grants, and students compete with each other for grades and jobs.

For example, the red flags hanging from the university building where I work celebrate that my university is 'Proud to be a top 10 UK and world top 100 university', as rated by the Academic World University Ranking 2017. Every day I go to work, the flags subtly remind me of the importance of branding, metrics and rankings to demonstrate our world-leading 'excellence'. As a teacher and researcher, I am made aware that the university culture is also an audit culture, which emphasises transparency and performance and in which 'we' are expected to boast about how great 'we' are in comparison with other institutions (Strathern, 2000). Institutions and individuals are regularly assessed using performance measures such as the Research Excellence Framework (REF) (previously Research Assessment Exercise (RAE)). Not only will my research be measured according to pre-established criteria but I am also required to grade my own publications according to a 'star' rating system, from one to four 'stars', depending on how nationally and internationally excellent, original and rigorous I deem them to be.

In the corporate university, it seems that no one is permitted to do what they are doing for its own sake, and nothing is allowed to stay as it is – we must always be 'performing' excellently in our teaching and research, and ideally better than everyone else, at least as measured by the latest metrics. This corporate ethos was made transparent to me during a lengthy 'Leading Teaching Teams' training course I attended. This, rather than teaching us lecturers how to lead teaching teams, seemed to be about turning academic staff into corporate managers. We were taught by an external consultant from the Leadership Foundation for Higher Education how to use our newly learnt 'New Public Management' skills to disseminate Universities UK (UUK) policies into academic colleges and schools, with the assistance of psychometric measurement tools taken from US corporations, and how to evaluate our 'leadership' styles and the 'team-working' abilities of our colleagues.

Colleagues in Western Europe are looking on the UK university system with a mixture of sadness and horror (Collini, 2012): sadness because they once deeply respected British higher education; horror because they know that the free higher education they take for granted will soon also be replaced by a system of tuition fees. They know that the marketisation of higher education is heading their way, pushed by politicians and vice chancellors. They fear the consequences of importing the corporate business models of the US and UK to their own countries. When viewed from the outside, British universities are looked upon as canaries in a coalmine, or guinea pigs in a massive experiment. The question is, to what extent can education, educators and students be turned into commodities to be bought and sold on the educational marketplace?

McMindfulness in the corporate university

The growth of New Public Management and neoliberalism in supposedly public sector institutions such as universities dovetails and has strong parallels with the rise of 'mindfulness' across an array of political, corporate and educational institutions. The parallel emergences of mindfulness and neoliberal capitalism might not be just a coincidence. When looked at from a historical perspective, it makes sense that university vice chancellors and senior managers should be getting increasingly interested in mindfulness and related contemplative practices. They are looking for tools not only to enhance performance and efficiency – cultivating 'self-care', 'work–life balance' and 'resilience' among their employees to further their institution's goals – but also to address what they see as a worsening 'mental health' crisis among staff and students during times of cuts and austerity. This was illustrated in the UK recently when the Leadership Foundation for Higher Education called for the creation of 'The Mindful University' (Leadership Foundation for Higher Education, 2017). The foundation trains future university leaders and managers in corporate business models, and collaborated with Universities UK and the Mindfulness Initiative to organise a one-day 'Mindfulness in Higher Education' conference with 'global leaders' in London in 2017 (see also Seldon & Martin, 2017).

Mindfulness, along with related concepts of resilience, happiness and wellbeing, has become a buzzword in educational circles. It is, I would argue, being sold as a panacea for the ills of competitive capitalism, and is rapidly being implemented across educational institutions and for all age groups, ostensibly to address worsening mental 'wellbeing' and enhance 'flourishing' among staff and students, but also to promote their productivity and efficiency. Much of the discussion of mindfulness and meditation in higher education revolves around their potentially beneficial therapeutic effects and putative promise to be able to enhance students' academic attainment. Therapeutic applications of mindfulness, taught either in group sessions or in one-on-one counselling, are targeted mainly at students but also at staff suffering from stress, anxiety and depression. This therapeutic mindfulness is commonly taught by staff in university counselling and wellbeing services, but also increasingly in university schools, departments and colleges, as part of professional programmes of medicine, education and social work.

In addition to therapeutic applications, mindfulness is also applied within generic performance enhancement and productivity workshops, framed within the broader aim of cultivating 'grit' and 'persistence' among students and staff, especially for the purpose of improving assessment scores, teaching and learning 'outcomes' and research 'outputs'. Such applications of mindfulness are illustrated, for example, in time management workshops, such as 'How to be a Productivity Ninja', which encourages a 'Zen-like calm' (Think Productive, 2017). From a commercial perspective, mindfulness can be employed to grow the institution and economy by producing more efficient graduates for the future workforce – employees who take less time off, have greater mental resilience, get better grades and are able to submit, and sometimes sacrifice, their lives to meet institutional economic and social goals.

However, while mindfulness is certainly being co-opted by neoliberal agendas, it is also being employed in the service of lobbying activities for more public funding and expenditure across a number of publically-funded sectors, especially mental health care and education – an example of which I will relate below. For, in its defence, it has also been suggested that mindfulness may in fact pose a challenge to the ideal of self-contained individualism, thereby exposing the limits of neoliberalism (Carvalho, 2014; Cook, 2016; Mamberg & Bassarear, 2015). It is said that mindfulness teachers may present mindfulness as merely a secular technique for self-improvement, but they may also present it as a 'spiritual' or 'sacred' practice and encourage social and political engagement and self-transcendence among their students, along with self-responsibility and self-improvement (Reveley, 2015). There is even an argument that mindfulness is also now being applied to further goals of sustainability, creativity and social change activism (Rowe, 2016).

Thus, matters of mindfulness might be more complex than its main proponents and critics suggest. Rather than assuming from the outset that mindfulness automatically represents an individualising practice of self-governance, should we be asking instead what kinds of social worlds are being imagined through cultural turns toward mindfulness (Illouz, 2008)? By simultaneously holding more lightly both progressive endorsements and cultural critiques of mindfulness, and by looking at the various contexts in which mindfulness is made manifest, we may find that its applications produce outcomes unexpected by proponents and critics alike.

Indeed, advocates of mindfulness – especially in educational circles – are themselves often also critics of the neoliberal reforms of education that are the subject of the 'McMindfulness' critiques. They are often turning to mindfulness precisely as a potential corrective to the corporate focus on competition and economic productivity. For example, the philosopher of education Terry Hyland (2013) promotes a mindfulness-based affective education (MBAE) in order to foster 'cognitive-affective' balance across the educational system. He regards MBAE as an 'education of the emotions' and a way of critically responding to the overly materialistic, rationalist and instrumentalist philosophies of education commonly found in institutions modelled on neoliberal values. In his vision, self-care and emotional and bodily awareness become prized over and above the mission statements of corporate universities. This kind of contemplative education has been described as an 'accelerating movement' in higher education, across sciences, social sciences, and humanities in North America (Bush, 2011).

McMindfulness on strike

The contradictions and paradoxes inherent in the application of mindfulness in universities to address 'wellbeing' and 'mental health' became starkly apparent to me during the 2018 pensions dispute, when thousands of university staff in the UK went on strike in response to proposed cuts to their pensions. During the pensions strike, some protestors employed critical (or social) mindfulness, turning their collective attentions to the organisational workings of the corporate university.

The university staff pensions strike is (at the time of writing) the largest and longest industrial dispute in the history of UK higher education. It is as significant as the massive public demonstrations against government increases in student tuition fees in 2010. The university managers who were proposing to cut staff pensions were the same managers who introduced, and continued to raise, tuition fees. University vice chancellors assumed that new university staff would prefer to be self-sufficient entrepreneurs, flexibly gambling their pension payments on the stock market, rather than wanting to collectively share with each other and their employing institutions the burden of financial risk.

The strike prompted staff and students alike to pose profoundly challenging questions, not only about pensions but also about the nature and purpose of higher education. How can we create cultures of care and value in the academy? How can we reclaim and democratise 'The University' as an institution in the face of managerialism and marketisation? How can we challenge and rethink audit culture – metrics, grading, and rankings – in our increasingly competitive times? How can we 'decolonise' our educational institutions, research and teaching? How can debates about worsening student and staff mental health be better linked with discussions about the conditions of 'academic capitalism', neoliberalism, precarious and casualised labour, rising tuition and student accommodation fees and endemic inequalities and injustices? How can we foster and sustain staff–student solidarity and resistance, along with members of other trades unions, in the face of 'austerity' and ongoing attacks on public services?

The rise of the corporate university charted above, along with the critical questions raised during the strike, clearly illustrate that 'The University' is also part of the 'real world' and not a collection of ivory towers. Universities are like a microcosm of the wider society and embody many of its inequalities, contradictions, paradoxes and hypocrisies. Universities themselves often fall short of the standards set by their own critical academic research, scholarship and teaching. But this is not a reason to give up on the idea of a university education as a freely available public good. For many educators and students who work in the UK Higher Education sector, the strike opened up rare and valuable spaces for practically rethinking and re-imagining universities outside of business models, as well as considering alternatives to marketised education, in 'teach-outs' and 'teach-ins' organised up and down the country.

The strike was not only about the issue of pensions. Protesters argued that, if we want higher education to have a future in the UK, we must challenge the elite privatisation of universities and find new ways of valuing higher learning, educators and students alike – along with those who support and facilitate teaching and learning – in more just, democratic and caring ways. While the strike exposed and put into sharp relief what we value and how we do so when it comes to higher education, the strike also prompted many of us to critically reflect on what have become our taken-for-granted and internalised cultures of competition and how we might start to cultivate in their place cultures of greater care and equality within the academy. It might be that mindfulness has a place in the revisioning of higher education, but mindfulness will arguably be most transformative when it is carried out in alliance with wider movements and campaigns to create a better world.

The paradoxical position of university vice chancellors' apparent concern to address my wellbeing while simultaneously cutting my pay and pension was personally brought home to me in a very direct way in the middle of the strike action. Returning to work for two days of Action Short of a Strike (ASOS) (actually just 'working to contract' – or doing the job I am paid to do within the hours I am paid to do it), I checked my pigeon hole and found a parcel I had been expecting. I had asked the university wellbeing service to send me the freebies given out during the recent university wellbeing week, which I had missed due to the flu. I eagerly opened the parcel. It contained a university-branded mindfulness colouring book, a pack of colouring crayons and a 'wellbeing' mug. It felt like Christmas had come early. The idea of the mug is that, to take care of myself and look after my wellbeing, I should have regular breaks for a cup of tea, and, as I pour hot water into the mug, see the plain black design morph magically into a colourful display of the university's key performance indicators (KPIs), as published in its strategic vision plan for 2018–2023. My favourite KPI was that the staff survey will show that 71% of staff think the university is a 'great place to work'. Not 70%, or 72%, but 71%. Sipping my lemon and ginger tea, I wondered just how many breaks it would take for me to 'feel great' and fully internalise the university KPIs enough to be motivated to achieve them. Working in universities is increasingly coming to feel like working in a real-life sitcom. You do not even need to make up the comedy any more.

We might ridicule the powers-that-be, and this can be one way of starting to imagine alternative ways of working and studying within universities. But we cannot seriously and maturely think about our mental health (or otherwise), or the shocking numbers of suicides taking place among university students and staff, without also simultaneously thinking about what is happening to us – the cuts, debts, competition, inequalities – and what we are in turn doing to ourselves and each other, as we attempt to live our lives within arguably inhospitable situations. Neglecting to sincerely understand how our mental wellbeing intersects with our social and economic situations means denying the basic contexts and conditions that give rise to our feelings of wellbeing in the first place.

University managers' responses to the pensions strike reflected a commercial spirit and ethos. In proper British tradition, they wanted students and non-striking staff to 'keep calm and carry on' through the disruption. Keep your head down and stay quiet, as if nothing is happening. Be professional. Or even better, 'be mindful' of the situation, because the therapeutic ethos poses no inherent challenge to the corporate ethos. However, by being mindful of the language used during the strike, we came to notice the somewhat Orwellian qualities of the discourse used by university managers. We found Orwell's essay *Politics and the English Language* (1946) particularly helpful for developing this critical language awareness or organisational mindfulness (Weick & Sutcliffe, 2006).

Our employers say they care deeply about 'the student experience' but it became increasingly apparent that this abstract concept, which is the recipient of vast sums of money, appears to mean that university vice chancellors are making massive investments in new building projects ('capital expenditure') and charging exorbitant rental fees for student accommodation. Meanwhile, the very idea of The University itself seems to refer to some place 'over there', in the distance. In the managers' discourse, The University was always taken to mean 'the managers', who really cared about 'our' students. The University was not 'us', the teaching and administrative and support staff and students. At a student's union-hosted question-and-answer session for students about the strike, two pro-vice chancellors were introduced as being representatives of The University, whereas two striking lecturers were not described as members of The University but as members of the University and College Union (UCU). The Twitter hashtag #WeAreTheUniversity became a rallying cry to those of 'us' who wanted to critically question the idea that The University was not 'us'. Where was The University, we asked, and whose interests did it represent?

One popular expression of resistance to neoliberal capitalism, explicitly framed as an alternative to 'fast-food' McMindfulness, has been the development of 'slow' culture. Arguments for slow culture often elide the positions of power and privilege in institutional hierarchies that, for example, 'slow professors' (Berg & Seeber, 2016) might be able to occupy at the expense of the exhausted, 'fast-food-style' casualised workers who cover their teaching. But, when allied with collective movements and campaigns for social change, slowness, silence and stillness can be applied as strategies and tactics of demonstration and protest, to powerful effect. During the strike, with colleagues and supporting students, we developed a series of interventions that adapted mindfulness meditation practices as forms of protest and demonstration.

We collectively staged a standing-still demonstration, protesting against our student union's failure to support striking staff. Around 50 staff and students stood for 10 minutes on the steps of the Student's Union, motionless, silently making their point, while in the background an old university building was being demolished to build a new 'Centre for Student Life'. This meditation 'flash mob' was recorded and broadcast on social media and the idea was taken on by other union branches. The following week, over 100 protestors silently walked around the perimeter of our university main building, where our vice chancellor's office is located. Guiding the walking meditation, which was also a demonstration, felt like leading a funereal march or procession in mourning for the death of the public university. These were powerful and affective displays of collective protest.

My suggestion is that mindfulness meditation might not automatically and inherently embody a corporate ethos – although it often does. Depending on how mindfulness is framed, contextualised and taught, it might also be recruited for the purpose of campaigning for social change, justice and equality. Such attempts to revision mindfulness as a civic, critical, public, relational and social practice are now proliferating on the margins of the mindfulness movement (Purser, Forbes & Burke, 2016). Mindfulness meditation, like Zen practice, potentially 'slows, erodes and makes visible the usual reality-building processes (personal and collective) used by all groups in everyday life' (Preston, 1988: 123).

To live up to these hopes, mindfulness meditation would need to be explicitly taught and framed as a practice of developing what David Smail (2005: 81) has described as 'outsight'. In addition to developing 'insight' about our psychological worlds, we also need to develop 'outsight' about the contexts and conditions that give rise to our inner worlds. This might require meditation practices to be taught in a way that explicitly topicalises our shared, collective and social realities. But to see these realities more clearly, we may also need to disrupt those realities, in sometimes extreme or subtle ways, such as by 'breaching' experiments that involve disrupting social norms to discover the background expectancies that create the sense of 'normality' in the first place (Stanley et al, 2015).

Minding mindfulness: in conclusion

If universities are to be imagined as critical institutions, existing independently and autonomously from corporate values, then academics and students alike have a moral obligation to become undisciplined and undisciplinable, to engage in critical thinking and to pose difficult questions about the world in which we are living, working and studying. These questions are difficult in the sense that they challenge us to see our world differently from how we might have seen it previously. Students and staff alike need to be prepared to take the risk of giving unpopular answers to the questions we are asked.

Challenges to the business model of universities are not new. There are long histories of developing alternative, radical, progressive, popular and public universities and contexts for higher learning that challenge corporate models (Fielding & Moss, 2011). A recent attempt is the *Manifesto for the University of the Future* (2018), which sets out an alternative vision of what our universities should be. The question then becomes how we practically act on such manifestos to change our everyday working lives in such a way as to challenge, or create alternatives to, the corporate ethos of universities. Critics of academic capitalism and New Public Management, such as the scholars working on critical university studies, have been slow to propose practical alternatives to 'business-as-usual' in higher education.

If many academics, university staff and students have learnt to internalise the corporate ethos of education as a business, then it must be possible to 'unlearn' that ethos. But that is difficult, not least because 'when we live in society, we are often unaware of society because we live inside society' (McGrane, 1994: 10). One potential source of resistance is, perhaps surprisingly, mindfulness meditation. While mindfulness has been justifiably critiqued as a politically pacifying activity that generates 'acceptance' of the status quo, it is also possible to reimagine mindfulness by tying its practice more explicitly to campaigns for social justice and equality, such as the universities pensions strike.

Critics of mindfulness and the expansion of therapeutic cultures within our contemporary institutions sometimes appear to be dismissive of the potential benefits of such practices for those who suffer the most – for example, those at the intersections of damaging classed, raced and gendered dynamics and those who have been subject to oppression and trauma (Berila, 2016). If mindfulness is revised to be a collective and social practice that explicitly topicalises people's differences as well as galvanising groups of people making a collective point, there might be hope for it still.

Yet, by practising mindfulness in this way, we should be aware of the potential risks and hazards of meditating differently. Our strike exposed how the UK university system, through being marketised, is being pushed to its breaking point. The pensions strike was publicised worldwide and, much to the embarrassment of university vice chancellors, so were the all-too-often 'hidden' injuries of academic capitalism, such as those discussed by Ros Gill (2010), and the toll they take on university workers and students. Coming to a fuller awareness of such hidden injuries is never going to be easy. Depending on how it is taught, there are potentially disturbing consequences of practising mindfulness in institutional settings such as workplaces, schools, colleges and universities that are rarely mentioned in the popular or academic literatures, or indeed at professional conferences and public talks. We might call these the hidden and potentially unsettling 'social side effects' of mindfulness meditation practice (see Lindahl et al, 2017).

Instead of becoming calm, relaxed and happy, with our stress accordingly reduced, we may find ourselves becoming 'stress induced' (Bazzano, 2013). We may actually find that, rather than making us 'fitter, happier, more productive' – as the Radiohead song goes – mindfulness meditation makes us more aware of the insufficiency and sense of 'lack' (Loy, 2003) that is cultivated in corporate institutions and that can lead us to feel like an 'empty self' – empty of community, tradition and shared meaning. There is a risk that we experience this sense of worthlessness, meaninglessness and confusion personally as an emotional hunger to be filled through consumption (Cushman, 1990).

By practising mindfulness, then, we might find ourselves:

- more aware of the 'hidden injuries' of the commercial culture of higher education, including the personal costs of studying, producing, competing, and performing beyond our human capacities (Gill, 2010)
- less willing to unreflectively reproduce that culture in our studying and working lives and better able to say 'no' to institutional demands, or become more aware of our lack of power to say 'no' without adequate working conditions, collective support and solidarity
- less productive and less efficient than our teachers and managers might want us to be.

Obviously, no popular self-help book on mindfulness – or, indeed, scientific publication – is likely to boast that practising mindfulness will make a person 'unproductive', 'obstinate' or even 'damaged'. But still, these are possible 'risks' of mindfulness meditation, if practised diligently in a corporate culture. Mindfulness practices should sensitise us to the violence, hurt and trauma of life, rather than numbing us to those realities. Instead of being applied to adapt us to our society or accommodate us to the dominant social mores and ethos, mindfulness meditation might be assigned to the task of developing a radical critique of the society in which we live. But there would need to be a very large health warning on this path. Rather than more productive, mindfulness practices may make practitioners less productive. Rather than well-adapted and well-functioning in society, the practitioner may find themselves unable to adapt or function in the ways they are expected to. And the diligent mindfulness meditator may find that its practice may damage, rather than enhance, their 'career' and future job prospects.

Such suggestions may not be comfortable reading or particularly good for the promotion of mindfulness in our increasingly commercial culture of higher education. Still, let us turn our critical, mindful attentions to our universities, and ask ourselves whether our loftiest goal is to become merely 'sane in insane places', or to resist adapting ourselves to institutions not worthy of our adaptation.

References

All-Party Parliamentary Group on Wellbeing Economics (2014). Wellbeing in Four Policy Areas: report by the All-Party Parliamentary Group on Wellbeing Economics. London: All-Party Parliamentary Group on Wellbeing Economics. http://b.3cdn.net/nefoundation/ccdf9782b6d8700f7c_lcm6i2ed7.pdf (accessed 7 January 2019).

American Mindfulness Research Association (2017). *AMRA Resources and Services.* [Online.] American Mindfulness Research Association. https://goamra.org/resources/ (accessed 7 January 2019).

Arthington P (2016). Mindfulness: a critical perspective. *Community Psychology in Global Perspective 2*(1): 87–104.

Bazzano M (2013). In praise of stress induction: mindfulness revisited. *European Journal of Psychotherapy & Counselling 15*(2): 174–185.

Becher T, Trowler PR (2001). *Academic Tribes and Territories: intellectual enquiry and the culture of disciplines* (2nd ed). Buckingham: The Society for Research into Higher Education/Open University Press.

Berg M, Seeber BK (2016). *The Slow Professor: challenging the culture of speed in the academy*. Toronto: University of Toronto Press.

Berila B (2016). *Integrating Mindfulness into Anti-Oppression Pedagogy: social justice in higher education*. London: Routledge.

Billig M (2013). *Learn to Write Badly: how to succeed in the social sciences*. London: Sage.

Brazier D (2013). Mindfulness reconsidered. *European Journal of Psychotherapy and Counselling 15*(2): 116–126.

Bush M (2011). Mindfulness in higher education. *Contemporary Buddhism 12*(1): 183–197.

Caring-Lobel A (2016). Corporate mindfulness and the pathologization of workplace stress. In: Purser R, Forbes D, Burke A (eds). *Handbook of Mindfulness: culture, context and social engagement*. New York: Springer (pp195–214).

Carrette J, King R (2005). *Selling Spirituality: the silent takeover of religion*. London: Routledge.

Carvalho A (2014). Subjectivity, ecology and meditation – performing interconnectedness. *Subjectivity 7*(2): 131–150.

Cederström C, Spicer A (2015). *The Wellness Syndrome*. Cambridge: Polity Press.

Chakrabortty A, Weale S (2016). Universities accused of 'importing Sports Direct model' for lecturers' pay. *The Guardian*; 16 November. www.theguardian.com/uk-news/2016/nov/16/universities-accused-of-importing-sports-direct-model-for-lecturers-pay (accessed 18 January 2019).

Cohen E (2010). From the Bodhi tree, to the analyst's couch, then into the MRI scanner: the psychologisation of Buddhism. *Annual Review of Critical Psychology 8*: 97–119.

Collini S (2012). *What Are Universities For?* London: Penguin.

Cook J (2016). Mindful in Westminster: the politics of meditation and the limits of neoliberal critique. *Journal of Ethnographic Theory 6*(1): 141–161.

Cromby J (2011). The greatest gift? Happiness, governance and psychology. *Social and Personality Psychology Compass 5*(11): 840–852.

Cushman P (1990). Why the self is empty: toward a historically situated psychology. *American Psychologist 45*(5): 599–611.

Davies W (2015). *The Happiness Industry: how the government and big business sold us well-being*. London: Verso.

Deem R (2004). Globalisation, new managerialism, academic capitalism and entrepreneurialism in universities: is the local dimension still important? In: Tight M (ed). *The RoutledgeFalmer Reader in Higher Education*. London: RoutledgeFalmer (pp287–302).

Eagleton T (1991). *Ideology*. London: Routledge.

Eaton J (2013). American Buddhism: beyond the search for inner peace. *(A)theologies* February 19.

Farb NAS (2014). From retreat center to clinic to boardroom? Perils and promises of the modern mindfulness movement. *Religions 5*(4): 1062–1086.

Fielding M, Moss P (2011). *Radical Education and the Common School: a democratic alternative*. London: Routledge.

Foresight Mental Capital and Wellbeing Project (2008). *Mental Capital and Wellbeing: making the most of ourselves in the 21ˢᵗ century*. [Online.] London: The Government Office for

Science. https://www.gov.uk/government/publications/mental-capital-and-wellbeing-making-the-most-of-ourselves-in-the-21st-century (accessed 7 January 2019).

Furedi F (2003). *Therapy Culture: cultivating vulnerability in an anxious age*. London: Routledge.

Gill R (2010). Breaking the silence: the hidden injuries of the neoliberal university. In: Ryan-Flood R, Gill R (eds). *Secrecy and Silence in the Research Process: feminist reflections*. London: Routledge (pp228–244).

Grafton A (2010). Britain: the disgrace of the universities. [Blog.] *New York Review of Books*; 9 March. www.nybooks.com/blogs/nyrblog/2010/mar/09/britain-the-disgrace-of-the-universities/ (accessed 7 January 2019).

Hyland T (2013). Moral education, mindfulness, and social engagement: fostering social capital through therapeutic Buddhist practice. [Online.] *SAGE Open*; 22 October. https://doi.org/10.1177/2158244013509253.

Illouz E (2008). *Saving the Modern Soul: therapy, emotion, and the culture of self-help*. London: University of California Press.

Jones SA, Oakley C (2018). *The Precarious Postdoc: interdisciplinary research and casualised labour in the humanities and social sciences*. [Online.] Durham: Working Knowledge/Hearing the Voice. www.workingknowledgeps.com/wp-content/uploads/2018/04/WKPS_PrecariousPostdoc_PDF_Interactive.pdf (accessed 7 January 2019).

Kabat-Zinn J (1994). *Wherever You Go, There You Are: mindfulness meditation for everyday life*. London: Piatkus.

Kucinskas J (2019). *The Mindful Elite: mobilizing from the inside out*. Oxford: Oxford University Press.

Langer E (2000). Mindful learning. *Current Directions in Psychological Science* 9(6): 220–223.

Langer E (1997). *The Power of Mindful Learning*. Reading, MA: Addison-Wesley Longman.

Langer E (1989). *Mindfulness*. Reading, MA: Addison-Wesley Longman.

Lasch C (1979). *The Culture of Narcissism: American life in an age of diminishing expectations*. London: WW Norton & Co.

Leadership Foundation for Higher Education (2017). *Mindfulness in Higher Education*, London; 19 June. www.lfhe.ac.uk/en/programmes-events/conferences/mindfulness-in-he/index.cfm (accessed 18 January 2019).

Lindahl JR, Fisher NE, Cooper DJ, Rosen RK, Britton WB (2017). The varieties of contemplative experience: a mixed-methods study of meditation-related challenges in Western Buddhists. [Online.] *PLOS ONE* 12(5): e0176239. https://doi.org/10.1371/journal.pone.0176239

Loy D (2003). *The Great Awakening: a Buddhist social theory*. Boston, MA: Wisdom Publications.

Mamberg MH, Bassarear T (2015). From reified self to being mindful: a dialogical analysis of the MBSR voice. *International Journal for Dialogical Science* 9(1): 11–37.

Manifesto for the University of the Future (2018). *Manifesto for the University of the Future*. [Blog.] University of the Future; 10 March. https://universityofthefuture.blog/2018/03/10/manifesto-for-the-university-of-the-future/ (accessed 7 January 2019).

McGrane B (1994). *The Un-TV and the 10 mph Car: experiments in personal freedom and everyday life*. Fort Bragg: The Small Press.

Mindfulness All-Party Parliamentary Group (2015). *Mindful Nation UK: report by the Mindfulness All-Party Parliamentary Group (MAPPG)*. [Online.] London: the Mindfulness Initiative. https://themindfulnessinitiative.org.uk/images/reports/Mindfulness-APPG-Report_Mindful-Nation-UK_Oct2015.pdf (accessed 19 January 2019).

Morone NE, Moore CG, Greco CM (2017). Characteristics of adults who used mindfulness meditation: United States, 2012. *The Journal of Alternative and Complementary Medicine* 23(7): 545–550.

Orwell G (1946). Politics and the English Language. *Horizon*; April.

Oxman AD, Sackett DL, Chalmers I, Prescott TE (2005). A surrealistic mega-analysis of redisorganization theories. *Journal of the Royal Society of Medicine* 98(12): 563–568.

Preston DL (1988). *The Social Organization of Zen Practice: constructing transcultural reality.* Cambridge: Cambridge University Press.

Purser RE (2015). Confessions of a mind-wandering MBSR student: remembering social amnesia. *Self & Society* 43(1): 6–14.

Purser R, Forbes D, Burke A (2016). *Handbook of Mindfulness: culture, context and social engagement.* New York, NY: Springer.

Purser R, Loy D (2013). Beyond McMindfulness. *Huffington Post* [Online.] www.huffingtonpost.com/ron-purser/beyond-mcmindfulness_b_3519289.html (accessed 7 January 2019).

Pykett J, Jones R, Whitehead M (eds) (2017). *Psychological Governance and Public Policy: governing the mind, brain and behaviour.* London: Routledge.

Reveley J (2015). School-based mindfulness training and the economization of attention: a Stieglerian view. *Educational Philosophy and Theory* 47(8): 804–821.

Rivers N, Webster D (2019). *Working out in the academy? Why the 'university is like a gym' metaphor is flawed.* [Blog.] Fruits of the Pedagogic Life. https://davewebster.org/2019/01/03/working-out-in-the-academy-why-the-university-is-like-a-gym-metaphor-is-flawed/ (accessed 18 January 2019).

Rowe JK (2016). Micropolitics and collective liberation: mind/body practice and left social movements. *New Political Science* 38(2): 206–225.

Ryan T (2012). *A Mindful Nation: how a simple practice can help us reduce stress, improve performance, and recapture the American spirit.* London: Hay House.

Samuel, G. (2014). Between Buddhism and science, between mind and body. *Religions* 5(3): 560–579.

Segal ZV, Williams JMG, Teasdale JD (2013). *Mindfulness-Based Cognitive Therapy for Depression* (2nd ed). New York, NY: The Guilford Press.

Seldon A, Martin A (2017). *The Positive and Mindful University*. HEPI Occasional Paper 18. London: Higher Education Policy Institute. www.hepi.ac.uk/2017/09/21/positive-mindful-university/ (accessed 18 January 2019).

Smail D (2005). *Power, Interest and Psychology: elements of a social materialist understanding of distress.* Ross-On-Wye: PCCS Books.

Stanley S, Barker MJ, Edwards V, McEwen E (2015). Swimming against the stream? Mindfulness as a psychosocial research methodology. *Qualitative Research in Psychology* 12(1): 61–76.

Stanley S, Purser R, Singh N (eds) (2018). *Handbook of Ethical Foundations of Mindfulness.* New York, NY: Springer.

Strathern M (ed) (2000). *Audit Cultures: anthropological studies in accountability, ethics and the academy.* London: Routledge.

Tan C-M (2012). *Search Inside Yourself: the unexpected path to achieving success, happiness (and world peace).* London: HarperOne.

Think Productive (2017). *Bringing mindfulness into your office.* [Blog.] Think Productive; 7 April. https://thinkproductive.co.uk/bringing-mindfulness-into-your-office/ (accessed 7 January 2019).

University and College Union (2018). *Boycott the NSS.* London: University & College Union. www.ucu.org.uk/boycott-the-nss (accessed 18 January 2018).

Weick T, Sutcliffe KM (2006). Mindfulness and the quality of organizational attention. *Organization Science 17*(4): 417–526.

Žižek S (2001). *On Belief.* London: Routledge.

PART 2
DOGMAS OF WORK AND HEALTH

6

The employment dogma

David Frayne

David Frayne is a writer and social researcher with a principal interest in the ethical, political and social dimensions of possible 'post-work' societies. He is the author of several online articles and the book The Refusal of Work *(Zed, 2015).*

Our health, wellbeing and happiness are inextricably linked to work.
Duncan Selbie, Chief Executive Officer, Public Health England
(Mason, 2016)

When a great number of individuals do not even question whether society can and should organise production and distribution differently, this ought to register as a loss of freedom.
James Chamberlain (2018: 12)

In the UK, evidence on the relationship between employment and health has been heavily publicised in recent times. If you accessed the UK Department for Work and Pensions website at a certain point in 2017, you would have seen a large diagram, reproduced from the government's *Improving Lives* Green Paper (Department for Work and Pensions/Department of Health, 2016). The diagram examined the relationships between work, health and disability. Imagine the diagram split into two sides. On the left side, in bold, black typeface, are the phrases '**good work**' and '**good health**'. A bi-directional arrow, in reassuring hospital green, links the two phrases to suggest that good work leads to good health and good health leads back to good work.[1] On the right-hand side of the diagram, in the same typeface, are the phrases '**worklessness**' and '**poor health**'. Another bi-directional arrow – blue this time – links the two phrases, illustrating the supposition that being jobless leads to poor health and poor health leads to joblessness. The visual simplicity of this diagram has an undeniable appeal. Work = health = good. Unemployment = illness = bad. These ideas have the reassuring ring of common sense, seeming to map on to what we know about the poverty, social isolation and misery that often accompany life without a job.

The purpose of this chapter is not to trivialise this suffering, nor to deny that employment can be rewarding. Even when its content is uninteresting, employment is still often valued as a chance to adopt new roles, forge new relationships and temporarily escape the intimacy of domestic and community life (Gorz, 1985: 54). The precise dispute here is with the suggestion (represented by the Public Health England quote above) that health and wellbeing are *inextricably* linked with employment. It is the 'inextricable' part that is most problematic, with its suggestion that the link between employment and good health is somehow natural or innate to human flourishing. Although this is often framed as an objective position, grounded in an evidence base, we must recognise that such a claim ultimately represents an ethical and political stance. It not only suggests that employment is linked to health, but also that we should accept this reality as normal and ideal and direct social policies towards providing and encouraging employment. My own position is that – even in light of evidence that employment has a strong relationship with wellbeing – we should still pose the question of whether it would be better to accept or change this reality. Given today's proliferation of poor-quality jobs, and the inability of a large section of the population to participate in employment, whether due to job scarcity, disability or the replacement of some workers by automated technologies, the collective challenge we might be facing is precisely to *extricate* ideals of health and wellbeing from the institution of paid work. The pragmatic path ahead might not be to prop up the employment-centred society for the sake of individual wellbeing but to loosen the connection between employment and health through policies designed to make life richer and more hospitable outside the sphere of employment.

---

1. For all the simplicity of the diagram, the actual claim being made here is quite unclear. What does the Department for Work and Pensions mean when it says that 'good health' leads to 'good work'? Is it that good health makes people do their jobs more effectively? That being healthy shapes the quality of employment? That it helps individuals to find the good jobs?

Jobs are good for you

On the political Left and Right, we find a strong commitment to the ethical and psychosocial value of employment. When the Conservative leader David Cameron became Prime Minister in the 2010 Coalition government, he rebranded his party as the party for the 'hardworking people' of Britain, promoting the idea that employment lies at the heart of a just and stable society. For an example from the Left, we can consider the Labour MP Chuka Umunna's remarks in a *Guardian* article about the elimination of jobs by automated technologies. Umunna worried that 'without [work] people are denied a sense of dignity and of community. When you lose work, the meaning and purpose of life are taken away from you' (Umunna, 2017). Work is equated with the meaning of life itself. Whether we approve or otherwise, it is clear that, in capitalist societies, employment far exceeds its function of distributing income. It is also idealised as a source of prestige, independence and dignity.

It is in this political context that claims about the importance of employment for people's health have been publicised. To date, one of the most widely-cited sources on the relationship between employment and health in the UK is the government-commissioned literature review, *Is Work Good for Your Health and Well-Being?* (Waddell & Burton, 2006). This review collated evidence from a range of empirical studies on the relationship between work and health, concluding that 'there is a strong evidence base showing that work is generally good for physical and mental health and well-being' (2006: 10). The report also gives special consideration to sick and disabled people, advising:

> ... when their health condition permits, sick and disabled people (particularly those with 'common health problems') should be encouraged and supported to remain in or (re)-enter work as soon as possible. (Waddell & Burton, 2006: 44)

Although the Waddell and Burton review has a reputation for being doggedly pro-employment, it is worth mentioning that the report itself includes details that muddy the picture. The definition of 'work' laid out at the beginning of the report, for example, is specifically *not* limited to paid employment, but includes 'unpaid or voluntary work, education and training, family responsibilities and caring' (2006: 3). The authors also hint at the socially contingent nature of the relationship between work and health, adding the qualifier that 'work meets important psychosocial needs in societies *where employment is the norm*' (2006: 31, my emphasis). Complicating the picture further, Waddell and Burton also suggest that the beneficial health effects of work depend on the nature and quality of the jobs in question, and that 'various physical and psychosocial aspects of work can... be hazards and pose a risk to health' (2006: ix). The authors opt out of elaborating on this important point, on the basis of 'insufficient evidence' (2006: x), but they do suggest that the characteristics of 'good' jobs and 'good' workplaces might include factors such as safety, fair pay, job security, personal fulfilment, opportunities for development, the absence of discrimination, a level of autonomy and good communications (2006: 35). For people with some common health problems, Waddell and Burton suggest entering and re-entering poor-quality jobs could cause further harm (2006: 35).

These details are referred to in the report as 'provisos' – they are noted, but in the final instance do not upset the overall conclusion that 'work is generally good for physical and mental health and well-being'. The message is clear: work is good for you. This is the headline finding, and the one that was cited by news outlets, mental health charities and the UK government, who would all interpret the conclusion in terms of the narrower definition of 'work' as employment, or a paid job. As the Royal College of Psychiatrists reported it:

> Studies show that work is generally good for health. As well as a financial reward, it gives many of us self-esteem, companionship and status... Some studies go so far as to conclude that the risk to health of being out of work, in the longer term, is greater than the risk of other killer diseases such as heart disease. (Royal College of Psychiatrists, 2018)

The way a piece of research is reported and used can often have a more significant impact than the finer details of its findings. Government ministers with responsibility for work and health matters have explicitly talked about the power of employment to help people recover from illness when justifying tightening welfare conditionality and the introduction of more punitive welfare policies (Mason, 2016). This is representative of the new synergy between the Westminster government's Department of Health (DH) and Department for Work and Pensions (DWP), for whom getting people into work is a key policy outcome, meeting the three goals of improving population health, reducing welfare spending and benefitting the national economy.

This new synergy was outlined in the joint DWP/DH *Improving Lives* documents (a Green Paper in 2016 and a subsequent White Paper in 2017). Citing Waddell and Burton's review, the Green Paper stated:

> The evidence that appropriate work can bring health and wellbeing benefits is widely recognised. Employment can help our physical and mental health and promote recovery. (Department for Work and Pensions/Department of Health, 2016)

The subsequent White Paper extended this line of thinking, outlining the state's commitment to 'join up work and health' (Department for Work and Pensions/Department of Health, 2017: 36), promote a greater level of collaboration between job centre and healthcare providers, and 'raise the profile of work as a health outcome amongst healthcare professionals' (p37).

> When working-age individuals consult with healthcare professionals, we want to see them receive work-related advice and supportive engagement as part of making work a health outcome. This is based on the understanding that good work is good for health. (p36)

This overall aim to 'join up work and health' has resulted in a number of policies, some implemented and some in the pipeline. These include the proposal to double the number of 'Work and Health Champions' – occupational therapists, embedded in health settings and 'trained to deliver work and health tools and techniques to healthcare professionals' (Department for Work and Pensions/Department of Health 2017: 37). Other policies include embedding employment outcomes into NHS evaluation measures (2017: 38); doubling the number of employment advisors placed in state-funded psychotherapy services (2017: 40) (see Jay Watts' Chapter 7 and Paul Atkinson, Chapter 8); rebranding the doctor's sick note to the 'fit note', to emphasise the importance given to returning to work (2017: 42); training job centre work coaches on the basics of mental health (2017: 53); introducing a 'health and work conversation' for claimants of disability benefits, 'to help people respond resiliently to challenges and overcome fixed beliefs about their abilities' (2017: 55) and implementing new 'three-way' conversations between patients, job coaches and health professionals (2017: 54).

Taken as a whole, the proposals in *Improving Lives* show the extent to which beliefs about the relationship between employment and health have taken hold at government policy-making level. In accordance with this belief, employment and health services are now being integrated, and more pressure is being placed on sick and disabled people to return to work. UK activist groups, under the banner of the Mental Wealth Alliance,[2] have candidly called this the era of the 'work cure', where employment is believed not only to sustain health but also to help sick people get better. Their important argument is that this upbeat assumption has trivialised and ignored the experiences of people living with long-term health conditions (Hume, 2016). In an open letter to the 'big five' UK psychology organisations,[3] who all endorsed the government's policy programme, the Mental Wealth Alliance expressed deep concern about the coercive aspects of these policies, many of which were intended to be mandatory for the ongoing receipt of benefits and all of which emphasised the virtues of employment over people's own ideas about health and recovery (Free Psychotherapy Network, 2016).

For neoliberal governments with a prior political commitment to dismantling the welfare state, evidence that employment is good for people's health indeed arrives like a gift, especially when that evidence carries the gravitas of scientific expertise. A political agenda may then be advanced wearing the disguise of objectivity. The evidence that 'work = health' also enables a harmful reform agenda to be carried forward under the cover of aims that, on the surface, sound benevolent. In an Orwellian move, coercing people to work, or imposing poverty through sanctions, can be framed through euphemisms like 'supporting' or 'helping' people to work, or 'remedying inequalities in work participation' (Department for Work and Pensions/Department of Health, 2016). It is in the context of these harmful realities that now, more than ever, it is important to recognise that evidence demonstrating the link between employment and wellbeing should not be taken at face value.

---

2. Groups in the alliance include Mental Health Resistance Network; Disabled People Against Cuts; Recovery in the Bin; Boycott Workfare; The Survivors Trust; Alliance for Counselling and Psychotherapy; College of Psychoanalysts; Psychotherapists and Counsellors for Social Responsibility; Psychologists Against Austerity; Free Psychotherapy Network; Psychotherapists and Counsellors Union; Critical Mental Health Nurses' Network; Social Work Action Network (Mental Health Charter); National Unemployed Workers Combine; Merseyside County Association of Trades Union Councils; Scottish Unemployed Workers' Network; National Health Action Party; Making Waves (Free Psychotherapy Network, 2016).

3. British Association for Behavioural and Cognitive Psychotherapies, British Association for Counselling and Psychotherapy, British Psychoanalytic Council, British Psychological Society, United Kingdom Council for Psychotherapy.

Incursions on freedom

The motivation to fund and carry out research on the relationship between work and wellbeing is the hope that this might guide the creation of social policies. The presumption is that, when we can find out what is good for wellbeing, we will know which political road to take. One of the glaring problems with 'wellbeing' as a guiding political ideal, however, is that it is perfectly possible for people to function adequately, or even report that they are happy and well, in situations that may be less than ideal. At risk of using a heavy-handed analogy, we can consider the philosophical problem of the 'happy slave', who is adequately acclimatised to their conditions and stops hoping for change, even when those conditions present a direct threat to their humanity. What is important in this situation is not the enslaved person's 'wellbeing', but whether their wellbeing is achieved at the expense of more pressing concerns, such as freedom, equality and justice.

In his key work, *The Sane Society* (1963), Erich Fromm describes the predominance of the 'adjustment view' of mental health found in psychiatry, which assesses mental health in terms of a person's ability to function within the dominant norms and structures of a particular social context. The problem with this adjustment view, of course, is that it leaves no space to question that social context, no room to think about whether its dominant norms and structures support or hinder the human requirements for mental health. What ultimately matters in the adjustment view is only whether the individual 'fits', regardless of whether this fitting-in involves accommodating to unreasonable demands or tolerating harms and incursions on freedom.

To illustrate this, we can consider the approach that is usually taken in the raft of workplace wellness initiatives (stress-busting programmes, mindfulness training and so on) discussed throughout this book. In line with the adjustment view of mental health, the question presented is not whether the working environment is conducive to the mental health of workers, but only how workers can adapt their behaviour and mindsets to fit the requirements of the working environment – requirements that from the offset are deemed to be unchangeable or even natural features of the workplace. The value of wellness coaches to the capitalist organisation – their skill, we might say – consists in how effectively they are able to place off-limits any notion that the workplace itself might be at fault. The purpose is to examine and optimise the individual's adaptation to the environment, not collectively scrutinise whether or not the environment itself is conducive to health.

If the adjustment approach to mental health discourages critique at the social and structural level, the value of Erich Fromm's work is that it does the opposite, invoking the feeling that it is really society, and not the individual, that needs to change. For Fromm, the central problem is not with a quantity of unadjusted individuals but with the possibility that the wider norms and structures of society are themselves unadjusted to certain basic requirements for human flourishing:

> ... mental health cannot be defined in terms of the 'adjustment' of the individual to his society, but, on the contrary, that it must be defined in terms of the adjustment of society to the needs of man, of its role in furthering or hindering the development of mental health. (Fromm, 1963: 72)

Fromm elaborates his theory of the 'needs of man' in some depth in *The Sane Society*, but it is not necessary to go down that complex path here. What is important for our purposes is Fromm's insistence that we should resist judging the standard of societies in terms of the extent to which people are adjusted or 'happy'. For it is perfectly possible for humans to experience wellbeing in an unhealthy society – a society 'which creates mutual hostility, distrust, which transforms man into an instrument of use and exploitation for others' (Fromm, 1963: 73). What we need is some additional criterion or benchmark that can reveal to us whether adjustment to the present situation is desirable or undesirable, healthy or pathological, sane or insane. If, by this other criterion, society is found to be inimical to human needs, the presence of 'wellbeing' might itself be seen as a problem – as a sign of what Fromm called the 'pathology of normalcy'. In such a situation, what we require is not a greater effort to incorporate individuals into the standards of normality but a greater effort to collectively change those standards for the benefit of everybody.

In *Undoing Work, Rethinking Community* (2018), James Chamberlain exposes the problems with the link between employment and wellbeing by assessing the situation according to a different criterion – not a standard of wellbeing, but a standard of *freedom*. Avoiding the dizzying number of philosophical debates on the nature of freedom, Chamberlain takes a relatively simple definition as 'the capacity of agents to act according to their own values, needs and desires, or ends, for short' (2018: 10). As he explains, this idea of freedom requires more than the absence of coercion or interference; it also requires a social context that allows people to satisfy their biological needs and provides scope for them to collectively express themselves, deliberate and experiment with different ways of living. Assessing today's employment-centred society from the vantage of freedom produces a very different picture than if we assess it from the standpoint of wellbeing, which is more amenable to the adjustment view of health. Chamberlain usefully groups the concerns of work's critics into four key areas.

1. The lack of choice about whether to participate in employment

In the commercial structures and dominant norms of capitalist societies, there are few opportunities to access what we need other than through a wage, and few ways to gain social recognition and respect without having a job (Frayne, 2015). The norm is that people work to earn in order to purchase the things they need and want on the market and – through these activities – gain recognition in the eyes of others and become 'good citizens'. This lack of genuine choice about whether or not to work is heightened by commercialisation, which reshapes our social and institutional environments in ways that make it harder to meet needs without income. It is also heightened by the stigmatisation of unemployed and disabled people, which has been given extension through workfare and psycho-compulsion (Friedli & Stearn, 2015). Workfare activities serve to monopolise people's time and energy with job-related efforts, even outside employment. Within this context, we do of course enjoy certain liberties – to criticise work privately, to escape work temporarily, change jobs or choose between consumer pleasures – but this liberty does not extend to a more fundamental freedom to protest against the fact that we are being forced to sell our lives simply in order to live. Ultimately, all but the most privileged in society face little choice about whether or not to work, and this is a major incursion on freedom.

2. The lack of freedom within workplaces

Deep changes in the nature of work, currently tied to forces like globalisation, deregulation and accelerated technological development, have functioned to decrease the power of workers to shape the terms and conditions of their work. Some of the most regularly reported excesses of this tendency include workers pushed to the brink as they struggle to meet performance targets in call centres (Woodcock, 2017); workers whose movements are tracked by handheld computers in Amazon warehouses, and those having to cope with unmanageable workloads in the corporate university (see Steven Stanley's Chapter 5 in this book). We can also include the incursions of insecure work, as the removal of basic worker protections like a living wage, guaranteed hours, sick leave and secure contracts leaves many people in a perpetual state of anxiety about making long-term plans and meeting needs. As I cited in my introduction to this book, an analysis of the Labour Force Survey from 2017 found that one in nine workers (or 3.8 million people) in the UK were employed in insecure jobs in the final quarter of that year – a category that includes temporary workers (like agency workers, casual workers, seasonal workers and so on), workers whose main job has a zero-hours contract and self-employed workers earning less than the National Living Wage (Trades Union Congress, 2018a).

This is perhaps a good point at which to note that the claim that 'health, wellbeing and happiness are inextricably linked to work' reflects a startling absence of comment on job quality. Both the aforementioned Waddell and Burton review and the government's *Improving Lives* policy papers do use the qualifier of '*good* jobs' when talking about the health benefits of employment, but this represents a weak gesture at best. There is no attempt to properly elaborate the features of a 'good job', nor any investigation into the extent to which these ideal forms of work are actually available in the capitalist present or likely to remain available in the future. We should also note the extent to which hopes for 'good jobs' conflict with capitalism's *raison d'etre*, which is essentially to squeeze the greatest productivity out of workers in the pursuit of private profit.

Responding to the need for a better grasp of job quality, some researchers *have* undertaken the tiring work of uncovering the metrics of job quality. In their critical survey of the literature, Bustillo and colleagues explore no less than 20 such attempts by a combination of academics, trade unions and international organisations (Bustillo et al, 2011). Their breakdown of indicators offers an intricate picture, including a range of variables encompassing both contractual conditions and the nature of the job itself. Such indicators include wages, level of workplace democracy, the job's skill level, level of worker autonomy, pace of work, presence of a sense of meaning, work environment, scope for job progression, presence of physical and psychological risks, work scheduling, workload and the flexibility of hours, among others. This quest to uncover the metrics of job quality could be a source of endless debate, but some attempt to incorporate an understanding of job quality is essential to temper the current enthusiasm for the health benefits of employment.

And yet, even if we do incorporate an understanding of job quality, we should still not lose sight of the bigger picture – namely, the essentially exploitative character of much work, meaning that even jobs that are rated as 'good quality work' can still involve relations of injustice. What Erich Fromm refers to as 'the use of man by man' is an incursion on freedom that transcends questions of job quality:

The basic concept of *use* has nothing to do with cruel, or not cruel, ways of human treatment, but with the fundamental fact that one man serves another for purposes which are not his own but those of the employer... The fact remains the same, that a man, a living human being, ceases to be an end in himself, and becomes the means for the economic interests of another man, or himself, or of an impersonal giant, the economic machine. (Fromm, 1963: 93)

3. The colonisation of time and energy by work

Chamberlain's third category of incursions on freedom describes the way in which our employment-centred society has reduced both the institutional spaces and the human reserves of time and energy required for participation in non-market activities. The key point here is that people do not simply step outside of work and into a world of freedom. Not only does work occupy a large proportion of the week's hours; the typical scheduling of work also divides people's leisure time into slivers, making it difficult to take part in activities that require a steadier investment of concentration or time. By exhausting people's energies, jobs also require people to spend a significant proportion of their leisure time recuperating, so they are ready to do it all again tomorrow (Adorno, 1991). What we might think of as the colonising power of work also extends to people outside and yet to enter employment, as they embark on the lifelong project to cultivate and maintain their 'employability', gaining credentials, networking and job-seeking in order to succeed in today's competitive labour market. The competition and insecurity of today's labour market have made this quest all-but compulsory for most people, leaving less time to engage in non-instrumental activities involving care, friendship, play or idleness. Chamberlain suggests that one of the biggest incursions of all of this residual economic activity is into people's time to *think*. The ability to engage in reflection, by oneself and with others, around questions of meaning, values, needs and desires is one of the key prerequisites for freedom: 'Only this reflexivity can shield the subject against the ever-present threat of unthinkingly conforming to tradition or the ends of others' (Chamberlain, 2018: 11-12).

4. The reproduction of inequalities

Last but not least, the final incursion of today's work-centred society on human freedom lies in the way it reproduces inequality (since any rigorous definition of freedom will always depend on a baseline of equality). Here we might consider the way in which socially valuable activities outside the economic sphere – particularly care work – remain under-recognised and unremunerated, often because they are associated with marginalised groups like women and migrant workers (Olorenshaw, 2016). We might also consider the way in which the ideology of work has withheld recognition from people who cannot work, such as disabled people, full-time caregivers or people living in areas with high unemployment. There is also the uncomfortable truth that whole sectors of employment exist primarily to benefit an elite section of society – people who are effectively able to purchase more time for themselves by offloading everyday tasks onto a poorer and less privileged group (Gorz, 1989: 157).

Drawing these insights together, we can see that, assessed according to an ideal of freedom, today's work-centred society falls short in deeply troubling ways. Indeed, perhaps the key problem with reports promoting an incontrovertible link between employment and individual wellbeing is that they are silent about the ways today's work-centred society harms people and restricts their autonomy. The literature on job quality has gone some way to resolving this, drawing our attention to the features of good work versus bad work, but even this more nuanced literature feels insubstantial in the context of broader problems like the exploitation of workers, the lack of choice people face about whether to work, the ways that employment takes over people's lives, and the way society marginalises people who cannot satisfy the social ideal of the good worker. I propose that, rather than responding directly to the question of whether employment is good for health and wellbeing, we need to redefine the terrain of the debate. The question is not 'Is employment good for wellbeing?' Rather, it is: 'Will we choose to tolerate and preserve the idea that jobs are essential to health, even when to do so costs so much in terms of our freedom?'

But isn't worklessness bad for health?

Even after the incursions of employment on freedom have been acknowledged, it may still seem sensible to defend the importance of employment for wellbeing, given the demonstrable fact that *un*employment can be so personally harmful for health. Researchers have shown time and time again that unemployment is associated with significant declines in both mental and physical health (for example, Paul & Moser, 2009). Further studies have also shown that people often fail to recover from these declines in health, suggesting that unemployment can have a long-term scarring effect on individuals (for example, Clark, Geogellis & Sanfey, 2001). In one prominent study from the 1930s, a team of social researchers temporarily settled in the Austrian town of Marienthal after the closure of a textile factory left 77% of the community's families without anyone in employment (Jahoda, Lazarsfeld & Ziesel, 1933/1972). Drawing on extensive surveys and observations, the researchers painted a bleak picture of the town's inhabitants on a slippery slope of despondency and resignation, with low expectations of the future, a dragging experience of time and feelings of apathy. The Marienthal study could indeed be describing any number of forgotten post-industrial communities in the UK today.

The Marienthal study would eventually be developed by social science researchers into what some know as the 'deprivation model', premised on the understanding that unemployment is harmful because it cuts people off from a number of essential psychosocial needs that are furnished by employment (see Cole, 2007). These include the needs for shared experience and a sense of collective purpose, for a structured experience of time, involving regular activity, and for a sense of status and self-identity (Jahoda, 1982). Thus, if unemployment is deemed harmful because it cuts people off from satisfying these essential needs, employment is deemed valuable because it can supply what is necessary to meet these needs and restore people to a state of healthy functioning. To this day, this logic of *unemployment as deprivation of employment* remains at the heart of many influential understandings of the relationship between work and health, but this represents a crude analysis. While studies on the experience of unemployment are valuable for inserting empathy and understanding (where there has often been only disdain and blame), researchers and policymakers must be careful about the conclusions they draw.

First of all, it should be emphasised that the experience of living without a job is influenced by a whole host of variables other than work deprivation. There are an untold number of mitigating factors that impact on people's experiences of unemployment, from personality to previous work experiences, financial resources, future prospects, the possession of social and cultural capital, the presence of stigma, the manner in which the job was lost, and whether or not the individual has access to activities that might compensate for the lack of employment. Indeed, the experience of employment *itself* could be classed as a factor in the misery that most people experience during unemployment, given the extent to which full-time working prevents people from cultivating other relationships and interests to fall back on. We might also reasonably ask why it continues to be deemed that worklessness is *intrinsically* bad for people, when retirement, sabbaticals and other periods of repose are presumed to be desirable.

One possible explanation is that it is the presence of the moral expectation to work, as opposed to work deprivation *per se*, that is partly responsible for the distress of unemployed people. What often upsets people is the feeling that they are transgressing a powerful and nurtured moral standard (Frayne, 2015: Chapter 7). A paper by Daniel Sage reminds us that 'unemployed people live in societies where paid work yields status, identity, respect and human worth' (2018: 3). Arguing that researchers have paid insufficient attention to this context, Sage cites studies that suggest unemployment is less detrimental to people's wellbeing in societies with a weaker commitment to the ethical value of work. He also conducts his own analysis of the European Values Study and finds that people with a weaker personal commitment to the work ethic suffer less during unemployment than those who believe strongly in the value of work (2018). Overall, it is important to recognise the degree of variance in people's experiences of unemployment. Losing a job can be a catastrophe or a blessing, depending on the person, their history and their broader cultural, economic and political context.

Rather than adopting the crude formulation that worklessness = poor health (and jumping to conclude that work = health), it is perhaps more accurate to say that it is the *consequences* of worklessness that lead to poor health. What truly matters are the conditions that surround worklessness, and the extent to which these enable or disable people in maintaining their dignity and capacity to act. One of the reasons this has not been more clearly understood relates to language. When the DWP and others talk about the link between 'worklessness' and ill health, what they should be stressing is the link between 'unemployment' and ill health. The distinction is crucial. 'Unemployment' is a phenomenon specific to capitalist societies, where commercial culture and the wage-relation (as outlined above) bind people into a dependent relationship with employment. We should readily expect unemployment to have miserable consequences when there is no robust welfare state to protect people from poverty, when a pervasive work ethic makes it difficult for people to achieve recognition without a job, and when the forces of commercialisation have made it difficult to access needs and enjoy leisure without a steady wage. 'Unemployment' refers to the condition of joblessness *within the norms and structures of work-based societies* – ie. within a particular historical and sociocultural configuration – and is hence distinct from worklessness *per se*. A simpler way of putting this is to say that worklessness is miserable because our current system is set up to make it that way. The good news is that there seems to be no convincing reason as to why, under a different arrangement of values and policies, time outside employment could not be rendered dignified, secure and rewarding (I will return later in this chapter to this point in more detail).

It is here that we begin to see that the vaunted claim that 'health, wellbeing and happiness are inextricably linked to work' – as much as its preachers may insist on its grounding in an 'evidence base' – is not really an objective claim at all, but a deeply political one. It is political because it is based on a foundational acceptance that there are no alternatives to the work-based society, no social system that could allow people to access key material and psychosocial needs or live a dignified life without participating in employment. It is based on that most classic of neoliberal ideas: that 'there is no alternative' to the capitalist present.

In the context of this political complacency and the refusal to consider alternatives, we might regard the evidence base on work and health in the same manner that the philosopher Michael Cholbi has treated evidence on people's stated preference for work: with a healthy dose of scepticism (Cholbi, 2018). Cholbi's argument is that, in the context of employment-based societies and their obvious incursions on freedom and justice, we should resist the temptation to take at face value an individual's stated preference for a job. The preference for employment may instead take the form of what philosophers call an 'adaptive preference': a preference for some state of affairs that is formed within a limited set of options, under unjust social conditions (Cholbi, 2018: 2). The theory of adaptive preferences rests on the idea that humans, in a spirit of necessity and self-preservation, will often adapt to, and even begin to state a preference for, situations that are less than ideal, or maybe even actively oppressive. Just as we might question a woman's indifference to education in a society where it is not available to them, we should treat with suspicion any suggestion that humans have an inviolable need to be employed, when this need is formed in an environment where people are more or less compelled to work in order to survive and have any status.

What is more, the adaptive nature of the need and preference for employment may be heightened because it is not simply the case that individuals in work-centred societies have limited practical options; it is also the case that many people *remain unaware that certain options have been placed off-limits*. Here I think of Max Weber's reference to the 'spirit of capitalism' as an established universe in which people feel destined to participate (Weber, 1904/2002), or of Kathi Weeks' discussion of the naturalised nature of today's work-centred societies, where 'the fact that... one must work to "earn a living" is taken as part of the natural order rather than as a social convention' (Weeks, 2011: 3). In my experience as a public speaker on these issues, part of the challenge is persuading people that the employment-centred society is eligible for debate in the first place.

The point I wish to make above all is that, just like the stated preference for work, the strong relationship between work and health is a *social construction* – a historically specific moment reflecting a particular configuration of social policies and values. We are told that there is an inviolable relationship between health and employment, and we are told that this is proven by credentialed experts and an evidence base. But we should remember that this is ultimately a political position, premised on a foundational reluctance to consider alternative ways in which humans might flourish, survive and feel valued outside employment. What the evidence on the relationship between work and health may reveal above all is not our inextricable dependence on employment for the fulfilment of psychosocial needs but the troubling dearth of political alternatives. Even if evidence shows that employment is integral to health, we still face a political choice as to whether to celebrate this or see it as an opportunity for critique and change. In the face of evidence that employment has become integral to health, a more valid response than acceptance might be a sense of disquiet about the extent to which our personal needs and the needs of capital have become so harmonised.

Exploring alternatives

We might rightly ask why there has been such complacency when it comes to exploring ways in which people could be supported to fulfil key psychosocial needs outside employment. This reluctance perhaps stems in some small part from the methodological difficulties of investigating social alternatives. The problem with alternatives is, of course, that they do not yet exist, and since we cannot investigate empirically what is not already there, investigators would be required to embody a different set of values. The current, positivist commitment to discovering the 'truth' about the psychosocial relevance of employment (seen in the key government policy papers but, notably, also in the papers of many of their critics) would need to be abandoned in favour of a different kind of investigative sensibility – one that tries to scope and assess the impact of possible alternatives. Such a research effort will always be a political exercise, explicitly aimed towards an ideal of greater human freedom.

Yet one suspects that the reluctance to explore alternatives has less to do with methodological issues and more to do with the ideological functions of the work ethic. In order to maintain the loyalty and productivity of labour power, especially in unfree and unjust conditions, capitalism depends on our ethical and existential submission to employment in order to keep functioning. To realise this, we need only consider the threat that would be posed to the maxims of profit and productivity were people given the scope to structure and define their lives around activities other than paid jobs.

Whatever the causes of the current political inertia, a loose coalition of writers and activists – broadly categorised in the tradition of 'post-work' thinking – are arguing that it must be challenged (for example, Gorz, 1999; Weeks, 2011; Srnicek & Williams, 2016). Some argue that this challenge is especially urgent given the difficulty of securing a steady income in today's insecure labour market. There are also predictions that such problems will be compounded as certain job sectors are transformed or eliminated by new developments in automated technology and artificial intelligence (for example, Frey & Osborne, 2017). What is more, from an ecological perspective, continuing to offset these job losses with an ongoing programme of economic growth is no longer a viable option (see Jackson, 2009; Schor, 2010).

Authors in the post-work tradition explore policies that would allow citizens to have more choice around employment participation and working hours, their work provoking us to explore other ways in which humans might co-operate, structure their time, achieve a sense of dignity and put a roof over their heads. Following their example, we should be ready to scrutinise proposals designed to shore up our current system: proposals for a universal job guarantee (a guaranteed, state-provisioned job for everybody), still more 'activation' policies for unemployed people, and the specious goal of full employment. Instead, we should investigate alternative proposals that could enable people to work less. These include proposals for alternative systems of welfare provision that could resource people to meet their needs and do something worthwhile outside of employment. The idea of a Universal Basic Income – the proposal to pay each person a liveable income as a basic social right – is gaining momentum in many advanced welfare states (Standing, 2017). There are also proposals for a society-wide reduction and redistribution of work, intended to share the resource of free time more equally among the population (this was recently endorsed in the UK by the Trades Union Congress (2018b)). The more progressive post-work writers also propose social changes to support and encourage people to be autonomous outside the sphere of employment. These might include rethinking urban design to provide well-maintained civic spaces in which people can congregate, co-operate and produce things outside the economic sphere. They might also include new educational priorities to prepare young people for a life of autonomy and multi-activity, as opposed to a life of employment in a single career path (Illich, 1971).

All of these proposals would also need to be accompanied by a new form of ethics that relaxes on the idea of busyness as a virtue, while also granting recognition and esteem to the many socially valuable activities that people perform outside the economic sphere, whether this is care work, community work, political activism, the work of self-maintenance, or any number of other activities that currently go unrecognised. Above all, this new ethics would recognise an individual's right to care and recognition, irrespective of their productive capacities.

The current discussion of alternatives represents an exciting field, full of liberating possibilities, unexplored avenues and difficult practical and ethical debates. But the discourse remains tethered until we let go of the idea of employment as an inviolable source of health and wellbeing. Only when we let this go can we have a concerted discussion about the possibilities of a less work-centred future. Instead of clinging to a system built around employment, might we instead explore more liberating social and economic forms, which could allow people to be productive and live a dignified life outside the employment relation?

To these ends, I would like to finish on the suggestion that the way forward cannot be revealed by a positivist research effort to discover the 'truth' about the relationship between employment and health. Positivist research can perhaps tell us *how things are,* but it is inadequate to the task of telling politicians and citizens *what to do* – a task that is not the exclusive domain of expert researchers but which properly belongs in the field of democratic discourse. The advantage of this is that you needn't be a credentialed expert to participate. There may be evidence to highlight the current psychosocial importance of employment, but there is still a great deal to discuss about how governments and citizens should respond to such evidence. It has hitherto been treated as proof that there is no alternative to the status quo, but what if we instead perceive it as an unsettling reflection of our existential dependency on being exploited? Or of how hostile society has become to people who do not or cannot participate in employment? Or of how dependent we have become on the market to meet our needs and structure our lives? To use a line from David Smail (2005), the problem we have is not one of insufficient evidence but of too much evidence in the context of too little thinking.

So, let us think. Let us ask whether our present work-centred society is a fair society, a free society, a society that treats people well, and a society most people would choose to live in, given the option. If researchers are to gather evidence, let them recognise that this is always a political exercise, and direct such efforts not only towards understanding the employment-centred present but also towards sketching out and investigating the probable impacts of social alternatives. Furthermore, let governments and academics stop using the prestige of positivist research to exclude dissenting voices from the debate. The feminist critique of science has highlighted the way in which appeals to the 'hard', 'objective', or 'serious' nature of quantitative research can serve as a way of positioning the layperson as ignorant (Shiva, 2014: 23). The government's failure to hear those who have suffered as a result of poor-quality work and cruel welfare reforms is a case in point.

Here, in this quagmire of stress, monotony and insecurity, we can no longer accept the dogma that work is inherently good for wellbeing. Our critiques may not always be premised on the hard data generated by positivist research and its sophisticated measuring tools, but it is valid. It comes from our ethical faculties, from the labour of critical thinking, and from the everyday strains and injustices we experience through our senses. To quote André Gorz, the task of our critique is to 'unravel the web of dominant discourse which reduces lived experience to silence' (1989: 87). Let our felt lack of freedom count for something. It is time for a change.

References

Adorno T (1991). Free time. In: Adorno T. *The Culture Industry*. London: Routledge (pp187–197).

Bustillo RM, Fernández-Macías E, Esteve F, Antón JI (2011). *E pluribus unum?* A critical survey of job quality indicators. *Socio-Economic Review* 9(3): 447–475.

Chamberlain J (2018). *Undoing Work, Rethinking Community: a critique of the social function of work*. Ithaca, NY: Cornell University Press.

Cholbi M (2018). The desire for work as an adaptive preference. [Online.] *Autonomy 04:* 1–17. http://autonomy.work/wp-content/uploads/2018/08/The-Desire-For-Work-As-An-Adaptive-Preference-V3.pdf (accessed 7 January 2019).

Clark A, Geogellis I, Sanfey P (2001). Scarring: the psychological impact of past unemployment. *Economica* 68(270): 221–241.

Cole M (2007). Re-thinking unemployment: a challenge to the legacy of Jahoda et al. *Sociology* 41(6): 1133–1149.

Department for Work and Pensions/Department of Health (2017). *Improving Lives: the future of work, health and disability*. London: The Stationery Office.

Department for Work and Pensions/Department of Health (2016). *Improving Lives: the work, health and disability Green Paper.* London: The Stationery Office.

Frayne D (2015). *The Refusal of Work: the theory and practice of resistance to work.* London: Zed Books.

Free Psychotherapy Network (2016). *Mental Wealth Alliance response to the psy professional bodies' statement on benefit sanctions and mental health 30/11/16.* [Online.] The Free Psychotherapy Network; 30 November. https://freepsychotherapynetwork.com/mwa-response-to-the-psy-professional-bodies-statement-on-benefit-sanctions-and-mental-health-301116 (accessed 7 January 2019).

Frey C, Osborne M (2017). The future of employment: how susceptible are jobs to computerisation? *Technological Forecasting and Social Change 114*: 254–280.

Friedli L, Stearn R (2015). Positive affect as coercive strategy: conditionality, activation and the role of psychology in UK government workfare programs. *Medical Humanities 41*(1): 40–47.

Fromm E (1963). *The Sane Society.* London: Routledge.

Gorz A (1999). *Reclaiming Work.* Cambridge: Polity Press.

Gorz A (1989). *Critique of Economic Reason.* London/New York, NY: Verso.

Gorz A (1985). *Paths to Paradise: on the liberation from work.* London: Pluto Press.

Hume J (2016) *Work won't set us free.* [Blog.] Medium; 31 October. https://medium.com/@jonathanhume/work-wont-set-us-free-1ef781eb9e1f (accessed 7 January 2019).

Illich I (1971). *Deschooling Society.* London: Marion Boyars Publishing.

Jackson T (2009). *Prosperity Without Growth: economics for a finite planet.* London/New York, NY: Earthscan.

Jahoda M (1982.) *Employment and Unemployment: a social-psychological analysis.* Cambridge: Cambridge University Press.

Jahoda M, Lazarsfeld P, Ziesel H (1933/1972). *Marienthal: the sociography of an unemployed community.* London: Tavistock.

Mason R (2016). Sick pay and work assessments to be reviewed, Jeremy Hunt reveals. [Online.] *The Guardian;* 31 October. www.theguardian.com/society/2016/oct/31/sick-pay-and-work-assessments-to-be-reviewed-jeremy-hunt-reveals (accessed 7 January 2019).

Olorenshaw V (2016). *All women's work and no pay: the maternal misfit in the neoliberal machine.* [Blog.] Autonomy. http://autonomy.work/portfolio/womens-work-no-pay-part-one/ (accessed 7 January 2019).

Paul K, Moser K (2009). Unemployment impairs mental health: metaanalyses. *Journal of Vocational Behaviour 74*(1): 264–282.

Royal College of Psychiatrists (2018). *Social inclusion.* [Online.] Royal College of Psychiatrists. www.rcpsych.ac.uk/usefulresources/workandmentalhealth/worker/isworkgoodforyou.aspx (accessed 19 January 2019).

Sage D (2018). Unemployment, wellbeing and the power of the work ethic: implications for social policy. [Online.] *Critical Social Policy;* 25 June. https://doi.org/10.1177/0261018318780910 (accessed 7 January 2019).

Schor J (2010). *Plenitude: the new economics of true wealth.* London: Penguin.

Shiva V (2014). Reductionism and regeneration: a crisis in science. In: Mies M, Shiva V. *Ecofeminism*. London: Zed Books (pp22–35).

Smail D (2005). *Power, Interest and Psychology: elements of a social materialist understanding of distress*. Ross-on-Wye: PCCS Books.

Srnicek N, Williams A (2016). *Inventing the Future: post-capitalism and a world without work*. London: Verso.

Standing G (2017). *Basic Income and How We Can Make It Happen*. London: Penguin.

Trades Union Congress (2018a). *1 in 9 Workers are in Insecure Jobs, Says TUC*. Press release. [Online.] Trades Union Congress; 10 May. www.tuc.org.uk/news/1-9-workers-are-insecure-jobs-says-tuc (accessed 7 January 2019).

Trades Union Congress (2018b) *A Future That Works for Working People*. [Online.] London: TUC. www.tuc.org.uk/sites/default/files/FutureofWorkReport1.pdf (accessed 7 January 2019).

Umunna C (2017). The machine age is upon us. We must not let it grind society to pieces. [Online.] *The Guardian;* 14 November. www.theguardian.com/commentisfree/2017/nov/14/post-work-world-age-of-robots-social-contract-jobs-artificial-intelligence (accessed 7 January 2019).

Waddell G, Burton K (2006). *Is Work Good for Your Health and Well-Being?* London: The Stationery Office.

Weber M (1904/2002). *The Protestant Ethic and the Spirit of Capitalism*. New York, NY: Charles Scribner's Sons.

Weeks K (2011). *The Problem with Work*. London: Duke University Press.

Woodcock J (2017). *Working the Phones: control and resistance in call centres*. London: Pluto Press.

7

Not in my name; not in my profession's name

Jay Watts

Jay Watts is a consultant clinical psychologist and psychotherapist. She has held many senior jobs in the NHS and academia, specialising in working with people experiencing distressing psychosis and long-standing interpersonal difficulties and trying to change organisational cultures for the better. Jay writes regularly for the Guardian *and* Independent, *is an activist and spends a frankly unhealthy amount of time tweeting as @shrink_at_large*

Therapy is about reducing suffering, right? Living a fuller life? Not according to current moves to place employment as a central aim of therapy. How come this move is so damaging? How does this link with psy-welfare? And what role does psychology have in this?

Clinical psychology in the UK has always been a conservative discipline, originating in the post-war period as a way of assessing and evaluating the population through psychometric testing (eg. Cheshire & Pilgrim, 2004). Clinical psychology training is funded by the state, unlike psychotherapy, and has often been used as an intermediary of government regulation, shaping subjectivities to fit societal ideals of what makes a good citizen. The implications of this are often neutralised by the argument that clinical psychology is a force for good, focused on talking to, rather than acting on, service users. There are many ways this positioning is achieved, but one is by contrasting clinical psychology with psychiatry, which is associated with punitive practices such as sectioning, restraint and enforced medication.

Yet clinical psychology has its violence too, not least in its shaping effects on ideology.

Psychological ideas shape what gets to be seen as significant and what gets missed – a practice that actively creates modern subjectivities. For example, locating normal developmental milestones is central to both child, clinical and 'abnormal' psychology. Defining normal has very real consequences – children diagnosed with autism have often been subjected to behavioural interventions to attempt to make them more like 'normal' kids. It is only now, as identity politics gain a prominence, that the neurodiversity movement rubbishes such damaging interventions, celebrating difference and locating psy-propaganda as a decades-long cause of distress (eg. Silberman, 2015). Similarly, people used to think life was quite difficult, that the best that could be expected was what Freud called 'ordinary unhappiness', and that distress was generally dis-ease, or dis-comfort with your lot. In the last 30 years, these ideas have been turned on their heads, with happiness proffered as a tantalising possibility; the psyche is re-presented as something that can be moulded and shaped using positive psychology techniques. As a consequence, more and more people identify as mentally ill (eg. Davies, 2015). For what other explanation for problems can there be?

Ideological violence is often seen by psychiatric survivors to be as damaging as physical violence, for it colonises thinking and is thus especially difficult to identify and resist. It is not 'out there' in the world but 'in here' in the mind, and is thus more difficult to call out. Many women with a diagnosis of 'borderline personality disorder' have found psychological formulation deeply pathologising; their desperate attempts to get help from a worker they trust, as opposed to another worker who is more rubbish, get labelled as 'splitting'. It is difficult to speak of something as oppressive when it is presented as benign, and even more so when structurally you have less power, as does the person in the role of the patient, provoking a double bind that is exaggerated by clinical psychology's perverse obsession with being the 'good guys'.

This chapter is about some ideas around work and responsibility that have a cultural currency that clinical psychology has partially enabled. They include the notion that worklessness is a symptom that needs to be cured through positive psychology, that employment is a legitimate outcome of a health intervention, and that a lack of commitment to these ideals takes away your entitlement to social support under 'rights and responsibilities' ideology. I write as a clinical psychologist – someone who both profits from its cultural position and also, as an activist, resists some of the effects of its power – namely, the devastating impacts of some of its ideas on claimants. The clinical psychology I am focusing on in this chapter is mainstream thinking that doesn't critique the effects of doing clinical psychology on public health, above and beyond individual clinical outcomes.

I also write as a survivor – someone who has been in the psychiatric system and has lived on disability benefits. I thank my lucky stars, often daily, that I am not on benefits at this point in history; the landscape has altered so much, I do not know whether I would still be alive. The culture is so belittling, so dehumanising, so shame inducing that, as the United Nations has declared, it goes against basic human rights (Lambert, 2017).

I hope this chapter will galvanise professionals to feel a greater responsibility for the current state of affairs, to push back the tyranny of work as a requirement for citizenship and to promote a culture where all of us can be seen as equal and interdependent on one another.

A very brief history of clinical psychology

Clinical psychology has a rather complicated relationship with science, psychotherapy and art. As mentioned earlier, clinical psychology arose as a scientific discipline to measure, assess and evaluate people's cognitive abilities in the post-war environment. It was the Other to psychoanalysis, the Other to psychotherapy, an initial fan of and proponent of behaviourism, and later firmly the champion of cognitive behavioural therapy (CBT). By this I mean that the profession's initial attempts to give itself a scientific legitimacy – often in contrast to psychoanalysis and other forms of psychotherapy – wedded it to the idea that clinical psychologists were/are 'scientist-practitioners'.

Clinical psychology has always prided itself on being evidence-based – it stands on the notion that human distress can be quantified, measured and evaluated meaningfully and objectively. This emphasis has given clinical psychology a power and prestige in the NHS and academia above and beyond its size. Although presenting itself as value-free, clinical psychology has been influenced by and influenced the rise of neoliberalism.

Neoliberalism is an ideology that has been espoused by all the political parties who have held power since Margaret Thatcher was elected prime minister (Harvey, 2007). In this ideology, state provision is situated as something that fosters a state of dependency. Dependency is seen as an impairment to individual growth and a drain on society (Watts, 2017). People who question these values are positioned as functioning under an illusion that the state has infinite resources and denying individuals their right to an upward journey. We find this idea most clearly in the dreadful phrase 'the nanny state', and in the promotion of 'recovery principles' that insist individuals can overcome their problems and 'thrive', disavowing the reality of many people's lives. If you object, say, to recovery, you are positioned as denying patients the right to achieve their true potential – a discursive move that has justified the closure of resources for those with long-term needs (eg. Watts, 2017).

Neoliberalism and therapy culture have risen hand in hand on the back of one another, with ideas from psychology used to stop those with less privilege rebelling. If the answer lies in downloading the latest meditation app, with its glistening evidence base, or developing a 'positive mental attitude' using CBT techniques, as millennials especially are conditioned to do, who would think to raise the socio-political causes of distress? The 1960s social justice movements changed our relation to the establishment forever (eg. Taylor, 1999). Yes, there had been anti-authoritarian movements before, but never had so many of the disaffected risen up to demand change. From the American civil rights movement to campaigns for women's rights, gay liberation, nuclear disarmament and so on, discontent appeared to foster both rage and hope that a better world was possible. By the mid-1970s, the mass social justice movements began to be drained of their radicalism – a shift that can be attributed to the rise of a certain atomised individualism. The usual suspect for this turn is neoliberalism. But this ideology could only develop hand-in-hand with the rise of therapy culture (Watts, 2016a).

Psychological ideas as a tool of regulation and self-audit had begun to permeate general culture in the 1950s, with psychoanalyst Donald Winnicott's much-loved radio programme guiding citizens on how to parent (Farley, 2012). But it gained a new currency in the 1960s with the rise of abnormal psychology and the human potential movement, which spread like wildfire to mould subjectivities (Stone, 1978).

Encounter groups (Rogers, 1970) emerged as an attempt to help individuals work together to tackle internalised oppression. For example, feminist encounter groups consisted of small collectives of women who met to tell their stories and link their distress to structural discrimination and emancipatory action. However, this kind of collective work soon became co-opted by ideas such as self-actualisation (Fitts, 1971). The inner world was to be explored now, not for the collective endeavour but in the pursuit of individual happiness. Mass activism began to wane as the sale of self-help books mushroomed (Bührmann & Ernst, 2010), carrying within their pages the message that responsibility for growth and happiness rested firmly with the individual. Why, after all, go to a feminist encounter group when you could find the tools for enlightenment in a self-help book you could read at home?

The side effect of the rise of therapy culture was a de-politicised understanding of embodied distress and a certain navel-gazing. The causes of anger and anxiety were located solely in individuals' childhoods or, as the 21st century beckoned, in their genes. Consideration of power relations and the structural causes of inequalities became a lefty side-project, getting in the way of developing 'brand me', or a footnote at the end of academic articles.

Mainstream psychology here served neoliberalism's ideals perfectly – making individuals feel responsibility for governing their own behaviour through proffering techniques such as cognitive behavioural therapy (eg. Beck, 2011), through which the individual could, supposedly, cut out personality traits that did not fit the market ideals and develop 'the right kind of affect'. Anger here is not a reasonable response to, say, sexual abuse, misogyny or poor social conditions, but something you must excise to be the perfect 'walking CV'. Sadness is something that doesn't fit the job market, so is to be managed via mindfulness. Clinical psychology here positions itself as an entity that can provide you with tools to help yourself in these endeavours and, in so doing, turns the gaze away from other approaches to conceptualising and helping with discontent. An ever-expanding number of mood conditions – from anger to anxiety – began to be framed as mental disorders, rather than as understandable reactions to impossible environments. There are hundreds of diagnoses available now, sold back to us via Big Pharma and psychiatric expansionist programmes such as Mental Health First Aid. Our internal worlds are being commodified.

Yet the idea of the self as atomised, which neoliberalism proffered and psychology helped produce, is deeply flawed (Rose, 1999). Our inner worlds are predominantly a product of the discursive and material environments that we inhabit: the opportunities open to us and those from which we are barred (Recovery in the Bin, 2015). For example, as a result of ableism, an individual may be positioned as lesser because they are disabled – an experience of the world underlined by structural discriminations that imprint on the body and psyche. Hopelessness, poverty, isolation, discrimination and lower social rank, for instance, are key predictors of mental stress. Although therapy was storied as a helpful solution to the problem, its models of the self were partly responsible for the current mental health epidemic.

To explore these issues, and the special responsibility professionals have to speak out right now, we need to go back in time to explore the rise of something Rimke has called psychocentrism (Rimke & Brock, 2012). Psychocentrism is a form of neoliberal governance that pathologises suffering and places its causes firmly within individuals, rather than in the structural inequalities, oppressions and experiences of trauma that make people mad. Psychocentrism is a form of governance that shapes subjectivities, moulding how we experience the inner world. Psychocentrism was and is neoliberalism's great enabler.

Psychocentrism in society has led to people voting for change-agents who support the ragged individualism we have been socialised into, even when such votes only serve to reinforce the conditions of oppression citizens think they are rejecting. Psychocentrism has also allowed the government to demonise those who are not in work.

In the past 11 years, this neoliberal psychology has become tied to the work agenda. This is a product of two things – the rise of the Improving Access to Psychological Therapies (IAPT) programme, and the emergence of behavioural economics.

The rise of IAPT

In 2006, the Labour government's popularity was waning. Something was needed to show a commitment to the welfare of the masses. Yet this intervention could not be too socio-political, for New Labour attributed its popularity to its relationship to the neoliberal ideology of rights and responsibility (Ball & Exley, 2010). You had, the new era would come to suggest, the right to resources only if you took responsibility for your situation through psychological modification.

Take a Tony Blair speech from 2001, 'Faith in Politics'. In this short speech, Blair mentioned the word 'responsibility' 10 times, declaring:

> A sharper focus on individual responsibility is going hand-in-hand
> with a great improvement in the support provided by government.
> Responsibility from all – security and opportunity for all. Not an idle
> slogan, but the only way forward as we break the old culture which left
> generations of families trapped in unemployment and poverty.

Blair was right – this was not an idle slogan but a policy move that enabled the Tories to develop these ideas into a system that denies welfare to people in need, and to justify this brutality by declaring they are 'saving' them from transgenerational poverty.

An economist, Professor Lord Richard Layard, presented a clever solution: *The Depression Report* (Layard & CEP Mental Health Policy Group, 2006). *The Depression Report* paved a way for IAPT, a national programme to roll out psychological therapy to the masses. Layard's Machiavellian genius was to sell this using an economic argument as much as a moral one. The 'one in six of the population suffer[ing] from depression and chronic anxiety disorder' could be:

> ... cured at a cost of no more than £750... For depression and anxiety
> make it difficult or impossible to work, and drive people onto Incapacity
> Benefits. We now have a million people on Incapacity Benefits because
> of mental illness - more than the total number of unemployed people
> receiving unemployment benefits... Can we afford the £750 it costs
> to treat someone? The money which the government spends will pay
> for itself. For someone on Incapacity Benefit costs us £750 a month in
> extra benefits and lost tax. If the person works just one month more as
> a result of the treatment, the treatment pays for itself! (Layard & CEP
> Mental Health Policy Group, 2006)

The rhetoric was zealous, evangelical and ultimately convincing. IAPT was piloted in 2007, and swiftly rolled out, explicitly committed from the off to reducing unemployment to pay the salaries of its employees. Employment as an outcome was central to this project, with pre-and post-therapy measures acculturating both therapist and patient to what was required. Employment advisers were to be available in each and every IAPT clinic, one for every eight therapists, as set out in the Department of Health *IAPT Implementation Plan* (2008). It is difficult to over-emphasise how radical a change this was to the mental health landscape in the UK. This was not just a change to service structure: the indexing of outcome to economics was hitherto unheard of. It was both a fast-forwarding of the 'auditable-surface' outcome culture that had been introduced into the NHS from the 1990s and a coupling of outcome with public good (the public purse) as opposed to individual good (what a specific patient wants).

The introduction of IAPT was met with some protest in clinical psychology circles (eg. Smail, 2006). This generally took the form of a rehashing of criticisms of CBT and the individualisation of distress it tends to promote, but dissent was remarkably absent. Most IAPT proponents and leads were clinical psychologists, and wasn't it just common sense that more therapy was better than less? Wasn't something better than nothing? How could you be against 'improving access to psychological therapies?' And wasn't this a chance for clinical psychology – one of the good guys, remember – to gain terrain?

This stopped detailed analysis of certain components of the IAPT programme – specifically, the emphasis on work as an indicator of good character and a pre-requirement to gain the benefits of citizenship. And this was not just any work; it was paid work. Voluntary work, a traditional goal for many, was presented as purposeless (and later became actively risky, given the 'if you are fit enough to volunteer ever, you can work always' discourse pushed out by Department for Work and Pensions (DWP) assessors). For example, Layard and colleagues (2006, above) argued that IAPT treatment would pay for itself if someone could hold down a job for even a month. Yet where is the consideration of what it means to be 'driven' into work? How might that affect mental health? How might it give claimants the impression that not working makes them expensive drains on the national economy? How might starting a job due to these pressures and then collapsing after a month because of the strain affect mental and physical health? Might the costs for the state end up being more?

These questions were largely invisible because of a resistance among the majority to looking at how cognitive behavioural therapy (CBT) serves the neoliberal dream. CBT, after all, has given clinical psychology its prominent place in the psy-workforce today.

Cognitive behavioural therapy

To make sense of this relationship, we need to take a small detour to explore what CBT is. Over the past 25 years, CBT has become the psy-treatment of choice in the UK. There are many reasons for this, including that it is relatively cheap, highly marketable, and it fits well with the grand narrative of the NHS – evidence-based care (Watts, 2016b).

CBT is explicitly storied as a therapy that is 'forward thinking' and 'positive', not 'endless nor backward-looking' (Layard & CEP Mental Health Policy Group, 2006: 1), which, presumably, other therapies are because they give time and space to hearing in detail what has happened to people. CBT thus focuses on the here-and-now, adding the 'C' of exploring cognitions (or thoughts) in response to ethical concerns about pure 'B' (or a focus on behaviourism).

Consider a standard session. A client is given a 'thought record' (eg. Hundt et al, 2013) and asked to identify the 'hot cognition' that is bothering them. This thought, or belief, is then rated for 'evidence for' and 'evidence against' it. Most often this jury-type examination will result in the writing of a new belief. Thus, 'I can't do anything' might be replaced by the belief, 'I can sometimes do things, but sometimes struggle'. In Beck's model, common problems like social anxiety or depression are seen as linked to certain dysfunctional ways of thinking and information biases (eg. Neenan & Dryden, 2005).

Thus, someone with anxiety might be seen as having 'danger-oriented beliefs' and be prone to 'jumping to conclusions'. Childhood experiences are not up for discussion. Rather, clients in this therapy are heavily socialised into certain ideas – that problems can be changed by thinking differently; that emotional difficulties like depression and anxiety can be cured, and that people can be trained to think in non-disordered ways (eg. Richards & Whyte, 2011). Socialisation into these ideas starts with information leaflets, posters and – crucially – the outcome measures that patients are often required to fill in at each and every therapy session. These materials shape the subjectivity of both patient and therapist – the 'right' goal is symptom reduction rather than understanding, for example (Watts, 2016b). The focus here is on creating what Foucault refers to as 'governable subjects' who construct their distress as an individualised problem, a 'private trouble' to be solved by therapeutic means (Giddens, 1992). This forecloses evidence that clearly links such distress to material conditions like poverty, job insecurity and insecure accommodation (eg. Psychologists Against Austerity, 2015).

The psychocentrism that Becksian CBT propagates pushes responsibility for mental health onto the individual, who must use CBT techniques to restore a less problematic equilibrium. The procedures used to achieve this have, for many, an echo of 'disciplinary power' (eg. Foucault, 1977). They prescribe new 'emotional rules' about which emotions are OK and to what degree, and impose self-help techniques, self-observation and the filling out of tables. While this is storied as free choice – 'collaborative empiricism', to use the CBT buzzword – the degree of socialisation into 'right messages' implies that this freedom is actually freedom within a certain ideology, based on norms. The power relations inherent within this are masked both by an obsession with the idea that CBT is collaborative and by ever-shorter trainings for its practitioners, now frequently focused just on CBT and so jam-packed with manuals for specific conditions that reflection outside the tenets of the model is near impossible.

Practitioners of CBT are keen to say that the goals of therapy are decided by clients (Tee & Kazantzis, 2011). However, this is a slightly bizarre claim. First of all, what we think we want is subject to the environment we live in and the cultural messages we receive. Most people on benefits, for example, feel they *ought* to pay tax, that they ought to work, that they have less value otherwise, because they have internalised these ideas from our wider culture. Given the current demonising of the workless as worthless (Coote & Lyall, 2013), given the neoliberal obsession with self-as-commodity, we would expect people in pain in the 2010s to see not working as a problem in a way they wouldn't have in the more open 1960s. This is why a key part of psychodynamic therapy, for example, is *not* presuming a person knows what they want from what they initially say. Indeed, the first part of psychodynamic work is often about pushing back this kind of discourse to find out where desire really lies, and saying 'no' to the performances of good citizenship and, indeed, illness that we have internalised and are enacting.

It is only in recent decades that the presenting symptom has been taken so literally and as a sign of pathology. In earlier traditions, there was space to see symptoms as double-edged – bearers of pain, yes, but also communicating something. Freud's idea of the 'compulsion to repeat', for example, recognises that traumatic flashbacks carry in them a desire for something to be responded to differently; a desire to place something unbearable into a narrative in order to make life liveable again (after Freud, 1936). Ignoring this, and shaping the therapeutic setting as a space to excise what is problematic, can, therefore, end up reinforcing what is oppressing the person – which, all too often, is their life in a society that pits people against one another, sets up impossible ideals and refuses to listen to how structural inequality and trauma skewer people.

These pressures and presumptions carry a new weight in the current climate, where claimants are constantly drip-fed messages that their worklessness is their symptom and work is their cure. And therapy can reinforce that damaging ideology. A client presents who is feeling hopeless and is on benefits. He feels guilt and shame for not being able to work, that he is failing as a man and is worth nothing. CBT focuses less on the problems with situating work as the one true goal of an individual right now in history, less on the connection between masculinity and 'being a breadwinner' and more on the individualised cognitions and behaviours that stop this man earning, as if the difficulties lay in him rather than the hate-fuelled, job-obsessed culture that neoliberalism propagates. This is not a politically neutral act, but a form of therapy that reinforces some of the damaging, individual-blaming cultural scripts that – as decades of evidence show – make people ill. What are the options for this man: to disengage from therapy, leaving him without help? To try to work, even when his disability makes this physically and mentally dangerous? Or to enact internally the outside world's rejection of his difficulties in the form of depressive collapse?

If clients are sold the idea that their problems are disorders, this is what they will present with. Some will have internalised these ideas; others will perform them to get something, even if it doesn't fit their own ideas. For example, I know many women with a diagnosis of 'borderline personality disorder' who say, if they go to IAPT for help, they have to pretend they haven't been abused because they know there is no space there to process trauma. So, they go and dissimulate because they need some help, desperately. This, of course, puts huge pressure on patients who have to pretend their anxiety, say, is due to the normal vicissitudes of life. It is also potentially dangerous for people with chronic trauma histories, who are supposed to have long therapies with highly skilled professionals. And of course, this way of conceptualising embodied distress is produced and reinforced by leaflets, psychoeducation and immersion in IAPT culture. Crucially, as mentioned earlier in this chapter, this culture includes subjecting clients to outcome measures at each and every session – measures that locate employment as a goal, shaping what it means to recover and what IAPT workers, as employees of the state, decide they will work on with clients. For example, there is a strong evidence base that behavioural couples therapy is effective for depressed women – a treatment that probably works for intersectional reasons, such as the excessive demands on women for emotional labour and caring. To not offer this treatment and, instead, offer one that encourages compliance with a regulated emotional life is a political act.

While CBT presents itself as worthy of its central place in culture due to its effectiveness evidence base, it in effect takes attention away from other equally valid evidences for why people suffer, reinforcing a neoliberal agenda that 'there is no such thing as society' and that everything is equally possible for everyone, if only they would just goddamn cultivate the right psychological mindset. The difference here is that CBT fits very well with one type of evidence base – the one based on outcome measures and randomised controlled trials – because it presumes knowledge of what needs to be changed for a client, based on problem clusters such as anxiety and depression, so can provide data that are good for crunching. Now, there are many good things to be said about quantitative evidence. However, to privilege it above other means of collecting evidence – for example, qualitative feedback and what patients actually say – is deeply problematic.

It is doubly so when most trials of CBT that show efficacy do so in comparison with something called 'treatment as usual', or TAU. This TAU is nearly always 'usual' GP or community mental health team care, rather than another active treatment – that is, another therapy, like psychodynamic therapy.

Further, because IAPT has put its worth firmly in the twin goals of savings to the public purse and better health outcomes, it is especially vulnerable to demands for ever-shorter forms of treatment. To my admiration, the BABCP – the main body representing CBT practitioners – put out a press release (BABCP, 2014) a few years ago explicitly condemning the pressure therapists were under to provide treatment in fewer sessions than the gold standard number recommended in the good-practice guidelines produced by the National Institute for Health and Care Excellence (NICE). But we have yet to hear that same critique when shorter treatments are tested for efficacy versus TAU in a service that provides substandard (ie. non-NICE-compliant) interventions. You cannot conclude from these studies that shorter forms of CBT are as effective as longer models, yet by omission this is the suggestion. This plays into the hands of the master – ie. neoliberalism – at the expense of quality of patient care (especially given that helping people is pretty much always financially beneficial in terms of the public purse, in the medium to long term).

It is, of course, important not to write off the entire IAPT programme; it has helped many, many people, as has clinical psychology. It is crucial, though, to hold this reality while taking a critical view of what IAPT systemically does: ie. the effects of the overplaying of its evidence base (as demonstrated in Paul Atkinson's Chapter 8) and its complicity with the DWP work programme.

Thus, while offering some assistance to some people in distress – for IAPT can help people, but with nothing like the efficacy its proponents suggest (eg. Ali et al, 2017) – it supercharges ideas that the causes of distress arise from dysfunctional cognitions and are thus easy to remedy. This allows the government to position people who struggle to succeed according to its terms as almost wilfully responsible for their situation, and so justify the structural violence against claimants we see today.

Subsequently, this emphasis on locating distress in individuals was further reinforced by the introduction of behavioural economics, as embodied in the Nudge Unit.

Behavioural economics

In 2010, the recently elected prime minister David Cameron ordered his cabinet to read over their summer holidays a book called *Nudge* (Thaler & Sunstein, 2008). *Nudge* sets out how behaviourism, a type of psychology, could be used to encourage people to make the 'right' decisions about how to live. Behaviourism at heart is quite simple, despite propaganda to the contrary. You need to reward behaviour deemed 'good' – the carrot approach – and punish that deemed 'bad' – the stick. 'A choice architect has the responsibility for organizing the context in which people make decisions,' the book's co-author Richard Thaler declares (Thaler & Sunstein, 2008): 'Roughly speaking, losses hurt about twice as much as gains make you feel good.'

Shortly after, the Behavioural Insights Team, known informally as the Nudge Unit, was established within the Cabinet Office, led by a psychologist, David Halpern. The Nudge Unit got a bit of stick from the psychology community, but not as much as you might hope. This was partly because of vested interests and partly because it was framed as being all about things like getting people to use fewer plastic carrier bags, and we all think saving the environment is a good idea. Its ideas about shaping 'right actions' spread like ideological wildfire across government departments. Citizens were seen as being motivated primarily by 'loss aversion', or a fear of losing what they have, in contrast to acting on what they might gain. The emphasis was thus on using people's fear that what they had would be taken away to shape their behaviour, resulting in the DWP's increased use of sanctions (Webster, 2013) – up 600% in the following four years (Stone, 2015) – to force claimants to do what the market required. Claimants were force-fed the idea that they were responsible for the causes of their distress (Friedli & Stearn, 2015) – for example, to see their worklessness as due to their having the 'wrong mindset' and that they required a short course of CBT to develop a 'positive mental attitude', after which everything would be OK. Placing the fault in individuals, rather than recognising, for example, the lack of jobs available, the quality of jobs as zero-hour contracts become a norm and the fact that many would never be able to work, was a brilliant way to quell resistance and let the government and tax-avoiding big business get off scot free.

But the casualties of this have, of course, been the people caught up in the resulting epidemic of mental distress, who are having to endure conditions so unbearable that many have killed themselves, some of them friends of contributors to this book (Calum's List, undated). Attempted suicide rates by disability benefit claimants have more than doubled since the introduction of fit-to-work benefits (Bulman & Polyanskaya, 2017), not just because of the material deprivations sanctions produce but due to the terror claimants experience from being made to feel under constant surveillance and that they are morally derelict. I've heard of claimants being asked, 'Well, why haven't you killed yourself by now?', with the suggestion that they are faking their problems.

The unholy alliance of behavioural economics and health outcomes

Some people have always argued that work is good for mental health, but the prominence and insistence on this idea are radically new. Some of the early treatments for mental health problems, such as the 19th century 'moral treatment' movement (for example, Borthwick et al, 2001), saw work as central to the cure. Sigmund Freud situated work and love as the 'cornerstones of our humanness' (Freud, 1930/2015). Early- and mid-20th century asylums saw work as crucial to stabilise patients. However, work as it is understood in the policies I will list below does not approximate to the kind of work these early pioneers were referring to. Work within these earlier contexts meant activity, or a project for its own sake; it could mean play and creativity. Its function was to occupy the mind (which would otherwise be obsessed with sin, sex or aggression, depending on the theorist). Work as understood within this context might be activism or voluntary work – both of which are activities disabled people now feel *less* able to do, due to the constant scrutiny of the DWP, who see *any* sign of ability as indicating that all benefits should be stopped.

Work in this neoliberal world means paid employment, with the one clear aim of making citizens economically viable in a society that places the market above all other aspects of the human experience, such as relationships, play, connection and hobbies. The argument that this is evidence based, that research shows work is good for your mental health, is used to warrant this move, unparalleled in history. Psychology and science in general are brought on board to make it appear an objective, apolitical move.

The evidence used for this, as critiqued in more detail in David Frayne's Chapter 6, is sketchy. It is based on one meta-analysis and relatively few studies of a small pool of participants receiving exceptional care and support in organisations that have predominantly shown their commitment to mental health (see Waddell & Burton, 2006). Other evidences (to misquote the Heineken advert) are available, including:

- that poor work is worse than no work (eg. Chandola & Zhang, 2017)
- that some people will never be able to work (eg. Holloway, 2010)
- that the pressure to work is making some people ill (eg. Dwyer et al, 2017).

Despite the dodgy evidence base, work as a health outcome has featured ever more centrally in government policy, as David Frayne's chapter describes, culminating in the Green and White Papers both titled *Improving Lives* (Department for Work & Pensions/Department of Health, 2016, 2017). This policy encourages Jobcentre Plus workers to signpost claimants into therapy, with employment advisors to be situated in each and every IAPT service (see also Paul Atkinson's Chapter 8). Claimants are forced to have 'health and work conversations' based on a questionnaire informed by positive psychology, and DWP advisors are now repositioned as 'job coaches', and use carrot and stick techniques to try to reinforce 'good' behaviours and undermine others deemed 'bad'. The fundamental conflict between the dual roles of coach and punisher goes unexamined.

At a time of unprecedented cutbacks across the NHS and social services, in 2017 the DWP announced a doubling of the number of employment advisers in IAPT services, backed with a £47.7 million cheque (Jarman, 2017). At the time of writing, no one knows what this is going to look like. However, a presentation at the 2017 New Savoy Conference – the annual get-together of IAPT, CBT and the power players in psychology – offers a clue. According to Kevin Jarman (2017), then Lead of the Work & Health Unit set up to operate across the DWP and Department of Health, IAPT therapists should:

- at assessment, identify whether employment support is required
- keep informed of the progress of employment support. In collaboration with the client, therapists should take the necessary action to ensure that employment support is successful by focusing on how to overcome emotional challenges of continuing in, starting or resuming work, for example, fear or anxiety around interviews, fear of returning to work after period of sickness absence, bullying, and so on
- work in conjunction with the client and employment advisor to produce a personalized package of care to address the emotional challenges of continuing in, starting or resuming work
- agree with the client and employment advisor shared goals, identifying psychological work/increasing activity/problem-solving skills that could contribute to achieving employment goals
- routinely review, during therapeutic contact, the client's need for employment support. This can be done at routine reviews of treatment plans or at each session, if routine reviews are not in place. (Jarman, 2017)

Anyone with even a superficial interest in how shaping, suggestibility and the structural power imbalance influence the therapeutic space can see how these demands, which come from the state, will affect the encounter between patient and clinician. Work is privileged, while accounts of trauma, oppression and distress are foreclosed. Therapy here is less about listening to the patient than shaping them into good, neoliberal subjects. This is simply professionally unethical.

The fightback

This move has not gone unchallenged. In the spring of 2015, then Chancellor George Osborne suggested in his budget (HM Treasury, 2015: 72) that IAPT workers should be co-located in job centres to target the million or so of claimants on Employment Support Allowance (ESA) with mental health problems. A number of us from the Alliance for Counselling & Psychotherapy contacted Disabled People Against Cuts[1] and Mental Health Resistance Network[2] to organise a meeting to see what we could do. Before then, truth be told, we had not worked as closely with survivors as we should have. However, the meeting that followed produced a collective loosely known as the Mental Wealth Alliance (MWA), which consisted eventually of 18 radical activist organisations.

We started off with organising a letter to the *Guardian* signed by 442 professionals calling for a stop to collusion between the DWP and the psy-professions (House et al, 2015). We began a correspondence with the psy-professional bodies, calling them out for their complicity and requesting a formal condemnation of sanctions and a clear delineation between therapy and DWP services (Free Psychotherapy Network, 2017). In 2015, MWA organised a protest outside the Streatham Jobcentre Plus, saying NO to psycho-compulsion, NO to forced treatment (Gayle, 2015). In 2016, we protested outside the New Savoy Partnership annual conference for two years in a row and contributed to two MHRN-led fanzines on psycho-compulsion (Disabled People Against Cuts, 2016). We held two major conferences – in Bermondsey and Liverpool – and, in 2017, lobbied outside the British Psychological Society conference (Free Psychotherapy Network, 2017).

The connections we have forged and the noise we have made have had an effect. The psy-professional organisations have come out publicly

1. https://dpac.uk.net
2. https://mentalhealthresistance.org

against sanctions and emphasised their commitment to informed consent, in response to our lobbying. In a joint statement, the British Psychological Society, the British Association for Counselling and Psychotherapy, the British Psychoanalytic Council, the British Association for Behavioural and Cognitive Psychotherapies and the UK Council for Psychotherapy jointly declared:

> Not only are we concerned that the sanctions process is undermining mental health and wellbeing – there is no clear evidence of pay-off in terms of increased employment and no commitment from the Government to investigate how the jobcentre systems and requirements may themselves be exacerbating mental health problems. (British Psychological Society et al, 2017)

This was repeated in June 2018, in response to a new report on welfare sanctions (BABCP et al, 2018). Yet this move has gone not nearly far enough. It has given some protection to what goes on in the therapy space. But the psychocentrism we are discussing in this book and the rise of the work agenda are more complicated than this. Clinical psychology and other psy-professions who profit from the discourses that propagate rampant individualism and the marketisation of the soul must take a greater responsibility for the current predicament it/we have partly caused. How?

1. Psychocompulsion is not something you can consent to

There are some among the psy-professions who have adopted the position that it is ethical to welcome DWP advisors into health settings because clients can still choose whether to see an employment advisor or not. This is at best naïve; it pays no heed to how power, suggestibility and identification operate. Claimants tell us repeatedly that their fear of the DWP is so great, its power to sanction so present, that they feel coerced into going along with what is 'suggested', because they don't want to risk losing their means of survival.

This is especially important to take seriously, because the decision-making around sanctions is somewhat opaque, subject to the whims of individual assessors and arbitration from the (equally unknowable) DWP decision-maker. Few claimants would risk turning down the 'suggestion' that they agree to have therapy to get them back to work, and nor do they have the social power to insist that the therapy concentrates on goals that are meaningful to them. If people entering IAPT are now not only to be asked once if they want to see a DWP employment advisor but to be signposted to it clearly throughout their therapy, it is very evident what the deal is. Middle-class professionals, who often have not experienced the operations of such power in the first place, may think consent is possible in such situations. Most claimants don't.

Further, all of us identify and internalise societal messages about who and what we are supposed to be. The internalisation of such attitudes means people come to regard their worklessness as the cause of their mental distress when it is the societal insistence on the moral value of work that has led to their guilt, anxiety, shame and depression (see David Frayne's Chapter 6). For example, claimants internalise the 'scrounger' narrative, which is super-boosted by the media in programmes such as *Benefits Street* and the notion that living on welfare is a 'lifestyle choice' (Patrick, 2016). Can informed consent really be seen to be possible when explicit messages shape and mould subjectivities in such a profound way? I think not.

2. Psychology is being used by the DWP away from the therapy room

The psy-professional bodies have made some progress towards understanding the situation claimants face. But what is missing is an understanding of, and campaigns against, the use of positive psychology and CBT techniques away from the therapy room. This includes the use of psychology in the new 'health and work conversations' insisted on for Universal Credit claimants, and the positive psychology courses they are obliged to sign up to. These and other devices serve to shape people's subjectivities to view worklessness as their fault and something they can easily rectify if they only make the effort to cultivate the 'right attitude'. The psy-professions should surely be lobbying to question whether consent is possible in these 'work and health conversations' that psychology has sold to the world. These kinds of interactions may not be therapy, but they take advantage of the therapy culture we have propagated in order to mask real, present, urgent concerns like long-term need, structural inequalities and oppressions, and the lack of decent work, for which government has a responsibility.

3. Choosing to focus health funding on work takes funding away from other places

As I have previously discussed, the evidence that work is good for your health is small. A strong case can be made to the contrary. And, indeed, to make any comments about work as a 'thing' is meaningless, stupid, ripe with moral assumptions and in denial of the absolute difference between work as a choice, work as rewarded and the soul-destroying, depersonalised nature of much work today. Differences in employment associated with class, gender, ethnicity and disability are all obscured in the gross statement 'Work is good for you', as is the fact that many people in work are also on benefits. Yet this has not stopped the government writing to GPs to tell them to tell patients this is a truth. 'Remember the long-term health risks of worklessness when advising your patient that they are not fit for work', as the official advice to GPs puts it (Department for Work and Pensions, 2015): 'As with other health advice, you should emphasise the advantages to the patient's health of being at work. This information will not always be embraced enthusiastically', it notes, without shame.

The evidence for treatments that focus on what those suffering mental distress want – to work through trauma, to improve quality of life, to have a space to speak – is far stronger and more substantial. In failing to critically explore claims for an evidence base for work as a health outcome, in failing to explore how the emphasis on work takes funding away from space to work through other goals, the psy-professions are complicit in the DWP's agenda to demonise a sector of the population. The time is surely here to point at what is not being funded in relation to what is.

In conclusion

We do not, would not tolerate the suggestion that chemotherapy should be funded by the state because it helps reduce welfare spending by getting people back to work.

Letting the idea that work is a health outcome into the mental health arena has been a disaster. As soon as you start privileging treatments that help the public purse, you are acting in the interests of neoliberalism rather than ethics. We should help and provide support for people because they matter and because recognising our interdependence helps everybody. Instead, the work agenda is part of the increasing focus on viewing people as atomised individuals who can either be shaped into the model that suits market economics or left to rot. The brutal nature of today's emphasis on productivity, as defined in economic terms above all else, allows claimants to be situated as workless scroungers and has caused uncounted deaths and brought many to despair. It has allowed the public and media to turn their gaze away from the plight of people society has not favoured and has fuelled policies that locate blame firmly in the individual – an idea they then internalise.

To remedy this disastrous predicament, we activists must turn the gaze back on the conditions that have allowed this turn of events, including the psychocentrism that psychology profits from. This means campaigning at a societal level to challenge the idea that paid work is central to the good life, challenging the idea that work is a health outcome, and recognising that psycho-compulsion, by definition, is not something individuals can consent to.

Psy-professionals like me, who profit from psychocentrism's central place in contemporary society, have a special responsibility to call out its misuse. Our activism, friends, must not take the polite, middle-class form of calling for enquiries or writing academic papers. No. It must take the specular, imagination-grabbing form that strikes at the heart, grabs the media's attention and speaks from a deep understanding of what it means to be human and to live well. It is time to declare, loudly, 'Not in my name, not in my profession's name.'

References

Ali S, Rhodes L, Moreea O, McMillan D, Gilbody S, Leach C, Delgadillo J (2017). How durable is the effect of low intensity CBT for depression and anxiety? Remission and relapse in a longitudinal cohort study. *Behaviour Research and Therapy 94*: 1–8.

BABCP et al (2018). *Response to welfare conditionality report on welfare sanctions.* Press release; 1 June. [Online.] Bury: BABCP. https://www.babcp.com/About/Press/Response-to-Welfare-Conditionality-Report-on-Welfare-Sanctions.aspx (accessed 24 January 2019).

BABCP (2014). *'Bullying cultures' in NHS mental health services putting vulnerable patients at risk.* [Online.] Press release; 25 September. Bury: BABCP. https://www.babcp.com/About/Press/Bullying-Culture-in-NHS-Mental-Health-Services-Putting-Vulnerable-Patients-at-Risk.aspx (accessed 7 January 2019).

Ball SJ, Exley S (2010). Making policy with 'good ideas': policy networks and the 'intellectuals' of New Labour. *Journal of Education Policy 25*(2): 151–169.

Beck JS (2011). *Cognitive Behavior Therapy: basics and beyond* (2nd ed). New York, NY: The Guilford Press.

Blair T (2001). *Faith in Politics.* Westminster Central Hall, London. Available from: British Political Speech. www.britishpoliticalspeech.org/speech-archive.htm?speech=280 (accessed 24 January 2019).

Borthwick A, Holman C, Kennard D, McFetridge M, Messruther K, Wilkes J (2001). The relevance of moral treatment to contemporary mental health care. *Journal of Mental Health 10*(4): 427–439.

British Psychological Society et al (2017). *BPS calls for the government to suspend its benefits sanctions system.* [Online.] www.bps.org.uk/news-and-policy/bps-calls-government-suspend-its-benefits-sanctions-system (accessed 7 January 2019).

Bührmann AD, Ernst S (eds) (2010). *Care or Control of the Self? Norbert Elias, Michel Foucault, and the subject in the 21st century.* Cambridge: Cambridge Scholars Publishing.

Bulman M, Polyanskaya A (2017). Attempted suicides by disability benefit claimants more than double after introduction of fit-to-work assessment. [Online.] *The Independent*; 28 December. https://www.independent.co.uk/news/uk/home-news/disability-benefit-claimants-attempted-suicides-fit-to-work-assessment-i-daniel-blake-job-centre-dwp-a8119286.html (accessed 7 January 2019).

Calum's List (undated). [Online.] http://calumslist.org (accessed 7 May 2018).

Chandola T, Zhang N (2017). Re-employment, job quality, health and allostatic load biomarkers: prospective evidence from the UK Household Longitudinal Study. *International journal of Epidemiology 1*(1): 47–57.

Cheshire K, Pilgrim D (2004). *A Short Introduction to Clinical Psychology.* London: Sage Publications.

Coote A, Lyall S (2013). Strivers v skivers: the workless and worthless. [Online.] *The Guardian;* 11 April. www.theguardian.com/commentisfree/2013/apr/11/strivers-v-skivers-divisive-notion (accessed 7 January 2019).

Davies W (2015). *The Happiness Industry: how the government and big business sold us well-being.* London/New York: Verso Books.

Department for Work and Pensions (2015). *Getting the Most Out of the Fit Note: GP guidance.* London: Department for Work and Pensions. https://assets.publishing.service.gov.uk/government/uploads/system/uploads/attachment_data/file/465918/fit-note-gps-guidance.pdf (accessed 24 January 2019).

Department for Work and Pensions/Department of Health (2017). *Improving Lives: the future of work, health and disability.* London: The Stationery Office.

Department for Work and Pensions/Department of Health (2016). *Improving Lives: the work, health and disability green paper.* London: Department for Work and Pensions.

Department of Health (2008). *Improving Access to Psychological Therapies Implementation Plan: national guidelines for regional delivery.* London: Department of Health. www.mhinnovation.net/sites/default/files/downloads/innovation/tools/IAPT-Implementation-Plan.pdf (accessed 20 January 2019).

Disabled People Against Cuts (2016). *Protest against work cure therapy 5th July, London.* [Online.] https://dpac.uk.net/2016/06/protest-against-work-cure-therapy-5th-july-london/ (accessed 9 January 2019).

Dwyer P, Jones K, McNeill J, Scullion L, Alasdair Stewart A (2017). *The Experience of Welfare Conditionality for People with Mental Health Issues.* Paper presented at Australian Social Policy Conference 25–27 September. www.welfareconditionality.ac.uk/wp-content/uploads/2017/09/26.09.17JMAustralian-Social-Policy-conference.pdf (accessed 24 January 2019).

Farley L (2012). Analysis on air: a sound history of Winnicott in wartime. *American Imago* 69(4): 449–471.

Fitts WH (1971). *The Self-Concept and Self-Actualization: studies on the self-concept.* Nashville, TN: Dede Wallace Center.

Foucault M (1977). *Discipline and Punish: the birth of the prison* (2nd ed). New York, NY: Knopf Doubleday Publishing Group.

Free Psychotherapy Network. (2017). *Some background to the MWA and the New Savoy demo and lobby Wednesday 15th March 2017.* [Online.] Available at: https://freepsychotherapynetwork.com/some-background-to-the-mwa-new-savoy-demo-and-lobby-25th-march (accessed 21 December 2017).

Freud S (1936). Inhibitions, symptoms and anxiety. *The Psychoanalytic Quarterly* 5(1): 1–28.

Freud S (1930/2015). *Civilization and its Discontents.* Peterborough, Canada: Broadview Press.

Friedli L, Stearn R (2015). Positive affect as coercive strategy: conditionality, activation and the role of psychology in UK government workfare programs. *Medical Humanities 41*(1): 40–47.

Gayle D (2015). Mental health workers protest at move to integrate clinic with job centre. [online] *The Guardian*; 26 June. Available at: www.theguardian.com/society/2015/jun/26/mental-health-protest-clinic-jobcentre-streatham (accessed 21 December 2017).

Giddens A (1992). *The Transformation of Intimacy: sexuality, love, and eroticism in modern societies.* Redwood City, CA: Stanford University Press.

Harvey D (2007). *A Brief History of Neoliberalism.* Oxford: Oxford University Press.

HM Treasury (2015). *The Budget 2015.* London: HM Treasury. https://assets.publishing.service. gov.uk/government/uploads/system/uploads/attachment_data/file/416330/47881_Budget_2015_Web_Accessible.pdf (accessed 20 January 2019).

Holloway F (2010). Rehabilitation psychiatry in an era of austerity. Editorial. *Journal of Mental Health 19*(1): 1–7.

House R, Totton N, Burnip L and 439 others (2015). Austerity and a malign benefits regime are profoundly damaging mental health. [Online.] Letter to the editor. *The Guardian;* 17 April. https://www.theguardian.com/society/2015/apr/17/austerity-and-a-malign-benefits-regime-are-profoundly-damaging-mental-health (accessed 9 January 2019).

Hundt NE, Mignogna J, Underhill C, Cully JA (2013). The relationship between use of CBT skills and depression treatment outcome: a theoretical and methodological review of the literature. *Behavior Therapy 44*(1): 12–26. doi: 10.1016/j.beth.2012.10.001.

Jarman K (2017). *Employment Advisers in IAPT: providing integrated IAPT and employment support.* [Online.] Presentation at The New Savoy 10th Annual Conference & Exhibition, Psychological Therapies in the NHS; 15–16 March 2017. London: New Savoy Partnership. www.newsavoypartnership.org/2017presentations/kevin-jarman. pdf (accessed 9 January 2019).

Lambert M (2017). Austerity has trampled over disabled people's rights. But the UK won't admit it. [Online.] *The Guardian;* 4 September. https://www.theguardian.com/commentisfree/2017/sep/04/austerity-disabled-people-rights-uk-un-government (accessed 9 January 2019).

Layard R, Centre for Economic Performance's Mental Health Policy Group (2006). *The Depression Report: a new deal for depression and anxiety disorders.* London: The Centre for Economic Performance's Mental Health Policy Group, London School of Economics.

Neenan M, Dryden W (2005). *Cognitive Therapy in a Nutshell.* London: Sage Publications.

Patrick R (2016). Living with and responding to the 'scrounger' narrative in the UK: exploring everyday strategies of acceptance, resistance and deflection. *Journal of Poverty and Social Justice 24*(3): 245–259.

Psychologists Against Austerity (2015) *The psychological impact of austerity.* [Blog.] Psychologists Against Austerity. https://psychagainstausterity.files.wordpress.com/2015/03/paa-briefing-paper.pdf (accessed: 4 February 2017).

Recovery in the Bin (2015). *RITB – Key Principles.* [Online.] Recovery in the Bin. https://recoveryinthebin.org/ritbkeyprinciples (accessed 24 January 2019).

Richards D, White M (2011). *Reach Out: national programme student materials to support the delivery of training for psychological wellbeing practitioners delivering low intensity interventions* (3rd ed). London: Rethink Mental Illness.

Rimke H, Brock D (2012). The culture of therapy: psychocentrism in everyday life. In: Brock D, Raby R, Thomas MP (eds). *Power and Everyday Practices.* Toronto: Nelson Education (pp182–202).

Rogers CR (1970). *Encounter Groups.* New York, NY: Harper & Row.

Rose N (1999). *Governing the Soul: the shaping of the private self* (2nd ed). London: Free Association Books.

Silberman S (2015). *Neurotribes: the legacy of autism and the future of neurodiversity.* London: Penguin.

Smail D (2006). Is clinical psychology selling its soul (again)? *Clinical Psychology Forum 168*: 17–20.

Stone D (1978). The human potential movement. *Society 15*(4): 66–68.

Stone J (2015). Benefit sanctions against people with mental health problems up by 600 per cent. [Online.] *The Independent*; 12 November. www.independent.co.uk/news/uk/politics/benefit-sanctions-against-people-with-mental-health-problems-up-by-600-per-cent-a6731971.html (accessed 9 January 2019).

Taylor E (1999). *Shadow Culture: psychology and spirituality in America from the great awakening to the new age.* Berkeley, CA: Counterpoint Publishing.

Tee J, Kazantzis N (2011). Collaborative empiricism in cognitive therapy: a definition and theory for the relationship construct. *Clinical Psychology: Science and Practice 18*(1): 47–61.

Thaler RH, Sunstein CR (2008). *Nudge: improving decisions about health, wealth and happiness.* New Haven, CT: Yale University Press.

Waddell G, Burton AK (2006). *Is Work Good for Your Health and Well-Being?* London: The Stationery Office.

Watts J (2017). As a psychologist I see the fantasy of neoliberal values having a devastating effect on mental health treatment. [Online.] *The Independent*; 4 December. www.independent.co.uk/voices/mental-health-treatment-tory-government-nhs-funding-access-work-benefits-a8037331.html (accessed 9 January 2019).

Watts J (2016a). Our mental health obsession has fuelled the politics of Donald Trump and Brexit. [Online.] *The Independent*; 12 September. www.independent.co.uk/voices/donald-trump-brexit-neoliberalism-individualism-cognitive-behavioural-therapy-a7413501.html (accessed 9 January 2019).

Watts J (2016b). IAPT and the ideal image. In: Lees J (ed). *The Future of Psychological Therapy: from managed care to transformational practice.* Abingdon: Routledge (pp84–101).

Webster D (2013). *The DWP's Updated Statistics on JSA Sanctions: what do they show.* Evidence presented to the House of Commons Work and Pensions Committee Inquiry into the Role of Job Centre Plus in the reformed welfare system. [Online.] London: House of Commons Work and Pensions Committee. www. spicker.uk/blog/wpcontent/uploads/2013/11/david-webster-evidence-to-hc-work-and-pensionscommittee-20-nov.pdf (accessed 24 January 2019).

8

The IAPT assembly line

Paul Atkinson

Paul Atkinson has worked as a psychotherapist for more than 30 years, mainly in independent practice in London. He was a political activist during the 1970s and in recent years has returned to campaigning, opposing the state regulation of psychotherapy and counselling, supporting protesters, organising psy-political events at Occupy St Paul's, campaigning for the NHS in East London, running men's therapy groups, and working with mental health activists against psycho-compulsion through Department for Work and Pensions 'work cure' policies. Paul is a member of the Free Psychotherapy Network, the Alliance for Counselling and Psychotherapy and Psychotherapists and Counsellors for Social Responsibility.

'England's mental health experiment: no-cost talk therapy.' This is how the *New York Times* described IAPT, the Improving Access to Psychological Therapy programme introduced in England a decade ago. The article (Benedict, 2017) presents it as a phenomenal mental health success story, 'offering virtually open-ended talk therapy free of charge at clinics throughout the country: in remote farming villages, industrial suburbs, isolated immigrant communities and high-end enclaves'. In 2017 the then Secretary of State for Health in England, Jeremy Hunt, writing in *The New Statesman*, called IAPT 'a paradigm shift in mental health provision' (Hunt, 2017). In this chapter, I will argue that IAPT is indeed a paradigm shift – a revolution in the deployment by the state of behavioural psychology in the pursuit of neoliberal agendas of social compliance and control. IAPT is a 'national nudge' into normative thinking and behaviour, with thousands of cognitive behavioural therapists and wellbeing coaches placed in primary care settings to offer quick-fix solutions for people's 'cognitive malfunctions', and sending them back into the workaday transactions of everyday life.

IAPT is not psychotherapy. It is an assembly line of behavioural adaptation and a perversion of the values and ethics of the counselling and psychotherapy profession.

The psy-professions have always had an intimate relationship with capitalism. Psychotherapy has at times been practised as a treatment for individual 'maladaptation' to the needs of the economy, and huge and diverse markets have arisen, seeking to extract a profit from people's psychological distress.[1] However, I want to suggest here that this is not the whole story. Psychotherapists have also been among the most outspoken critics of capitalism, practising psychotherapy as a critical and progressive means of personal, social and political transformation (Totton, 2000). In terms of IAPT, the roll-out of this programme has taken the political history of psy-practice into a new phase in the construction of 'governable subjects' for capitalism.[2] Yet it has also prompted new alliances among political activists, campaigners and critical theorists, all of whom recognise the evolving political links between the psycho-emotional and the socio-economic strategies of neoliberal capitalism. So, for example, when the then Chancellor George Osborne announced in his 2015 spring budget a plan to place IAPT therapists in 350 job centres (HM Treasury, 2015: 72), for the first time in the UK, psychotherapists, counsellors, psychologists and social workers joined activists and campaigners around mental health, disability and welfare reform to take direct action against the deployment of psychological therapy as a tool of violence and compliance.

Does IAPT have a future beyond its brief to get people back into work and realign them with the norms of neoliberal society? In this chapter, I will examine IAPT's collaboration with consecutive governments' welfare-to-work policies to illustrate its role as a neoliberal state tool. In the process, I will consider whether IAPT's brand of therapy (cognitive behavioural therapy (CBT)) truly qualifies as a talking therapy and the harm that IAPT's assembly line process can cause the therapist, as well as the patient. I will finish by charting how IAPT has also generated new and vibrant political alliances

---

1. See, for example, Katz (2006). See also Postle (2013) on the psy-professions and the enclosure of the psy-commons.

2. Much of what follows owes a debt to Rose (1999).

and activism, bringing together psy-professionals with mental health system survivors and disability activists to protest against the effects of such neoliberal policies on the human rights and everyday lives of UK citizens.

Is IAPT talking therapy?

The IAPT programme is the brain-child of economist Lord Richard Layard and psychologist David Clark. Layard has a long history of involvement in government policy on employment and welfare. In 1979, as founder of the Centre for Economic Performance at the London School of Economics, he contributed to Department for Education and Employment policy reviews on unemployment and the benefits system. He was an early advocate of mandatory workfare, making the case first to Thatcher's government and then to the New Labour government under Tony Blair. David Clark is a leading proponent of CBT in the UK, a professor of psychology at Oxford University, director of the Centre for Anxiety Disorders and Trauma at the Maudsley Hospital, and a national clinical adviser to the Department of Health.

The first fruit of Layard's collaboration with Clark[3] was *The Depression Report: a new deal for depression and anxiety disorders*, published by the Centre for Economic Performance in 2006 (Layard & CEP Mental Health Policy Group, 2006). This report brought together the state of the country's mental health, the claimed efficacy of evidence-based psychological therapies, the costs to the Treasury of sickness and unemployment benefits, and the possibility and economic value of making return to work an outcome of therapy. If therapy could be targeted specifically and successfully at the return-to-work goal, the costs of a six-week course of CBT would be precisely covered by the corresponding savings in welfare benefits, Layard argued. His solution to the mounting mental health-related welfare bill was a closer marriage between therapy and employment support, backed by the argument that work is of itself 'good for our mental health':

> Crippling depression and chronic anxiety are the biggest causes of misery in Britain today... That is the bad news. The good news is that we now have evidence-based psychological therapies that can lift at least a half of those affected out of their depression or their chronic fear... For many patients, work is an essential element in recovery and it is vital

3. For their narrative of IAPT's conception and rationale see Layard & Clark 2015: 115–128. See also Evans (2013).

that they keep their jobs or are helped to get back into work. Each team should therefore include an employment adviser working closely with Jobcentre Plus, a benefit adviser and an adviser on housing. (Layard et al, 2006: 1)

The report maps out the ambition of the project: teams of therapists trained in manualised therapies on state-funded courses to be placed throughout the country, offering short-term talking therapies to hundreds of thousands of people:

> The typical team might cover a population of about 200,000 – meaning 250 teams nationally. Each team would have a central office but most of the therapy would be done in GP surgeries, job centres, workplaces or premises provided by voluntary organisations. Patients could be referred through any of these organisations and would be assessed by the team before being allocated to a suitable therapist. (Layard et al, 2006: 8)

New Labour responded by funding and rapidly rolling out the IAPT programme from 2008, more or less according to Layard's template. By March 2012, IAPT had taken over most existing primary care psychological therapy services in England, including GP-attached counsellors; more than a million people had been referred to IAPT services across England, and, it was claimed, '45,000 people [had] moved off benefits' (IAPT/Department of Health, 2012).

Referrals through GPs, other agencies and, increasingly, via self-referral have rapidly increased. IAPT teams now provide talking therapies on behalf of every Clinical Commissioning Group in England, either replacing existing counselling and psychotherapy provision, absorbing them, or working alongside the few services that survive in the voluntary sector.

By 2015, IAPT had a workforce of around 7,000 therapists, including trainees and employment advisors (NHS England, 2015). Its annual reports provide an avalanche of statistics that are considered to prove the efficacy that justifies its funding. The 2016–17 report, for example, records 1,391,360 new referrals, of whom 965,379 entered treatment; 567,106 finished a 'course of treatment' (defined as having attended at least two sessions), and 49.3% of these achieved 'reliable recovery' (NHS Digital, 2018).[4]

---

4. IAPT's use of terms like 'reliable recovery' is intended to suggest a medical model of statistically reliable outcomes. For an NHS definition of 'reliable recovery', see www.nhs.uk/Scorecard/Pages/IndicatorFacts. aspx?MetricId=6208. For a radical critique of the use of 'recovery' terminology by the NHS, see Recovery in the Bin (2016).

The roll-out of IAPT was less an evolutionary process than a palace coup. While IAPT is badged as providing talking therapies, services are only allowed to provide therapies judged by the National Institute for Health and Care Excellence (NICE) to be clinically and financially effective, as proven by 'gold-standard' randomised controlled trial evidence. Most IAPT treatments are, therefore, forms of CBT.[5] This is unsurprising, as CBT has been well ahead of the rest of the psy-therapies in establishing an evidence base for its effectiveness, and its modus operandi is much more readily manualised and measured than the more relational, humanistic therapies. Counselling and psychotherapy are available in most IAPT services, but less so, and in forms that have been moulded to fit a manualised, medical model based on diagnosis and a standardised treatment plan, to be delivered within a tightly limited number of sessions. Outcome measures are recorded on a tick-box form at every session to ensure the patient is progressing steadily and evenly towards their predefined goal.[6] Such an approach caters to neoliberal public management's need for an 'evidence base' to demonstrate clinical effectiveness and financial efficiency.

In their book, *Thrive: the power of evidence-based psychological therapies* (2015), Layard and Clark proclaim the manifesto of the IAPT 'revolution':

> Until the 1950s there were no scientifically validated treatments for most mental health problems. But then came striking drug discoveries, and in the following decades major advances in psychological therapy. These advances were made by using the same standard methods of scientific experiment as are used in treating physical illnesses. As a result, we now have a range of treatments for mental health problems which have high success rates – as high as the success rates in treating many physical problems. To ensure that people get the best treatments, England has a remarkable institution called NICE – the National Institute for Health and Care Excellence. (pp115–128)

Antidepressant prescribing and developments in psychological therapy driven by 'scientific experiment' are both key features of the neoliberal era, as is the

---

5. See Fenn & Byrne (2013) for a succinct introduction to the principles of CBT.

6. For depression, for example, the Patient Health Questionnaire (PHQ-9) is used to ask the client before or after each session to describe the frequency of nine states of mind and behaviour over the previous two weeks ('not at all', 'several days', 'more than half the days', 'almost every day') – for example, 'Little interest or pleasure in doing things'; 'Feeling bad about yourself'; 'Trouble concentrating on things'. See an example of the PHQ-9 form at https://patient.info/doctor/patient-health-questionnaire-phq-9#ref-5

reframing of the psychological stresses of life under capitalism as individual mental health problems requiring medical treatment (Cain, 2018). Prozac was developed in the mid-1970s and launched in 1988, initially in the US but spreading fast to the UK, followed by a clutch of other SSRI antidepressants. Thirty years later, antidepressant prescribing has increased to the equivalent of one prescription a year for every single person in the Western world. Prescriptions for antidepressants are at an all-time high in England at 64.7 million (Campbell, 2017) – a 108.5% increase on the 31 million prescriptions for antidepressants that pharmacies dispensed a decade earlier, in 2006.

The first randomised control trials of CBT treatment for anxiety and depression date back to the 1960s and 1970s, but its status as an evidence-based, medical model of psychotherapy grew rapidly in subsequent decades. It is not surprising that CBT, like the commercially successful, supposedly side effect-free SSRIs, has come to be regarded as a tool to adapt individuals to the norms of capitalism. It is often described innocuously as a short course in positive thinking:

> The aim of CBT is to help you think more positively about life and free yourself from unhelpful patterns of behaviour. In CBT, you set goals with your therapist and may carry out tasks between sessions. (NHS Choices, 2016)

Or as one of its chief progenitors, Aaron Beck, puts it:

> The therapist helps a patient to unravel his distortions in thinking and to learn alternative, more realistic ways to formulate his experiences. (Beck, 1979: 3)

In IAPT, courses of treatment are so short that they can hardly be called talking therapy at all. For those lucky enough to have progressed through the stepped care structure to attain one-to-one, face-to-face therapy with a therapist, therapy comprises, on average, six sessions of some form of CBT. Most IAPT services allow the number of sessions to go up to 12, and some even to 16. A fifth of all courses of treatment in 2013–14 consisted of just two sessions (NHS Digital, 2015: 17). Most non-CBT forms of talking therapy regard the symptoms of psychological conflict, pain and distress as expressions of deeper experiences whose meaning is relatively opaque and may be gradually uncovered over time. Person-centred, humanistic and psychodynamic therapy make much of the quality of relationship between client and therapist as the medium through which the client may gradually come to risk making meaningful change. It is not clear what kind of relationship can develop through IAPT's relatively few sessions.

Talking therapy, where the therapist and client sit together and talk, makes up a minority of IAPT's provision of psychological therapies. Almost half of referrals who finish a course of treatment receive what IAPT calls 'low-intensity treatment', a quarter of which consists of various forms of self-help, guided or non-guided, via books or computer. The average number of sessions for this treatment is between 1.7 and three. Online CBT is a growing industry. Reportedly, there was a 900% rise in webcam and instant messenger appointments in IAPT services between 2012/13 and 2015/16, in the context of a 144% rise in appointments overall (Kraemer, 2017). When IAPT talks about psychological therapies, very little of what its services actually deliver qualifies under pre-IAPT definitions of 'talking therapy' in primary care.

Supporters of CBT dispute this.[7] They claim that CBT, done well, is delivered, just like other talking therapies, within a concerned and caring human relationship. They argue that CBT has a sophisticated philosophical base (Herbert, Gaudiano & Forman, 2013) and that, in fact, what gets called CBT is a wide family of so-called third-wave CBT therapies, many of which are 'holistic' and do not place so much emphasis on symptoms and simple measurements of recovery (Gilbert, 2009; Watts, 2015). Anecdotally, I've also heard many high-intensity IAPT therapists say their work is relational and tailored to the client's process because, regardless of the IAPT model, they work to their own sense of the ethics of psychotherapy, and fudge the statistics.

This may well be true. A high proportion of high-intensity IAPT therapists came into IAPT already trained in their preferred model of therapy, and have undertaken CBT training on top (Surviving Work, 2017). Nevertheless, the important point is that IAPT is a factory system within which attention to its clients' emotional and spiritual lives is closely audited, target-led, and only paid for by results. If there are decent therapeutic relationships, they have to be created *despite* its assembly-line culture.

The IAPT factory system

IAPT's organisational and managerial framework has many of the classic features of New Public Management (NPM), a form of public service

7. For a discussion for and against CBT, see Loewenthal & Proctor (2018).

administration pioneered by the UK and Australia during the 1980s (Gruening, 2001). NPM introduced private sector models of budgeting, competitive internal markets, tendering, customer service, efficiency measurement, privatisation, the privileging of managerialism over professionalism, and an audit culture of evidenced outcomes and payment by results. It is:

> ... based upon a cultural paradigm formed from a view promoting the primacy of the individual over social needs. The cultural paradigm lying behind this view is rooted in the belief that unfettered free enterprise, elevating self-interest over social needs, will optimally organise every facet of society, including economic and social life. (Simpson, 2016)

The collection of data that keeps the IAPT funding flowing has generated a pressure on its therapists comparable to that more commonly found on assembly lines or in call centres, with their intensive cultures of efficiency, output and auditing (Booth, 2016). This is emblematic of the acceleration of transactions in neoliberal markets more generally (Virilio, 2012: 58) – an acceleration that is, arguably, itself a source of the emotional distress to which IAPT was originally a response. One of the ironies of this therapy juggernaut is the toxicity of its own workplace culture, to the detriment of its own workers' mental health and the quality of service it provides. The truth about the impact of the IAPT work regime on the mental health of its practitioners has begun to emerge into the public realm (The Future of Therapy, 2017). The 2016 New Savoy Partnership's annual staff wellbeing survey found that 48% of the 1,200 psychological therapists surveyed had felt depressed in the previous week, 46% had felt a failure, and 92% found their job stressful some or all of the time (Rao et al, 2017). Nine out of 10 therapists said they felt under pressure to meet targets some or all of the time, 56% said they felt under pressure to work long hours some or all of the time, and a significant minority said they didn't get enough support and supervision or opportunities for professional development. Another study found a 68.6% prevalence of burnout among IAPT psychological wellbeing practitioners (PWPs – the least skilled, frontline graduate workers who carry out initial assessments and deliver the low-intensity therapies) and 50% among high intensity therapists (Westwood, 2017).

IAPT workers are often scared to speak out in public – scared for their jobs and of the stigma among colleagues (The Psychologist, 2017). In a Guardian article, psychologist Jay Watts describes a fellow clinical psychologist, Rachel, who was off sick with depression and anxiety from her

NHS job, having had to tell one of her clients, who had a history of abuse and being dropped from previous services, that they only had four more sessions together. 'Rachel now feels a failure because she had to put service targets above the needs of the client and above her own values' (Cooke & Watts, 2016).[8] Such conflicts between the personal values of the therapist and the practical pressures imposed by guidelines have become routine among IAPT workers (Proctor & Brown, 2019).

As reported above, the low-intensity therapy in IAPT is mostly provided by PWPs. These are mostly graduate psychologists who receive a one-year training in basic CBT and guided self-help skills. For many, the work is precarious. Dearbhaile Bradley, a counsellor, trained and worked as a PWP. In a vivid description of the stresses and ethical compromises of working for IAPT, she explained how the experience undermined her own mental health and led to burn-out.

> In PWP work, you either shape up or ship out. It is ironic just how many people I worked with ended up off work with stress-related illness in a service that is supposed to help people suffering. I don't know which was worse, watching those who toughen up or those who fell apart. The attrition rate in PWP work is shocking. But there is always another crop of young graduates eager to take this first step on the career ladder. Which means that the front-line workers in the NHS mental health service continue to be generally young, inexperienced, inadequately trained and overworked. (Bradley, 2017)

If the voices of IAPT workers are almost completely absent from the public realm, IAPT's service users seem to have no voice at all; we have only the aggregations of IAPT statistics to testify to the IAPT experience. Despite the apparently client-centred nature of its evaluation raw data, IAPT is a top-down programme, with top-down diagnosis, treatment options, definitions and measurements of desirable outcomes (Recovery in the Bin, 2016). We do know that less than 18% of people who are referred or who self-refer to the service complete a course of treatment and achieve 'reliable recovery'[9] (see further below). We know that IAPT's take-up and recovery rates are significantly reduced in more socially and economically deprived

---

8. See also Rizq (2011, 2013).

9. Data based on the author's unpublished analysis of the IAPT annual report for 2016-17 (NHS Digital, 2018). See also Grant & Rodger (2018).

communities (Delgadillo et al, 2016). We also know that a growing body of evidence suggests the relapse rate from low intensity treatments is very high (Ali et al, 2017; Johnsen & Friborg, 2015).

Anecdotal evidence from within IAPT, as well as from independent therapists working with former IAPT clients, suggests that client dissatisfaction with its assembly-line culture is rife. For example, one IAPT psychologist describes a client who made a complaint that he 'felt utterly uncared for, I was treated like a number' after receiving the service's standard initial assessment by telephone, being asked to complete (over the phone) what he felt were irrelevant questionnaires, and being told that he would not be offered any service if he refused (Rizq, 2011: 7). Another IAPT therapist reports a potentially suicidal client who was deemed unsuitable for treatment because of 'anger problems' – despite her history of emotional abuse by her partner (Watts, 2016: 96). As one respondent to an NHS psychological services staff survey said: 'We [therapists] are leaving people feeling worse because they feel like they failed rather than they are being given something that doesn't work' (The Future of Therapy, 2017).

As far as CBT's and IAPT's much-vaunted evidence base is concerned, it is a case of 'lies, damned lies and statistics' (Atkinson, 2014). Critiques of the methodology of CBT randomised controlled trials are abundant (Shedler, 2014; Dalal, 2014; Scott, 2018). IAPT's assembly-line diagnostic procedures, its measurement of outcomes, its adoption of 'recovery' language, its claims for waiting time reductions, its rate of relapse and failure to produce follow-up statistics have all been criticised (Timimi, 2014, 2015; Scott, 2018; Cooper, 2018).

Perversely, the avalanche of data generated by the IAPT programme in its own annual reports clearly reveals a service that is failing communities all over England. Its headline claim, for example, is a 50% 'reliable recovery' rate. This in itself would not be particularly impressive if we were to take seriously IAPT's application of the political rhetoric of 'parity of esteem' (in which mental health must be given equal priority to physical health). But this is *not* 50% of its total referrals: it is 50% of *referrals who finished a course of treatment*. Only a third or so (37%) of everyone referred to IAPT in 2016–17 completed a course of treatment, and it is half of *this* number who 'recovered'. In other words, less than a fifth of 1.4 million referrals 'reliably recovered'.[10] IAPT's champions have nothing to say about the 870,000 people who dropped out.

---

10. In 2012–13 only 12% of all referrals 'reliably recovered' (Atkinson, 2014).

What is more, for many Clinical Commissioning Groups, the IAPT 'reliable recovery' rate is significantly lower than the national average of 17.7%. In 2016–17 nearly 60 CCGs returned a rate of under 15%, and 14 scored less than 10%.[11] The annual reports also quantify referrals and outcomes by levels of deprivation, ethnic community, gender and sexual orientation. Sixty per cent of referrals in 2016–17 were from more deprived communities. From the 10% with the highest deprivation rates, the 'recovery' rate was 11%, compared with 23% among referrals from the 10% of least deprivation. In Tower Hamlets, only three per cent of referrals from the Bangladeshi community 'recovered'. A very small minority of IAPT services do follow-up surveys after treatment. Last year only 1.5% of all referrals finishing a course of treatment were contacted for a six-month follow-up. The results are not published. Academic research into rates of relapse after treatment suggest the story is far from encouraging.[12]

Work becomes a mental health outcome

IAPT's status as neoliberal state therapy becomes clearest when we consider its role in successive governments' drives to dismantle the post-war social contract and replace welfare with workfare. 'Welfare to work' has been adopted as a mantra by all the main political parties, by the mental health establishment, including IAPT, and by many of the big mental health and welfare charities. Becoming dependent on the state and the social contract has been treated as a psychological disorder of the individual, rather than a structural outcome of political-economic realities. Getting into, returning to and staying in work has become the funding priority of 'new initiatives' for welfare and mental health policy (Department for Work and Pensions, 2014, 2017a, 2017b). Further (as described in detail in David Frayne's Chapter 6 in this book), participation in employment has been treated as a cure for mental ill health and a major goal for state therapy (Watts, 2018).

In the UK, as in other developed economies, 'mental disorders' are the most common reason for receiving welfare benefits.[13] Driven by a multitude

---

11. Islington 9.9%; Wiltshire 9.7%; Central Manchester 7.8%; South Worcestershire 6.5%; Leicester City 5%; Barnsley 1.5%.

12. Data based on the author's unpublished analysis of the IAPT annual report for 2016-17 (NHS Digital, 2018). See also Grant & Rodger (2018).

13. In 2014, 47% of claims were attributed to a mental disorder. The number of long-term claimants (claiming for more than five years) with mental disorders increased by 87% from 2000 to 2011. Two-thirds of mental disorder claimants were classified as having a depressive or anxiety disorder (Viola & Moncrieff, 2016).

of forces – ideologies of the capitalist work ethic, the privileging of activities that take place in the economic sphere, popular prejudice against both mental illness and benefit claimants (de Vries & Reeves, 2017; Maddox, 2017; British Social Attitudes, 2016; Jensen & Tyler, 2015), the delusions of austerity politics (Atkinson, 2016; Thomas, 2016) – welfare reforms by neoliberal governments since Thatcher and Reagan have tightened eligibility to all social security benefits. Welfare payments have been cut and increasingly coercive burdens have been placed on welfare claimants to be active 'job seekers', with harsh sanctions for non-compliance.

The DWP and the healthcare establishment say that most benefit claimants with mental health issues *want* to work and need to be given opportunities and support, and yet at the same time support the idea that people need to be 'motivated' into work by threats of benefit cuts, mandatory job-search activities and training in workplace discipline and behaviour. The work of Lynne Friedli and Robert Stearn (2015) on the 'psycho-compulsion' of benefit claimants by the DWP has been invaluable in shedding light on current realities. Work capability assessments and welfare sanctions start from a deep-rooted assumption that welfare claimants are social delinquents, criminals even, who care nothing for the common good and must be policed and punished into adopting the appropriate attitude towards employment. To many mental health survivors, the government's welfare to work policies have very little to do with wanting them to be in work and more to do with creating a convenient political scapegoat (Friedli & Stearn, 2015).

As we have seen, the goal of getting people off benefits and into work was the primary rationale behind the IAPT programme – why else would any government risk investing so much money in an untried service development? And this goal continues to lead the government's linkage of work and health. However, despite IAPT proponents' insistence on an 'evidence base' for its offerings, there is no real evidence that work is good for people with mental health difficulties, especially those with more severe and enduring conditions.[14] Waddell and Burton's 2006 report remains the most often quoted root source for evidence that work is good for you, and yet a closer reading of the report reveals that it is quite ambivalent about the efficacy of employment for helping people with mental health difficulties.[15]

---

14. For a fuller discussion of the 'work cure' argument, see Atkinson (2018).

15. For an analysis of Waddell's work in connection with the biopsychosocial model of Work Capability Assessment, ATOS, and the Centre for Psychosocial and Disability Research, University of Cardiff, see Stewart (2016). On the influence of Waddell and Burton on US welfare policy and campaigning, see Fremstad (2018).

> The current review shows that work is not harmful to the psychiatric condition or mental health of people with severe mental illness although, conversely, it has no direct beneficial impact on their mental condition either. However, the balance of the indirect evidence is that it is beneficial for their overall well-being. (Waddell & Burton, 2006: 21)

Likewise, there is no good evidence to support the claim that 'as many as 90% of workless people who use mental health services wish to work' (see, for example, Lelliott et al, 2008: 17). There *is* evidence, however, that welfare to work programmes have simply not worked (Butler, 2013). And it is extraordinary that, in this era of 'bullshit jobs' (Graeber, 2013), zero-hour contracts, poverty wages and non-unionised labour without basic rights and protections, such massive pressure is being brought to bear on exactly those people who are the *least* likely to be able to sustain themselves in the madhouse of modern working environments (Marstas et al, 2017). Studies have also shown that moving from unemployment to bad employment is certainly not good for your mental health (Chandola & Zhang, 2018). Often those advocating that 'work is good for you' qualify the statement by pointing out that it has to be 'good' work, work people are interested in, work that is supportive of the worker's mental health, work that is sustainable. Everyone knows, however, that such jobs are increasingly rare, and are unlikely to be on offer to anyone bearing the stigma of a 'mental health' label (Reavley, 2016) or those most desperate to find work, any work, to keep the DWP off their backs.

The IAPT programme unashamedly supports the ideology of 'work is good for you' and uses psychological therapies as a tool to get people with mental health issues off benefits and into employment. This is bad enough, but what is utterly outrageous is the extent to which this support has been sustained in parallel with the violent (sometimes literally lethal) attacks by the government on benefit claimants with physical and mental disabilities. We know that benefit claimants with mental health difficulties are more likely to be sanctioned by the DWP. In 2013–14, 47% of claimants on Employment and Support Allowance suffered mental health difficulties, but the same group received 62% of DWP sanctions, and between July 2011 and March 2017, claims categorised as 'mental and behavioural' had the highest rate of sanctions (Webster, 2017).

To receive Employment and Support Allowance, claimants undergo the feared Work Capability Assessment, introduced by New Labour in 2007 and outsourced to private sector companies including the Franco-Dutch company Atos and the US corporation Maximus. Both these organisations use the now-infamous biopsychosocial model of fitness-for-work assessment developed by the US insurance company UNUM and adapted by Professor Sir Mansel Aylward, Chief Medical Officer, Medical Director and Chief Scientist at the DWP under Tony Blair's prime ministership (Pring, 2016). As the reporter Mike Sivier has written:

> The new test aggressively disputed whether the claimant was ill, questioning illnesses that were 'self-reported', labelling some disabling conditions as 'psychological', and playing up the 'subjective' nature of 'mental' and 'nervous' claims. The thinking behind it was: Sickness is temporary. *Illness is a behaviour* – all the things that people say and do that express and communicate their feelings of being unwell. The degree of this behaviour is dependent on the attitudes and beliefs of the individual, as well as the social context and culture. *Illness is a personal choice*. In other words: 'It's all in the mind; these people are fit to work.' (Sivier, 2013, original emphasis)

The combination of the Work Capability Assessment and the DWP's sanctioning regime, alongside cuts to Employment and Support Allowance and other benefits, have generated enormous fear and despair among claimants with long-term mental health difficulties. Suicides and attempted suicides by claimants driven to the end of their tether have been regularly reported in mainstream and social media since 2010. Calum's List – an online memorial for people who have died at the hands of welfare reform – reports 4,000 recorded welfare reform deaths and estimates a possible total of 80,000 in the UK (Calum's List, 2017; Barr et al, 2016). The proportion of people claiming the main out-of-work disability benefit who have attempted suicide also doubled between 2007 and 2014 (Pring, 2017). As the claimant activist Johnny Void so aptly puts it:

> This government [the Conservatives] do not give a shit about people with mental health conditions, and neither did the last one. Whilst politicians of all parties offer soundbites and fake sympathy, the treatment of people with a mental health condition by the benefits system now amounts to little more than psychological torture. This is not hyperbole. Whilst the medical establishment has stood idly by, and mental health charities have veered between mild disapproval and outright collaboration, the DWP has launched an all-out war on the most marginalised people in society. (Void, 2015)

Activism

The emotional and psychological difficulties of living in the UK and other neoliberal economies are becoming increasingly visible and alarming. We see it in our workplaces, in our schools and colleges and in our families, in response to the strains of economic insecurity. Capitalism has always generated toxic side effects in its exploitation of people's psychological resources in the service of profit and accumulation for the few. Capitalism's neoliberal iteration seems to be generating an accelerating pandemic of fear, insecurity and anxiety that is splintering and dividing our communities. Employment remains the critical mechanism of social control. Those who cannot work, or choose to focus on other things, are dangerous and to be treated as pariahs. In response to neoliberalism's psychological dysfunctions, governments are generating new partnerships with the health and social care professions, private providers and charities, through legislation, funding policies and the controls of New Public Management reform. IAPT is both a symptom of and a state response to a society that seems to be losing its mind.

On the Left, we need to build our own alliances and open up new discussions about what is generating so much fear, anxiety and depression, as well as how we should change our society and public services in response. Historically, we psy-practitioners have tended to see ourselves as broadly liberal or apolitical at work, as concerned with the inner psychological world of our clients rather than their socio-economic conditions. Most therapy practitioners initially greeted IAPT as a 'good thing' – it did at least offer free 'talking therapies' to a much larger group of people than ever before in the history of the NHS – and surely some talking therapy was better than none at all? I have heard psy-practitioners argue that 'It may not help everyone but it will surely help a lot more'; 'People who would never dream of seeing a therapist now get to experience therapy'; 'You can get round the rules of the system; you can fudge the stats; your work with the client can stay the same.' Many IAPT therapists were originally employed in the NHS or in GP surgeries and have a strong commitment to the public service ethos – but they need to earn a living and it is risky to speak out publicly against an employer as large and well networked as the NHS. Political criticism of IAPT has either been in the academic sphere or voiced privately, or within professional circles.

But things are beginning to change. Far more counsellors, psychologists and psychotherapists are becoming campaigners and activists around a range of socio-economic and political issues. On the issue of 'work cures' for benefit claimants, new campaigning and direct action alliances have begun to emerge.

Since 2010 at least, groups like Disabled People Against Cuts (DPAC), the Mental Health Resistance Network (MHRN) and Boycott Workfare[16] have been organising demonstrations, occupations and other direct actions against welfare cuts, benefit sanctions, the Work Capability Assessment, unpaid workfare and the growing psychological pressure of 'work-preparation' and job-search activities. Although left-leaning healthcare professionals have always campaigned alongside psychiatric and mental health care service users, there has been understandable suspicion about their motives. Much of the radical energy of survivors of the psychiatric system, for example, was aimed for decades at the injustices and inhumanity of psychiatric treatment regimes (McKenna, 2016).

When George Osborne's 2015 budget announced the introduction of IAPT therapists to job centres, a group of counsellors and psychotherapists in the Alliance for Counselling and Psychotherapy and Psychotherapists and Counsellors for Social Responsibility (PCSR) decided to contact welfare and mental health activists and form a political alliance to take joint action against the government welfare reforms. It was a key turning point for the therapists. In 2016, we joined Disabled People Against Cuts and the Mental Health Resistance Network in a protest at Streatham Jobcentre,[17] where co-location of IAPT and DWP services was to be piloted; outside an Islington GP surgery, where the placement of DWP job advisors was to be trialled,[18] and at the headquarters of the mental health charity Mind.[19] Twenty-three organisations of service users, survivors, welfare campaigners, social workers, psychologists, therapists and mental health charities joined forces to write an open letter to the main psy-professional bodies deploring their participation in welfare-to-work policies and calling for their withdrawal.[20] Since 2017, we have organised regular demonstrations at the New Savoy Conferences – the annual get-togethers for IAPT and government policy-makers – calling for IAPT to withdraw from its partnership with DWP around the 'work cure'.

---

16. See https://dpac.uk.net; https://mentalhealthresistance.org; www.boycottworkfare.org (accessed 14 January 2019).

17. https://johnnyvoid.wordpress.com/2015/06/26/streatham-jobcentre-besieged-by-protesters-demanding-no-forced-treatment (accessed 14 January 2019).

18. https://www.opendemocracy.net/ournhs/dr-lynne-friedli-robert-stern/why-we-re-opposed-to-jobs-on-prescription (accessed 14 January 2019).

19. https://www.disabilitynewsservice.com/mind-boss-lies-to-protesters-over-dwp-contracts(accessed 14 January 2019).

20. For a list of these 23 organisations, see Alliance for Counselling and Psychotherapy (2016).

Mental health services need more resources. Yet the hypocrisy of every political party in declaring their distress at the lack of such services, while continuing to cut health funding further and default on the pledge for parity between physical and mental health services, is shocking. Yes, we need more safe spaces for people with acute and severe mental health problems. We will continue to need more people with specialist trainings. And yes, we need more talking therapy, without a doubt, for all age groups, and not just the 'working-age' population. But top-down, prescriptive mental health services like IAPT, administered by psychiatrists, psychologists, therapists, nurses and other professionals, tend to disempower and isolate people. Services need to be designed, managed and developed by service users and survivors in genuinely democratic collaboration with the psy professions. Professional services need to be in the *service* of people's pain and suffering, not driven by managerial ambitions, profit making, the fear of losing funding or the fear of losing your own job. Fundamentally, we need a very different understanding of the kind of society and the kind of relationships that promote and support our mental wealth.

References

Ali S, Rhodes L, Moreea O, McMillan D, Gilbody S, Leach C, Lucock M, Lutz W, Delgadillo J (2017). How durable is the effect of low intensity CBT for depression and anxiety? Remission and relapse in a longitudinal cohort study. *Behaviour Research and Therapy* 94(July): 1–8.

Alliance for Counselling and Psychotherapy (2016). *Jobcentre therapy: MWF exchange letters with the big psy-organisations*. [Blog.] Alliance for Counselling and Psychotherapy; 28 April. https://allianceblogs.wordpress.com/2016/04/28/mwf_letters_2/ (accessed 11 January 2019).

Atkinson P (2018). *Is work a health outcome?* [Blog.] Free Psychotherapy Network. https://freepsychotherapynetwork.com/workcure (accessed 11 January 2019).

Atkinson P (2016). In the land of Austeria. *Self and Society* 44(4): 478–481.

Atkinson P (2014). *The sorry state of NHS provision of psychological therapy.* [Blog.] Free Psychotherapy Network; 9 March. https://freepsychotherapynetwork.com/2014/03/09/the-sorry-story-of-state-provision-of-psychological-therapy (accessed 11 January 2019).

Barr B, Taylor-Robinson D, Stuckler D, Loopstra R, Reeves A, Whitehead M (2016). 'First, do no harm': are disability assessments associated with adverse trends in mental health? A longitudinal ecological study. *Journal of Epidemiology & Community Health* 70: 339–345.

Beck A (1979). *Cognitive Therapy and the Emotional Disorders*. New York, NY: Plume.

Benedict C (2017). England's mental health experiment: no-cost talk therapy. *The New York Times;* 24 July.

Booth R (2016). Can call centre therapy solve the NHS mental health crisis? *The Guardian;* 25 January.

Bradley D (2017). *What's wrong with IAPT?* [Blog.] Free Psychotherapy Network. https://freepsychotherapynetwork.files.wordpress.com/2017/03/zine-online2.pdf (accessed 11 January 2019).

British Social Attitudes (2016.) *British Social Attitudes 34: tax avoidance and benefit manipulation.* [Online.] British Social Attitudes. www.bsa.natcen.ac.uk/latest-report/british-social-attitudes-34/tax-benefit-manipulation.aspx (accessed 11 January 2019).

Butler P (2013). Welfare to work scheme failing to get people work, say figures. *The Guardian;* 27 June.

Cain R (2018). How neoliberalism is damaging your mental health. [Online.] *Medical Express;* 30 January. https://medicalxpress.com/news/2018-01-neoliberalism-mental-health.html (accessed 11 January 2019).

Calum's List [Online.] http://calumslist.org (accessed 7 May 2018).

Campbell D (2017). NHS prescribed record number of antidepressants last year. *The Guardian;* 29 June.

Chandola T, Zhang N (2018). Re-employment, job quality, health and allostatic load biomarkers: prospective evidence from the UK Household Longitudinal Study. *International Journal of Epidemiology 47*(1): 47–57.

Cooke A, Watts J (2016). We're not surprised half our psychologist colleagues are depressed. *The Guardian;* 17 February.

Cooper K (2018). The devastating cost of treatment delays. [Online.] *BMA News;* 5 February. www.bma.org.uk/news/2018/february/the-devastating-cost-of-treatment-delays (accessed 11 January 2019).

Dalal F (2014). *Statistical Spin, Linguistic Obfuscation: the art of overselling the CBT evidence base.* [Video.] The Limbus Critical Psychotherapy Conference 2014. www.limbus.org.uk/cbt/videos.html (accessed 11 January 2019).

Delgadillo J, Asaria M, Ali S, Gilbody S (2016). On poverty, politics and psychology: the socioeconomic gradient of mental healthcare utilisation and outcomes. *British Journal of Psychiatry 209*(5): 429–430.

Department for Work and Pensions (2017a). *Government sets out plan to see more disabled people in work.* [Online.] Department for Work and Pensions. www.gov.uk/government/news/government-sets-out-plan-to-see-more-disabled-people-in-work (accessed 11 January 2019).

Department for Work and Pensions (2017b). *Improving Lives: the future of work, health and disability.* London: Department for Work and Pensions. https://assets.publishing.service.gov.uk/government/uploads/system/uploads/attachment_data/file/663400/print-ready-improving-lives-the-future-of-work-health-and-disability.pdf (accessed 11 January 2019).

Department for Work and Pensions (2014). *Health, Work and Wellbeing. Evidence and research: evidence, research and policy papers related to the health, work and wellbeing initiative.*

[Online.] Department for Work and Pensions. www.gov.uk/government/collections/health-work-and-wellbeing-evidence-and-research (accessed 11 January 2019).

de Vries R, Reeves A (2017). Why do people care more about benefit 'scroungers' than billions lost to the rich? *The Guardian;* 15 November.

Evans J (2013). *David Clark on Improving Access for Psychological Therapy (IAPT).* [Blog.] Philosophy for Life; 31 May. www.philosophyforlife.org/david-clark-on-improving-access-for-psychological-therapy-iapt (accessed 20 January 2018).

Fenn K, Byrne M (2013). *The key principles of cognitive behavioural therapy.* [Online.] *InnovAiT* 6(9): 579–585. DOI: 10.1177/1755738012471029.

Fremstad S (2018). *No, forced labor is not good for your health.* [Blog.] Talk Poverty; 19 January. https://talkpoverty.org/2018/01/19/no-forced-labor-not-good-health (accessed 11 January 2019)

Friedli L, Stearn R (2015). Positive affect as coercive strategy: conditionality, activation and the role of psychology in UK government workfare programmes. *Medical Humanities* 41: 40–47.

Gilbert P (2009). Moving beyond cognitive behaviour therapy. *The Psychologist 22*: 400–403.

Graeber D (2013). *On the phenomenon of bullshit jobs.* [Blog.] Libcom.org; 20 August. https://libcom.org/library/phenomenon-bullshit-jobs-david-graeber. (accessed 11 January 2019).

Grant R, Rodger J (2018). *How Poorer People in Birmingham Struggle to Recover from Mental Health Problems.* [Online.] Birmingham Mail; 7 March. www.birminghammail.co.uk/news/midlands-news/how-poorer-people-birmingham-struggle-14380185 (accessed 11 January 2019).

Gruening G (2001). Origin and theoretical basis of New Public Management. *International Public Management Journal 4*: 1–25.

HM Treasury (2015). *The Budget 2015.* London: HM Treasury. https://assets.publishing.service.gov.uk/government/uploads/system/uploads/attachment_data/file/416330/47881_Budget_2015_Web_Accessible.pdf (accessed 20 January 2019).

Herbert J, Gaudiano B, Forman E (2013). The importance of theory in Cognitive Behavior Therapy: a perspective of contextual behavioral science. *Behavior Therapy 44*: 580–591.

Hunt J (2017). Planning for a new mental health paradigm. *New Statesman;* 13 October.

IAPT/Department of Health (2012). *IAPT Three-Year Report: the first million patients.* [Online.] Department of Health. www.uea.ac.uk/documents/246046/11919343/IAPT+3+year+report.+The+first+million+patiets.pdf/0e0469ff-0884-4203-99de-4b61601e69dd (accessed 11 January 2019).

Jensen T, Tyler I (2015). Benefits broods: the cultural and political crafting of anti-welfare commonsense. *Critical Social Policy 35*(4): 1–22.

Johnsen T, Friborg O (2015). The effects of cognitive behavioral therapy as an anti-depressive treatment is falling: a meta-analysis. *Psychological Bulletin* 141(4): 747–768.

Katz C (2006). Partners in crime? Neoliberalism and the production of new political subjectivities. In: Laurie N, Bondi L (eds). *Working the Spaces of Neoliberalism: activism, professionalisation and incorporation.* Chichester: Wiley-Blackwell (pp227–235).

Kraemer D (2017). Huge surge in online mental health appointments attacked by specialists. *The Independent;* 20 March.

Layard R, CEP Mental Health Policy Group (2006). *The Depression Report: a new deal for depression and anxiety disorders.* CEP Special Papers 15. London: Centre for Economic Performance, London School of Economics. https://ideas.repec.org/p/cep/cepsps/15.html (accessed 11 January 2019).

Layard R, Clark D (2015). *Thrive: the power of evidence-based psychological therapies.* London: Penguin.

Lelliott P, Tulloch S, Boardman J, Harvey S, Henderson M, Knapp P (2008). *Mental Health and Work.* London: Royal College of Psychiatrists. https://assets.publishing.service.gov.uk/government/uploads/system/uploads/attachment_data/file/212266/hwwb-mental-health-and-work.pdf (accessed 11 January 2019).

Loewenthal D, Proctor G (eds) (2018). *Why Not CBT? Against and For CBT revisited.* Monmouth: PCCS Books.

Maddox D (2017). Tough benefits cap stops scroungers claiming thousands of pounds. *Daily Express;* 3 February.

Marstas N, Mullen K, Powell D, von Wachter T, Wenger J (2017). *Working Conditions in the United States: results of the 2015 American Working Conditions Survey.* Santa Monica, CA: RAND Corporation. www.rand.org/pubs/research_reports/RR2014.html (accessed 14 January 2019).

McKenna D (2016). *Welfare reforms and mental health.* [Blog.] Recovery in the Bin. https://recoveryinthebin.org/2016/03/10/welfare-reforms-and-mental-health-resisting-sanctions-assessments-and-psychological-coercion-by-denise-mckenna-mental-health-resistance-network-mhrn/ (accessed 14 January 2019).

NHS Choices (2016). *Types of Talking Therapies.* [Online.] NHS Choices. www.nhs.uk/conditions/stress-anxiety-depression/types-of-therapy/#behavioural (accessed 14 January 2019).

NHS Digital (2018). *Psychological Therapies: annual report on the use of IAPT services. England, further analyses on 2016–17.* [Online.] NHS Digital. https://files.digital.nhs.uk/publication/s/n/psyc-ther-ann-rep-2016-17_add.pdf (accessed 14 January 2019).

NHS Digital (2015). *Psychological Therapies: annual report on the use of IAPT services - England 2014–15.* [Online.] NHS Digital. https://digital.nhs.uk/data-and-information/publications/statistical/psychological-therapies-annual-reports-on-the-use-of-iapt-services/annual-report-2014-15 (accessed 14 January 2019).

NHS England (2015). *2015 Adult IAPT Workforce Census Report.* [Online.] London: NHS England. www.england.nhs.uk/mentalhealth/wp-content/uploads/sites/29/2016/09/adult-iapt-workforce-census-report-15.pdf (accessed 14 January 2019).

Postle D (2013). *The psyCommons and its Enclosures: professionalized wisdom and the abuse of power.* [Video.] YouTube; 21 December. www.youtube.com/watch?time_continue=2&v=pxuFnUuLqyc (accessed 14 January 2019).

Pring J (2017). 'Staggering' ESA suicide figures prompt calls for inquiry and prosecution of ministers. *Disability News Service;* 17 December. www.disabilitynewsservice.com/staggering-esa-suicide-figures-prompt-calls-for-inquiry-and-prosecution-of-ministers (accessed 20 January 2019).

Pring J (2016). Disabled researcher's book exposes 'corporate demolition of welfare state'. [Online.] *Disability News Service;* 15 September. www.disabilitynewsservice.com/disabled-researchers-book-exposes-corporate-demolition-of-welfare-state (accessed 20 January 2019).

Proctor G, Brown M (2019). Industrialising relational therapy: ethical conflicts and threats for counsellors in IAPT. In: Jackson C, Risq R (eds). *The Industrialisation of Care: counselling, psychotherapy and the impact of IAPT.* Monmouth: PCCS Books.

Rao A, Clarke J, Bhutani G, Dosanjh N, Cohen-Tovee E, Hacker Hughes J, Neal A (2017). *Workforce Wellbeing Survey 2014–2016.* London: BPS/New Savoy Conference.

Reavley N (2016). People with a mental illness discriminated against when looking for work and when employed. [Online.] *The Conversation;* 3 February. https://theconversation.com/people-with-a-mental-illness-discriminated-against-when-looking-for-work-and-when-employed-52864 (accessed 14 January 2019).

Recovery in the Bin (2016). *Mental Illness and UnRecovery.* [Online.] https://recoveryinthebin.org/2016/03/05/mental-illness-and-unrecovery/ (accessed 14 January 2019).

Rizq R (2013). *Perverting the course of therapy: the fetishization of governance in public sector mental health services.* [Online.] University of Roehampton. https://pure.roehampton.ac.uk/portal/files/631251/Perverting_the_course_of_therapy_pdf_for_PP_journal.pdf (accessed 14 January 2019).

Rizq R (2011). IAPT, anxiety and envy: a psychoanalytic view of NHS primary care mental health services today. *British Journal of Psychotherapy 27*(1): 37–55.

Rose N (1999). *Governing the Soul: the shaping of the private self* (2nd revised ed). London: Free Association Books..

Scott MJ (2018). Improving Access to Psychological Therapies (IAPT) – the need for radical reform. *Journal of Health Psychology 23*(9): 1136–1147.

Shedler J (2014). *Where is the evidence for evidence-based therapy?* [Video.] The Limbus Critical Psychotherapy Conference 2014. Pwww.limbus.org.uk/cbt/videos.html (accessed 14 January 2019).

Simpson I (2016). Containing anxiety in social care systems and neo-liberal management dogma. In: Lees J (ed). *The Future of Psychological Therapy: from managed care to transformational practice.* Abingdon: Routledge (pp51–68).

Sivier M (2013). *Unum, Atos, the DWP and the WCA: who gets the blame for the biopsychosocial saga?* [Blog.] Mike Sivier. https://mikesivier.wordpress.com/2013/01/18/unum-atos-the-dwp-and-the-wca-who-gets-the-blame-for-the-biopsychosocial-saga/ (accessed 14 January 2019).

Stewart M (2016). *Cash Not Care: the planned demolition of the UK welfare state.* London: New Generation Publishing.

Surviving Work (2017*). Precarious work.* [Online.] Surviving Work. http://survivingwork.org/wp-content/uploads/2017/11/Precarious-Work-short.jpg (accessed 14 January 2019).

The Future of Therapy (2017). *The IAPT juggernaut.* [Blog.] The Future of Therapy: a national survey of working life. https://thefutureoftherapy.org/iaptjuggernaut (accessed 14 January 2019).

The Psychologist (2017). Silence, power, evidence and a debate with no clear answers. Letters to the editor. *The Psychologist 30*(March): 02–05. https://thepsychologist.bps.org.uk/volume-30/march-2017/silence-power-evidence-and-debate-no-clear-answers (accessed 14 January 2019).

Thomas P (2016). Psycho politics, neoliberal governmentality and austerity. *Self and Society 44*(4): 382–393.

Timimi S (2015). Update on the improving access to psychological therapies programme in England: author's reply. *Psychiatric Bulletin 39*: 252–253.

Timimi S (2014.) No more psychiatric labels: why formal psychiatric diagnostic systems should be abolished. *International Journal of Clinical and Health Psychology 14*(3): 208–215.

Totton N (2000). *Psychotherapy and Politics.* London: Sage.

Viola S, Moncrieff J (2016). Claims for sickness and disability benefits owing to mental disorders in the UK: trends from 1995 to 2014. *BJPsych Open 2*(1): 18–24.

Virilio P (2012). *The Great Accelerator.* Cambridge: Polity Press.

Void J (2015). *A government that permits the psychological torture of benefit claimants does not give a fuck about mental health.* [Blog.] Johnny Void. https://johnnyvoid.wordpress. com/2015/02/06/a-government-that-permits-the-psychological-torture-of-benefit-claimants-does-not-give-a-fuck-about-mental-health/ (accessed 11 January 2019).

Waddell G, Burton K (2006). *Is Work Good for Your Health and Well-Being?* London: Department for Work and Pensions. The Stationery Office. https://assets.publishing. service.gov.uk/government/uploads/system/uploads/attachment_data/file/214326/ hwwb-is-work-good-for-you.pdf (accessed 14 January 2019).

Watts J (2018). Employment must not be the aim of mental health treatment. [Blog.] *Huffington Post;* 4 July. https://www.huffingtonpost.co.uk/dr-jay-watts/mental-health _b_10769174.html?guccounter=1&guce_referrer_us=aHR0cHM6Ly93d3cuZ29vZ2xl LmNvbS88&guce_referrer_cs=uYBxIW26R4EjUjtzKM6c2w (accessed 20 January 2019).

Watts J (2016). IAPT and the ideal image. In: Lees J (ed). *The Future of Psychological Therapy: from managed care to transformational practice.* Abingdon: Routledge (pp84–101).

Watts J (2015). *Cognitive behavioural therapy does not exist.* [Online.] Mad in America; 19 March. www.madinamerica.com/2015/03/cognitive-behavioural-therapy-not-exist/ (accessed 14 January 2019).

Webster D (2017). *Briefings on the DWP's JSA/ESA (and UC from 22 Feb 2017) sanctions statistics release.* [Online.] Child Poverty Action Group; 22 September. http://www.cpag. org.uk/david-webster (accessed 14 January 2019).

Westwood S (2017). Predictors of emotional exhaustion, disengagement and burnout among improving access to psychological therapies (IAPT) practitioners. *Journal of Mental Health 26*(2): 172–179.

9

The social and political origins of wellbeing: a critique of Action for Happiness

Psychologists for Social Change

*This chapter was written by **Christopher Jones**, **Vanessa Griffin**, **Sinead Peacock-Brennan**, **Rachel H Tribe**, **Chris O'Mahony** and **John Cheetham**, representing Psychologists for Social Change, a UK network of applied psychologists, academics, therapists, psychology graduates and others who are interested in applying psychology to social policy and political action. We believe that people's social, political and material contexts are central to their experiences as individuals and that psychologists have a responsibility to use the power that comes with their profession to take action to prevent suffering (McGrath, Walker & Jones, 2016).*

In this chapter we focus on the literature that has been used to support the Action for Happiness movement. In particular, we discuss how happiness has been understood in this literature, and the political consequences of this understanding. We focus on the work of Professor Lord Richard Layard and colleagues, who propose measures of societal wellbeing as central to the evaluation of national policies. Drawing on psychological, survivor and activist literature, we suggest the construction of wellbeing in this literature is not only erroneous but also dangerous when applied at a political and societal level.

The political pursuit of happiness

Richard Layard is an economist and a key proponent of the NHS primary care Improving Access to Psychological Therapies (IAPT) programme, which offers talking therapy (primarily cognitive behavioural therapy (CBT)) for people presenting with 'anxiety' or 'depression'. As explored by Jay Watts and Paul Atkinson in Chapters 7 and 8, IAPT services use a range of measures to define successful treatment, and one of their desirable outcomes is that the client is able to return to employment. Layard persuaded the Westminster government to invest heavily in IAPT with the argument that successful treatment of 'common mental disorders' would enable large numbers of people to move from 'benefit dependence' into employment (Layard & the CEP Mental Health Policy Group, 2006).

Layard continues to be active in this field, through his involvement in the Action for Happiness movement and research. Action for Happiness purports to be a movement committed to building a happier society and states that its top priority is to reduce unemployment because worklessness is one of the greatest enemies of happiness. Action for Happiness was launched in 2011 by Layard, with Geoff Mulgan (now Chief Executive of the Nesta think-tank) and Sir Anthony Seldon, right-leaning historian and political commentator – all proponents of positive psychology. It became a registered charity in 2018. The Action for Happiness initiative encourages people to take the 'happiness pledge' and, by addressing 10 key deficits in their life, increase happiness and decrease misery in their own life and the lives of others. The charity's activities include creating happiness toolkits, corporate consultancy, a happiness course, lobbying government and mobilising volunteers to open happiness cafés. The campaign website reports that the movement has gained momentum, attracting 25,000 people to face-to-face events and 3,000 to lead local community courses, and establishing an online community of more than one million people.

In addition, Layard has co-authored a number of books, including most recently *The Origins of Happiness: the science of well-being over the life course* (Clark et al, 2018). A central argument of the book is that economic explanations for happiness are not as compelling as often claimed. Reporting on data from a small number of surveys, the authors argue that, contrary to previous analysis in research such as Wilkinson and Pickett's *The Spirit Level* (2010), income inequality accounts for less than two per cent of the variation in happiness in the population. They propose that mental illness has a much stronger impact on life satisfaction than income and that the architects of national policies that target wellbeing should focus not on economic policy but on people's private lives.

The Origins of Happiness is part of a wider trend that proposes direct interventions to improve individual wellbeing without adequately acknowledging the social and political contexts that are required to achieve it. Given Layard's involvement in this research, it is likely to be politically influential. This is worrying, due to a number of highly debatable assumptions on which the research is based:

- that wellbeing is a simple and concrete construct that can be reliably used in policy work
- that poverty, mental health, misery and employment are all independent phenomena
- that the relationship between work and happiness is simple and linear
- that the best way to tackle mental distress is through individualised treatments.

The Office for National Statistics (ONS) (2011) distinguishes between 'wellbeing' and 'happiness' in its measures of national wellbeing. Happiness belongs among subjective measures of wellbeing (such as feeling that what you do is worthwhile), distinct from more objective measures (such as life expectancy and educational achievements). In their book, Layard and colleagues use questions about life satisfaction to obtain their measures of happiness. We think the distinctions between the terms 'wellbeing', 'life satisfaction' and 'happiness' are important – something we will explore later in the chapter. However, first we are interested in why this area of research has become politically popular and what this might tell us about our current social and political context.

It may seem surprising that a group of psychologists advocating for wellbeing at a societal level are questioning an initiative that puts happiness at its centre. In response to this, we affirm our belief that the idea of happiness does capture something important about how people understand their lives, and stress that we are certainly not against it. We are, however, concerned about the ethical and political implications of the research that fuels the Action for Happiness initiative and the policies that have been suggested on the basis of related studies. We question the legitimacy of arguments that happiness should be the predominant concern for policy-makers, and in this chapter will point to areas that have been neglected in the research and the impact of some of these oversimplifications on policy proposals. Our argument is that the concept of happiness is neither conceptually strong enough nor operationalised adequately enough for happiness-oriented policies to make a positive difference to people's lives. More than this, these conceptual limitations could actually lead to negative outcomes for wellbeing, because the narrow focus on happiness blocks from consideration other indicators of social advantage that could inform the development of more equitable social policies.

The centrality of happiness

Often under the influence of utilitarian thought, welfare economics in the UK has long been concerned with ideas about maximising happiness (Sen, 2009). Two questions arising from this have a bearing on the science of happiness. First, should happiness be a central consideration in government policy and, if so, to what extent? Second, is there any conceptual clarity on what we really mean by happiness?

To the first question, Layard (2005) has said it is self-evident that happiness should be considered the primary aim of human life. This line of reasoning can be traced back to Jeremy Bentham's (1789/1996) exposition, and John Stuart Mill's defence, of utilitarianism (Mill, 1863/2014). Although there are a number of different versions of utilitarianism (see Kymlicka, 2002), it essentially states that the rights or wrongs of an action or policy should be judged by its consequences. For Bentham, whose version of utilitarianism much of the happiness research supports, humans are primarily motivated to pursue or avoid objects by an apprehension of pleasure or pain. Utilitarian ethical arguments grounded in this form of psychological hedonism maintain that a course of action is good to the extent that it produces the most pleasure for the most people. For Bentham and Layard, happiness is *self-evidently* the central goal of human life and this does not need to be demonstrated. The closest that Layard gets to offering a rationale for this assertion is when he argues for the need to justify our social goals by how people feel, in order to avoid paternalism (Sen, 2009).

However, the problem with making arguments for the centrality of happiness on the basis that it is obviously desirable is that people often desire outcomes in their lives other than happiness. For example, people can bear certain uncomfortable psychological states in the short term if there is a realistic prospect of meaningful social change in the long term. There is no criterion in this theory about how we rank and choose between what we desire. Second, it is also clear that people sometimes desire to dominate those around them, but it does not then follow that domination on a global scale is desirable. Thus, the argument that happiness is self-evidently good is somewhat unconvincing. No theoretical grounding for this position is offered beyond a vague appeal to intuition, and we are left with only the unsupported assertion that happiness *should* be central to our lives and our social policies, just because.

Another argument that questions the political centrality of happiness relates to its limitations as an indicator for social policy. There are two lines of thinking here. The first is Robert Nozick's famous thought experiment relating to the type of psychological hedonism promoted by Bentham (and, latterly, the Action for Happiness movement). Nozick (1974) asked us to imagine that neuropsychologists had invented a machine that could give us whatever pleasurable experiences we wanted. What would we choose? Life in the machine, with constant pleasure on tap, or real life? If individual happiness were truly our primary desire, then everyone would surely choose to live in the machine, feeling nothing but happiness (Kymlicka, 2002). However, Kymlicka argues that very few people would choose life in the machine because, far from representing the best life we could lead, it would hardly represent a life at all.

Sen (2009) uses a similar logic to demonstrate why social goals based on happiness can overlook grave social injustices. He argues that judgements about a person or a society that are based exclusively on the metric of happiness or desire fulfilment have serious limitations. This is because those with the fewest opportunities may be more easily reconciled to deprivation than others raised in more fortunate and affluent circumstances. The measurement of happiness may therefore distort the extent of deprivation that oppressed minorities experience in intolerant societies or that workers feel in exploitative circumstances (Sen, 2009). It is not enough to consider happiness on its own, without a discussion about rights and freedoms, because we do not want just to be a society of happy slaves (Sen, 2009). Measuring happiness can, therefore, give a misleading impression of social equality when other, more objective measures of social advantage would present a very different picture.

Ultimately, because the Action for Happiness movement foregrounds happiness as the key indicator for social policy, it says nothing about access to material resources, social justice, human rights and substantive freedoms. To advocate for intervention at the level of individual psychology in an environment where, in many cases, people do not have the means to meet their basic needs, is unethical and likely to fail. That the authors of *The Origins of Happiness* do not consider these important factors in their definition of happiness represents a major problem with the Action for Happiness initiative more generally.

The nature of happiness

In everyday speech, we have different conceptions of happiness (Haybron, 2008). It is important to question how happiness is understood in the research that supports the science of happiness (eg. Layard et al, 2014; Clark et al, 2018). This research into the determinants of wellbeing devotes very little attention to the conceptual difficulties with defining happiness. For example, the terms 'life satisfaction', 'wellbeing' and 'happiness' are used interchangeably throughout, without any acknowledgment of their differences. Based on data from the British Cohort Study, in both studies, the authors use a measure of 'life satisfaction' to draw conclusions about an individual's 'wellbeing'. In Layard and colleagues' study (2014), respondents were asked to rate how dissatisfied or satisfied they were about the way their life had turned out so far, on a scale where 0 was 'completely dissatisfied' and 10 was 'completely satisfied'. In the later research, involving many of the same authors and based on the same dataset, Clark and colleagues (2018) discuss wellbeing and happiness interchangeably as a measure of life satisfaction:

> In our view we should evaluate people's happiness as they themselves evaluate it. People are often asked, 'Overall, how satisfied are you with your life these days?'... In many countries the question has been asked in unofficial surveys for up to 50 years. But now it is asked of large samples in regular official statistics in most European countries. When people answer this question, they are evaluating their own overall wellbeing. (p2)

However, it is problematic to move between wellbeing and life satisfaction, as they refer to different aspects of human life and can run in the opposite direction from one another (Haybron, 2007, 2008). Haybron (2007) argues that it is possible to be deeply unhappy but report being satisfied with life. This is because life satisfaction questions actually ask about our attitude to life, rather than our emotional response. Consider a young man who is precariously employed on a zero-hours contract and is struggling to pay his bills each month. After six months of working for his employer, he arrives at work one day and is notified that the company is no longer able to employ him. Haybron argues that, if we gave the young man a questionnaire asking whether he was satisfied with his life, his response would be governed by ethical norms. For example, if he believed that you should accept your lot in life, then he would be more likely to say he felt satisfied with his life. This is consistent with the happiness authors' claims about life satisfaction surveys necessitating a cognitive component to answer them (Layard et al, 2014). Haybron (2008) argues that this means 'you might reasonably be satisfied with your life, not because it is going well for you, but because you have or aspire to such virtues as gratitude or fortitude'. In short, we would not want to say that this young man's wellbeing is 'high' just because he has scored highly on a measure of life satisfaction. Furthermore, Suh and colleagues (1998) suggest that culture exerts a significant influence on the construct of life satisfaction. In particular, a person's emotional experiences will influence their judgement of life satisfaction more strongly in individualist cultures than in collectivist cultures. Therefore, it is important to take into account the influence of cultural understandings of selfhood in the response to questions about life satisfaction.

Another central problem for researchers whose work feeds the Action for Happiness position is that they ignore conceptual problems with the pursuit of happiness. John Stuart Mill, arguably, developed a more critical and sophisticated philosophy of happiness than the Benthamite arguments that guide the academic writings considered above. In his autobiography, Mill (1873/1989) reflected on how a 'mental crisis' led him to reappraise his thoughts on the centrality of happiness in human life:

> I never, indeed, wavered in the conviction that happiness is the test of all rules of conduct, and the end of life. But I now thought that this end was only to be attained by not making it the direct end. Those only are happy (I thought) who have their minds fixed on some object other than their own happiness; on the happiness of others, on the improvement of mankind, even on some art or pursuit followed not as a means, but as itself an ideal end. Aiming thus at something else, they find happiness by the way. (p117)

What is significant about this passage is that, while Mill still holds onto the importance of happiness, the pursuit of individual happiness is no longer central to his philosophy or thinking. Our individual happiness is fundamentally linked with the happiness of our family, group or community. Mill also held that happiness is not simply the ability to accumulate as many pleasures as possible but derives from the cultivation of a deeper understanding of the aesthetic, moral and intellectual aspects of our lives. The foregrounding of these kinds of higher qualitative pleasures marks the acme of Mill's intellectual maturity, where he was able to distance himself from the opinions of Jeremy Bentham and his father, James Mill. He also questions the extent to which happiness can be an aim in human life, and indeed in policy proposals, proposing instead that happiness flourishes in meaningful engagement with others.

In a similar vein, more recently, critical psychologist David Smail (1993) argued that our modern pursuit of happiness is perhaps, ironically, one of our biggest sources of unhappiness. The ethical expectation that we should be happy, along with the endless process of reflection on whether our life is meeting this expectation, may itself cause of a lot of our distress. It is also important, at this point, to briefly mention the political significance of unhappiness. Unhappiness often has a political significance, as a legitimate response to inequality, poor working conditions and other socio-political adversities. It should not merely be 'cured', brushed away; sometimes it is a signal that change needs to happen at the environmental or societal level.

Finally, even if you argue from the position that happiness can be measured and correlated with other variables using quantitative statistical methods, there are some clear problems. The authors of *The Origins of Happiness* often use a technique called multiple regression to learn about the relationship between several predictor variables and an outcome. The power of regression as a method relies on the assumption that all relevant 'predictor' variables have been included. When factors that affect the outcome we want to look at are missed, their predictive power can be wrongly attributed to the things that *were* included. Clark and colleagues (2018) note that they do not include certain societal factors like environment, housing or 'ethnic differences' as factors influencing life satisfaction. This means differences in life satisfaction that are related to these issues can be wrongly attributed to variables they have included (notably, for the purposes of their argument, mental illness diagnosis).[1]

Especially notable here is Clark and colleagues' (2018) conclusion that policies aimed at increasing income will not affect total happiness, because happiness is more affected by relative income. This is a controversial position

---

1. Clark et al (2018) do not clearly state the method they have used to choose the order of entry of predictors. As literature in the area already exists, the correct choice would have been hierarchical regression. Other ways of choosing to enter variables, if they have been used, can mean that the results are biased by random sampling variation. If hierarchical regression has been used, this means the authors should have made choices, based on past research, about the order in which predictor variables are entered. The reason for the order of entry of predictors in *The Origin of Happiness* models is not explained. This means it might just reflect the beliefs of the writers about the most 'important' predictors, and those entered first tend to be most closely correlated to the outcome. For example, if the authors believe mental illness diagnosis influences life satisfaction, entering mental illness diagnosis first would tend to produce that result.

and economists have shown sharply contrasting findings in studies using multiple datasets across many countries (Stevenson & Wolfers, 2008). Stevenson and Wolfers' analysis found a relationship between subjective wellbeing and income that was robust within countries (as societies became richer/poorer over time), between countries, and between rich and poor members of the same societies.

The myth of political neutrality

Overall, we would argue, the research by Layard and colleagues cannot draw firm enough claims about population wellbeing to provide the basis for substantive policy decision-making. This is primarily because it foregrounds the *meaning* that people attribute to what happens to them in their lives. While meaning is of undeniable importance for psychologists (Pilgrim, 2014), policy decisions need to also focus on how people's lives are *actually going* for them. Without a thorough analysis of this (which we will elaborate on later in this chapter), social policies will not work towards improving people's lives.

The decision to downplay and deny the socio-political contexts of life satisfaction requires Layard and his co-authors to ignore the substantial epidemiological evidence for the link between social inequality and poor mental health (Friedli, 2009; McGrath, Walker & Jones, 2016; Rogers & Pilgrim, 2003, 2014; Smail, 1993, 2005; Wilkinson & Pickett, 2010). In *The Origins of Happiness,* the authors state that their goal is to prioritise human happiness over income. In the introduction they say they hope to achieve this by creating a metric for happiness to enable policy-makers to prioritise allocation of scarce public funds: for example, choosing 'between care for the elderly and support for young mothers' (Clark et al, 2018: 2). This suggests that an unstated assumption of the research is that *policy-makers will always be unable or unwilling to redistribute wealth* – by, for example, raising taxes and funding public services. This is fundamentally a political position, deeply grounded in the neoliberal[2] mantra of 'no alternative'. The assumption seems to be that any policy proposal needs to fit with the prevailing political climate in which the wealthy are not asked to transfer any of their income or wealth to the less well off. In advising policy-makers, we believe we should try to

---

2. Bell and Green (2016) highlighted the varied use of the term 'neoliberal' in critical health research. It can broadly be thought of as a deregulation of markets with the intention of achieving economic growth and public welfare (Maskovsky & Kingfisher, 2001). A Foucauldian understanding of the term can also be used in which the state is understood to govern from a distance, via shifts in the subjectivity of its citizens (Ward & England, 2007).

influence political norms, rather than just accepting the prevailing political climate.

The authors of *The Origin of Happiness* mask their political adherences, whether deliberately or otherwise, by couching their account in the language of science and neutrality (a rhetorical move also explored by David Frayne in Chapter 6). This tendency can be seen in the Action for Happiness movement more widely. Their website states that they have no hidden agenda, despite Anthony Seldon, one of its founders, conversely stating that bringing happiness into governmental policy should be welcomed by the Right because it 'promotes productivity' (Seldon, 2011). The Action for Happiness campaign promotes as 'fact' that only 10% of happiness can be accounted for by our environment. The vastly greater influence derives, we are told, from our genes (50%) and our daily activities (40%) (Action for Happiness, 2018). This dismissal of the significance of environmental factors informs the campaign's promotion of its key ideas – that our actions as individuals can influence our level of happiness, along with small acts of kindness and changing our attitude to our situation.

The campaign website states that a top priority of Action for Happiness is to reduce unemployment because it is one of the greatest 'enemies of happiness' – a claim that effectively erases factors like ethnicity, gender, disability, sexuality and class from the discussion. Yet a huge body of evidence and common sense suggest that each of these has a profound relationship with individual happiness. For example, Williams and colleagues (2015) analysed follow-up data from the Southall and Brent Revisited (SABRE) study to find that Black Caribbean and South Asian first-generation migrants have almost double the prevalence of depressive symptoms than their White European counterparts, and that socio-economic disadvantage and chronic disease are partly responsible. In terms of gender, an OECD report on wellbeing (2013) has found that women report higher life satisfaction than men but are more likely to experience negative emotions. Findings like these highlight how the Action for Happiness agenda inadvertently, or perhaps deliberately, denies the role that factors like gender and ethnicity play in our individual happiness. This is in no way politically neutral. We would argue that, unless the oppressions that some groups face in society are acknowledged and addressed through political and social action, the individuals within those groups stand much less chance of realising the happiness towards which we are all entitled to aspire. If the proponents of the Action for Happiness campaign were really concerned to promote happiness, they would be organising societal action instead of promoting the 'work cure'.

Rediscovering the social determinants of wellbeing

The research in *The Origins of Happiness* is based on the assumption that poverty, mental health, misery (defined in the text as low life satisfaction) and employment are all independent variables, and thus can be measured against one another. We contend that this is invalid. Health and wellbeing outcomes exist on a social gradient, as levels of health and wellbeing are linked to social status: people from socio-economically disadvantaged groups are more likely to suffer poorer health and die younger than the more affluent (Rogers & Pilgrim, 2003). Poverty, mental health, misery and employment intersect and interact in many ways. For example, poverty can limit access to resources that can protect and promote mental health and also increase the likelihood of exposure to experiences that can damage mental health (Williams & Keating, 2005).

The World Health Organization has recognised the importance of social determinants of health and has called on governments to 'tackle the inequitable distribution of power, money and resources' (2014: 2) to improve health outcomes and reduce health inequalities. There are many social determinants of health, but we will focus on three key ones: income inequality, employment status and working conditions.

High income inequality has been consistently found to have a negative impact on societies and individuals. A comparison of national surveys across 12 developed countries found that more unequal countries had worse outcomes across many measures, including physical health, life expectancy, mental health, education, drug abuse and imprisonment (Wilkinson & Pickett, 2010). The epidemiological analysis found that levels of mental illness were three times higher in countries with high levels of income inequality. It is important to note that, 'for all its limitations, social psychiatric knowledge provides us with a database to discuss madness and misery in society' (Rogers & Pilgrim, 2003: 9). Income inequality has been associated with increased prevalence of experiences that have been labelled as schizophrenia (Burns, Tomita & Kapadia, 2014), psychosis (Burns & Esterhuizen, 2008) and depression (Hiilamo, 2014). Income inequality also does not affect all people equally. People from ethnic minority backgrounds, women, LGBT people, people with disabilities and people with mental ill health are all more likely to live in poverty (Equality and Human Rights Commission, 2010: 19; Joseph Rowntree Foundation, 2014; Williams et al, 2015).

Forms of disadvantage and discrimination do not act independently of each other; rather, they intersect and are shaped by one another in a way that compounds social injustice (Hatch et al, 2016; Wallace, Nazroo & Bécares, 2016; Williams et al, 2015). While we know that people in disadvantaged minority groups are at higher risk of mental ill health, evidence suggests the existence of a 'triple jeopardy': having multiple minority statuses (eg. class, race and gender) places people at particularly high risk of mental ill health (Rosenfield, 2012). *The Origins of Happiness* treats inequalities in income, employment, physical and mental health as if they were distinct, independent of one another and separable, rather than phenomena that interact with each other in complex ways. In a magazine article, Layard asks: 'If we wanted to reduce the numbers in misery, what change would have the biggest effect – raising incomes, ending unemployment, improving physical health or abolishing depression and anxiety?' (Layard, 2017: 13). Although compellingly straightforward, the question vastly oversimplifies and misrepresents the reality. The appeal of the model being articulated here is twofold: it is simple to grasp, and it doesn't demand any real deviation or change to our social structure and political norms.

The authors of *The Origins of Happiness* assert that employment is vital for wellbeing and functions as an important mental health intervention on its own (see David Frayne's Chapter 6 for a critique of this position). In discussing this, the authors make a further assumption that the relationship between work and happiness is simple and linear. However, research suggests that having any job is not necessarily better than having no job, and that poor working conditions can be equally or even more detrimental to mental health than unemployment. The majority of the research evidence that the authors of *The Origins of Happiness* draw on to support their point dates from before the rapid expansion of precarious employment, zero-hours contracts and the so-called gig economy. A recent longitudinal study following 1,000 unemployed adults found that those who got good-quality jobs enjoyed large improvements in their mental health, but those who found jobs with low pay, low security and low control had no better mental health than those who remained unemployed, and actually had higher levels of chronic physical stress (Chandola & Zhang, 2017).

Worryingly, these poor-quality jobs are the fastest growing employment sector in the UK. Almost 10 million people, or one third of the workforce, are in some form of precarious employment, according to the GMB Union (Butler, 2017). Previous studies have found that, when people have low levels of social support at work, few opportunities to use their skills and experience and little variety and control, they tend to experience lower wellbeing and greater emotional distress (Stansfeld et al, 1995; Link, Lennon & Dohrenwend,

1993). In their strategic review of health inequalities in England post-2010, Marmot and colleagues conclude (2010: 26): 'Getting people off benefits and into low paid, insecure and health-damaging work is not a desirable option'.

A case for alternative policy indicators

So far we have outlined our concerns about the research conducted by Lord Layard and colleagues to inform the broader Action for Happiness campaign. To summarise, we set out our position that:

- It is not self-evident that happiness should be considered the primary aim of human life. Making this the focus of social policy silences other discussions about the importance of human rights and freedoms in policy-making.

- The construct of happiness is not coherent in the research literature, and using concepts of happiness, wellbeing and life-satisfaction interchangeably oversimplifies a complex area of research. These discussions also make a worrying link to mental distress, implying that psychotherapy can 'cure' societal ills.

- The research methodology used to promote the wellbeing agenda is not sound, resulting in important discrepancies between the findings of work such as *The Origins of Happiness* and other research in this field.

- Poverty, mental health, misery and unemployment are not independent of each other and cannot be compared in terms of their potency to increase wellbeing. Income inequality and working practices are also important factors to consider, as they have important implications for policy-making.

It is our view that wellbeing is not the magic bullet that Layard and his colleagues in the Action for Happiness movement believe, and society would be far better served by attending to problems like structural inequalities and discrimination. The focus of change should not be individual wellbeing, happiness or satisfaction but problems of injustice, discrimination and inequality. Based on our review of psychological research literature, we propose that policy-makers need to evaluate the impact of proposed policies using five interconnected markers of a 'healthy society': agency, security, connection, meaning and trust (Psychologists Against Austerity, 2015). We offer these as a possible replacement for individualistic notions of wellbeing.

Agency

Having a sense of agency is a component of wellbeing and is strongly linked with physical and mental health outcomes (Frenkel et al, 1995; Jang et al, 2002; Lefcourt, 1991; Pudrovska et al, 2005; Welzel & Inglehart, 2010). Agency can be understood as a subjective sense of control over one's life and the capacity to make purposeful choices. Issues that restrict and limit one's sense of agency are associated with structural inequalities relating to the disempowerment of people according to class, education, gender identification, sexuality, race, ethnicity, age and (dis)ability. Policy action is needed to disentangle people from these inequalities, such as living in poverty or being employed in low income jobs (Landsbergis et al, 1992; Lefkowitz, Tesiny & Gordon, 1980; Stansfeld, Bosma & Marmot, 1998).

Security

Living in fear and insecurity in childhood is associated with poor mental health outcomes in adulthood. A sense of security includes believing that your community is safe. We know that people living in communities with greater rates of, for example, vandalism, litter and vacant buildings tend to have higher rates of mental health problems (Green, Gilbertson & Grimsley, 2002; Wanderman & Nation, 1998). Mothers who are living with more life stressors, poorer quality work and housing and lower socio-economic status have been found to be less sensitive in response to their baby's needs, which in turn negatively affects the baby's emotional development (Bakermans-Kranenburg, van IJzendoorn & Kroonenberg, 2004); dysfunctional attachment in infancy is a predictor of worse psychological wellbeing in adulthood. If they grow up in similar environments, these children will face the same structural inequalities as their parents. Given this evidence, the introduction of 'healthy minds' resilience training workshops for children, as suggested in *The Origins of Happiness*, is an incomplete intervention at best. Although it is clearly important to strengthen children and young people's resilience to life stressors, this becomes problematic if they continue to live in a toxic environment.

Connection

Having a sense of connection and belonging is a basic human need (Bowlby, 2005). We experience social exclusion as painful and this is strongly associated with the increased risk of developing mental health problems (Caxaj & Verman, 2010; Williams, 2007). The 'work cure' relies on the notion that, if an individual is not contributing to the economic productivity of the nation by engaging in paid employment, then they are shirking their responsibilities as a citizen and draining resources. A narrative shift is needed to take us away from the notion that those who do not enter into waged labour are 'shirkers', not part of society and make no contribution to their fellows and communities. Pilgrim, Rogers and Bentall (2009) have described the central role that relationships play in the creation and amelioration of mental health problems. Policies are needed that promote contact across different demographic groups, generating connections between people and strengthening communities. People who are in receipt of social security benefits should be recognised as being able to hold many roles in society that connect them with others – a new point of view that would promote a more holistic idea of health (Dupere & Perkins, 2007).

Meaning

The ability to live a meaningful life is central to wellbeing (Antonovsky, 1979; Sen, 1999). As mentioned above, access to work has been deemed a key route to developing a sense of meaning, purpose and value in society. However, the quality of this work is crucial, and we must support political and trade union efforts to improve working conditions. We might also want to engage in a deeper questioning of the extent to which the institution of employment can realistically cater to wellbeing. In this context, the concept of meaningful *occupation* perhaps becomes a far more useful concept than that of employment. Meaningful occupation might include volunteering, taking care of family members, political activism and civic participation, developing and maintaining a garden, or any number of other activities that are of interest and value to the individual.

Trust

Central to the notion of building a more trusting community is the concept of equality. Societies that are more equal and socially cohesive create citizens who are more trusting of each other (Kawachi, Sankaran & Kin, 2008; Wilkinson & Pickett, 2010). Greater levels of trust in a society are associated with a range of positive physical and mental health outcomes and higher rates of subjective wellbeing (Helliwell & Putnam, 2004). Trust helps develop and maintain our social bonds and keeps communities strong (Putnam, 1993). Trusting societies are better at bridging links between groups and are more able to work together to achieve collective goals (Fukuyama, 2002). Policies that empower local communities to use their own social and human capital to drive their local economies are essential to improving wellbeing.

What can psychologists do?

On the basis of these key goals, we call psychologists to take action in the following domains.

Research

In terms of reviewing and synthesising research, it remains important for consumers of research to note how often studies are based on unquestioned assumptions and political agendas. In terms of how research is used, it also appears that, on their own, facts don't change public opinion and we need better narratives to inform public thinking and put pressure on policy-makers. A good example of research that challenges current narratives of employment as a mental health cure is Friedli and Stearn's (2015) work, which amplifies the voices of those most affected by these narratives. They describe the coercive and punitive nature of psycho-policy interventions by drawing on personal testimonies of people subjected to workfare, policy analysis and social media records of campaigns against what they term 'psycho-compulsion'. The power of the psychological research sector could be better used to formulate and present alternative policy proposals to those with the power to implement them.

Research and applied psychologists also could commit to a more critical deconstruction of research and policies that draw a simplistic link between employment and mental health. Powerful organisations such as the Behavioural Insights Team (BIT), which works in partnership with the Cabinet Office to apply behavioural science to policy-making, should be scrutinised (see Cromby & Willis, 2014). These critiques should be shared within the psychology community and with campaigning allies. Psychologists and anyone interested in mobilising psychological knowledge could join campaigning organisations such as Psychologists for Social Change, the Psychotherapy and Counselling Union and Psychotherapists and Counsellors for Social Responsibility, which work alongside activist organisations such as Boycott Workfare,[3] the Centre for Welfare Reform[4] and Disabled People Against Cuts.[5] In a previous article (McGrath, Walker & Jones, 2016), we discussed the importance of research that engages with social action and social movements to bring about the possibility of change. It is through

---

3. Boycott Workfare – www.boycottworkfare.org (accessed 14 January 2019).

4. Centre for Welfare Reform – www.centreforwelfarereform.org (accessed 14 January 2019).

5. Disabled People Against Cuts – https://dpac.uk.net (accessed 14 January 2019).

developing broader research alliances with the people and groups affected by social policies that the work of psychology might be pushed in a more radical and socially progressive direction.

Therapy

Drawing on ideas from Liberation Psychology (Martín-Baró, 1996), psychologists should resist being 'value-neutral' and instead work towards challenging psychology's complicity in wider structural inequalities and oppression. When working therapeutically, clinicians should also be aware of the social policy climate and its harmful impact on many of those who attend mental health services. Access to benefits and the constant pressure to return to employment can be heard in the stories told to therapists in mental health services everywhere, and these should be incorporated into a formulation of their presenting problems that includes social and political factors.

Smail (1993), for example, has highlighted the importance of therapies in supporting people to develop 'outsight' – a perspective that acknowledges the significance of a person's material reality and social environment for their wellbeing. Further guidance on how to do this is found in Hagan and Smail's (1997) work on power-mapping. This critical perspective is essential to encourage service users not to blame themselves for their troubles. In 2018, the British Psychological Society and its Division of Clinical Psychology published *The Power, Threat, Meaning Framework* (Johnstone & Boyle, 2018), which offers a framework for understanding and responding to personal distress in its wider social, material and cultural context. There are several other therapeutic approaches that provide helpful frameworks through which to explore the broader social context of people's experiences (eg. Morgan, 2000; Seikkula & Arnkil, 2006; White, 2000).

If social context and related policies are included in the formulation of problems, it follows that psychological interventions should also attempt change at this level. Holland's (1992) consciousness-raising and social action work with women on the White City estate is a great example: the women who had attended individual therapy followed by group work went on to set up a self-help counselling and advocacy group called Women's Action for Mental Health. More recently, Holmes (2010) wrote about supporting people to consider the roots of their problems, followed by social action at local community, national and international policy-levels to transform these causes of distress.

Policy-making

It is not enough to critique dominant 'evidence-based' policy-making without suggesting an alternative. Psychologists for Social Change, for example, have produced a briefing paper evaluating the psychological research evidence for Universal Basic Income – a minimum regular payment given to each person as a right of citizenship (2017). Although there is still some complex debate on the merits of Universal Basic Income (with difficult questions to answer on the policy's official purpose, what amount would be sufficient, and whether the policy should completely replace means-tested benefits), it is important to go beyond critique and present 'psychologically healthy' policy proposals that acknowledge the vast and complex impact of social and structural inequality on mental health.

Health workers, including psychologists, counsellors, nurses and doctors, can work through their professional associations and trade unions to lobby UK parliaments, assemblies, non-governmental organisations and international bodies. It has been noted that academics become influential in policy if their work chimes with the ideology of the moment and it 'plays publicly' (Cairney, 2015). It is important, therefore, to consider which alternative political narratives might better meet the needs of the public who are currently being impacted by workfare and the 'work cure'. Evans (2017) describes the triumph of narrative over rationally presented facts and evidence, and suggests that we make sense of ourselves and the world through stories. He explains that we tell powerfully resonant stories that create a wider sense of a 'we', with whom the public empathise, and thereby demonstrate that an alternative way is possible.

Wider society

Given that psychologists are trained to be skilled in developing relationships and engaging in difficult discussions, they should be active citizens and encourage the public to question the assumptions underpinning harmful social policies. As citizens, psychologists can contribute to radio call-ins, write letters to local and national newspapers and present their critiques to the public in an accessible and informed style. Conversations within local community groups of which psychologists are members, from school parent-teacher associations to church groups, can widen an awareness of damaging practices and support members of the public to engage with these issues.

Psychologists Against Austerity (2016), for example, offers guidance on how we talk about inequality. These principles could be applied to conversations about societal problems that the public think are impossible to change. The overall aim is to introduce the possibility of an alternative. In this case, it might be by highlighting that, although more funding for individual therapy is much needed, without changes to policies and practices that damage the wellbeing of the most vulnerable in society, 'happiness' will not improve.

Conclusions

To conclude, the call by Layard and colleagues in *The Origins of Happiness* (Clark et al, 2018) for increased investment in mental health services and consideration of wellbeing in governmental policy-making appears well-intentioned. However, the assumption that 'mental illness' is something that occurs in individuals, unrelated to their physical and social contexts, has dangerous implications for policy. Furthermore, it leads to individual therapeutic solutions, which, in the context of ever-increasing social inequalities, can only be considered reactive – a 'sticking plaster' remedy that does little to contribute towards longer-term solutions, and may even discourage people from thinking about their problems in structural and political terms.

In this chapter we have highlighted our concerns about the definition and framing of 'happiness' in policy-making, and in particular the use of scientific and apolitical narratives when presenting recommendations for national policy. Importantly, we have highlighted that the methods of treatment proposed in *The Origins of Happiness* and the Action for Happiness movement all individualise the issues. There is a place for such interventions; as psychologists, we work therapeutically with people experiencing distress on a daily basis and we know the benefits of these approaches and how they can help people through times of difficulty. However, we also know their limitations, because such interventions do not proactively address the fact that the causes of distress are not only individual but also social, relational and material.

Without action to minimise the poverty and social inequalities that cause and worsen distress, the effects of psychological treatments are at best short-lived. They can be damaging to the individual, placing responsibility on them to change and exacerbating their feelings of shame and distress, while maintaining the systems that continue to oppress us. We believe other policy indicators should be considered to promote a more psychologically healthy society, such as agency, security, connection, meaning and trust. Psychologists have an important role in creating and critiquing research and social policies with this in mind. We need to begin a concerted discussion about how, as citizens and not just professionals, we can advocate for policies that hold these indicators more centrally.

We finish with an alternative account of happiness from the feminist Lynne Segal (2017). In her response to economistic happiness research, Segal describes an alternative idea of happiness as a complex emotional state that is always fleeting and always connected to our relationships with others. Segal points in particular to the role of neoliberalism in undermining happiness by reducing hope for a better future, as well as increasing inequality and undermining solidarity. Describing her participation in a range of political movements throughout her lifetime, Segal talks about hope and collective endeavour towards a different kind of future as making us feel more alive, and hence happier. Segal concludes that collective and public experiences are ultimately essential to happiness, especially when these involve working together for change.

References

Action for Happiness (2018). *Why Happiness?* [Online.] Action for Happiness. www.actionforhappiness.org/why-happiness (accessed 14 January 2019).

Antonovsky A (1979). *Health, Stress and Coping.* London: Jossey-Bass.

Bakermans-Kranenburg MJ, van IJzendoorn MH, Kroonenberg PM (2004). Differences in attachment security between African-American and white children: ethnicity or socio-economic status? *Infant Behavior and Development 27*(3): 417–433.

Bell K, Green J (2016). On the perils of invoking neoliberalism in public health critique. *Critical Public Health 26*(3): 239–243.

Bentham J (1789/1996). *The Collected Works of Jeremy Bentham: an introduction to the principles of morals and legislation.* Oxford: Clarendon Press.

Bowlby J (2005). *A Secure Base: clinical applications of attachment theory.* New York, NY: Routledge.

Burns JK, Esterhuizen T (2008). Poverty, inequality and the treated incidence of first-episode psychosis. *Social Psychiatry and Psychiatric Epidemiology 43*(4): 331–335.

Burns JK, Tomita A, Kapadia AS (2014). Income inequality and schizophrenia: increased schizophrenia incidence in countries with high levels of income inequality. *International Journal of Social Psychiatry 60*(2): 185–196.

Butler S (2017). Nearly 10 million Britons are in insecure work, says union. [Online.] *The Guardian*; 5 June. www.theguardian.com/business/2017/jun/05/nearly-10-million-britons-are-in-insecure-work-says-union (accessed 14 January 2019).

Cairney P (2015). *The Politics of Evidence-Based Policy Making.* London: Palgrave.

Caxaj C, Verman H (2010). Belonging among newcomer youths: intersecting experiences of inclusion and exclusion. *Advances in Nursing Science 33*(4): 17–30.

Chandola T, Zhang N (2017). Re-employment, job quality, health and allostatic load biomarkers: prospective evidence from the UK Household Longitudinal Study. *International Journal of Epidemiology 47*(1): 47–57.

Clark AE, Flèche S, Layard R, Powdthavee N, Ward G (2018). *The Origins of Happiness: the science of well-being over the life course.* Oxford: Princeton University Press.

Cromby J, Willis ME (2014). Nudging into subjectification: governmentality and psychometrics. *Critical Social Policy 34*(2): 241–259.

Dupere V, Perkins DD (2007). Community types and mental health: a multilevel study of local environmental stress and coping. *American Journal of Community Psychology 39*(1–2): 107–119.

Equality and Human Rights Commission (2010). *How Fair is Britain? The first triennial review.* London: Equality and Human Rights Commission.

Evans A (2017). *The Myth Gap.* London: Penguin Random House.

Frenkel E, Kugelmass S, Nathan M, Ingraham LJ (1995). Locus of control and mental health in adolescence and adulthood. *Schizophrenia Bulletin 21*(2): 219.

Friedli L (2009). *Mental Health, Resilience and Inequalities.* Geneva: World Health Organisation

Friedli L, Stearn R (2015). Positive affect as coercive strategy: conditionality, activation and the role of psychology in UK government workfare programmes. *Medical Humanities, 41*: 40–47.

Fukuyama F (2002). Social capital and development: the coming agenda. *SAIS Review 22*(1): 23–38.

Green G, Gilbertson JM, Grimsley MF (2002). Fear of crime and health in residential tower blocks: a case study in Liverpool, UK. *The European Journal of Public Health 12*(1): 10–15.

Hagan T, Smail D (1997). Power-mapping – 1: Background and basic methodology. *Journal of Community & Applied Social Psychology 7*(4): 257–267.

Hatch SL, Gazard B, Williams DR, Frissa S, Goodwin L, Hotopf M, SELCoH Study Team (2016). Discrimination and common mental disorder among migrant and ethnic groups: findings from a South East London Community sample. *Social Psychiatry and Psychiatric Epidemiology 51*(5): 689–701.

Haybron DM (2008). *The Pursuit of Unhappiness: the elusive psychology of well-being.* Oxford: Oxford University Press.

Haybron DM (2007). Life satisfaction, ethical reflection, and the science of happiness. *Journal of Happiness Studies 8*(1): 99–138.

Helliwell JF, Putnam RD (2004). The social context of well-being. *Philosophical Transactions of the Royal Society B: Biological Sciences 359*(1449):1435–1446.

Hiilamo H (2014). Is income inequality 'Toxic for Mental Health'? An ecological study on municipal level risk factors for depression. *PloS One 9*(3): e92775.

Holland S (1992). From social abuse to social action: a neighbourhood psychotherapy and social action project for women. In: Ussher J, Nicolson P (eds). *Gender Issues in Clinical Psychology.* London: Routledge (pp68–77).

Holmes G (2010). *Psychology in the Real World: community-based groupwork*. Ross-on-Wye: PCCS Books.

Jang Y, Haley HE, Small BJ, Mortimer JA (2002). The role of mastery and social resources in the associations between disability and depression in later life. *The Gerontologist 2*(6): 807–813.

Johnstone L, Boyle M with Cromby J, DIllon J, Harper D, Kinderman P, Longden E, Pilgrim D, Read J (2018). *The Power Threat Meaning Framework: overview*. Leicester: British Psychological Society.

Joseph Rowntree Foundation (2014). *Reducing Poverty in the UK: a collection of evidence reviews*. York: Joseph Rowntree Foundation.

Kawachi I, Sankaran SV, Kim D (2008). *Social Capital and Health*. London: Springer.

Kymlicka W (2002). *Contemporary Political Philosophy: an introduction*. Oxford: Oxford University Press.

Landsbergis PA, Schnall PL, Deitz D, Friedman R, Pickering T (1992). The patterning of psychological attributes and distress by 'job strain' and social support in a sample of working men. *Journal of Behavioural Medicine 15*(4): 379–405.

Layard R (2017). Origins of happiness. [Online.] *Centrepiece 22*(1): 13–14. http://cep.lse.ac.uk/pubs/download/cp497.pdf (accessed 14 January 2019).

Layard R (2005). *Happiness: lessons from a new science*. London: Penguin.

Layard R, CEP Mental Health Policy Group (2006). *The Depression Report: a new deal for depression and anxiety disorders*. CEP Special Papers 15. London: Centre for Economic Performance, London School of Economics.

Layard R, Clark AE, Cornaglia F, Powdthavee N, Vernoit J (2014). What predicts a successful life? A life-course model of well-being. *The Economic Journal 124*(580): F720–F738.

Lefcourt HM (1991). Locus of control. In: Robinson JP, Shaver PR, Wrightsman LS (series eds). *Measures of Social Psychological Attitudes Series Vol 1: measures of personality and social psychological attitudes*. San Diego, CA: Academic Press (pp413–499).

Lefkowitz M, Tesiny E, Gordon N (1980). Childhood depression, family income, and locus of control. *Journal of Nervous & Mental Disease 168*(12): 732–735.

Link BG, Lennon MC, Dohrenwend BP (1993). Socioeconomic status and depression: the role of occupations involving direction, control, and planning. *American Journal of Sociology 98*(6): 1351–1387.

Marmot M, Allen J, Goldblatt P, Boyce T, McNeish D, Grady M, Geddes I (2010). *Fair Society, Healthy Lives: the strategic review of health inequalities in England post-2010*. London: UCL Institute for Health Equity.

Martín-Baró I (1996). *Writings for a Liberation Psychology*. New York, NY: Harvard University Press

Maskovsky J, Kingfisher C (2001). Introduction: global capitalism, neoliberal policy and poverty. *Urban Anthropology and Studies of Cultural Systems and World Economic Development 30*: 105–121.

McGrath L, Walker C, Jones C (2016) Psychologists against austerity: mobilising psychology for social change. *Critical and Radical Social Work 4*(3): 409–413.

Mill JS (1873/1989). *Autobiography*. New York, NY: Penguin.

Mill JS (1863/2014). *Utilitarianism.* Cambridge: Cambridge University Press.

Morgan A (2000). *What is Narrative Therapy? An easy-to-read introduction.* Adelaide: Dulwich Centre Publications.

Nozick R (1974). *Anarchy, State and Utopia.* New York, NY: Basic Books.

OECD (2013). *How's Life 2013: measuring well-being.* Paris: OECD Publishing. www.oecd.org/sdd/3013071e.pdf (accessed 20 January 2019).

Office for National Statistics (2011). *National Statistician's Reflections on the National Debate on Measuring National Well-being.* London: the Stationery Office.

Pilgrim D (2014). *Understanding Mental Health: a critical realist exploration.* London: Routledge.

Pilgrim D, Rogers A, Bentall R (2009). The centrality of personal relationships in the creation and amelioration of mental health problems: the current interdisciplinary case. *Health 13*(2): 235–254.

Psychologists Against Austerity (2016). *Improving Public Discussion about Inequality: a briefing paper.* [Online.] Psychologists Against Austerity. www.psychchange.org/uploads/9/7/9/7/97971280/talking-about-inequality.pdf (accessed 20 January 2019).

Psychologists Against Austerity (2015). *The Psychological Impact of Austerity: a briefing paper.* [Online.] Psychologists Against Austerity. https://psychagainstausterity.files.wordpress.com/2015/03/paa-briefing-paper.pdf (accessed 14 January 2019).

Psychologists for Social Change (2017). *Basic Income: a psychological impact assessment.* [Online.] Psychologists Against Austerity. www.psychchange.org/basic-income-psychological-impact-assessment.html (accessed 14 January 2019).

Pudrovska T, Schieman S, Pearlin LI, Nguyen K (2005). The sense of mastery as a mediator and moderator in the association between economic hardship and health in late life. *Journal of Aging and Health 17*(5): 634–660.

Putnam R (1993). *Making Democracy Work: civic traditions in modern Italy.* Princeton, NJ: Princeton University Press.

Rogers A, Pilgrim D (2014). *A Sociology of Mental Health and Illness.* Maidenhead: McGraw-Hill.

Rogers A, Pilgrim D (2003). *Inequalities and Mental Health.* London: Palgrave Macmillan.

Rosenfield S (2012). Triple jeopardy? Mental health at the intersection of gender, race, and class. *Social Science and Medicine 74*(1): 1791–1796.

Segal L (2017). *Radical Happiness: moments of collective joy.* London: Verso.

Seikkula J, Arnkil TE (2006). *Dialogical Meetings in Social Networks.* London: Karnac.

Seldon A (2011). Action for happiness: it's time the Right looks beyond its prejudices and understands what this agenda is about. [Online.] *Daily Telegraph;* 12 April. www.telegraph.co.uk/news/uknews/8445576/Action-for-Happiness-its-time-the-right-looks-beyond-its-prejudices-and-understands-what-this-agenda-is-about.html (accessed 14 January 2019).

Sen A (2009). *The Idea of Justice.* Cambridge, MA: Harvard University Press.

Sen A (1999). *Development as Freedom.* Oxford: Oxford University Press.

Smail D (2005). *Power, Interest and Psychology: elements of a social materialist understanding of distress.* Ross-on-Wye: PCCS Books.

Smail D (1993). *The Origins of Unhappiness.* London: Constable.

Stansfeld SA, Bosma H, Marmot MG (1998). Psychosocial work characteristics and social support as predictors of SF-36 health functioning: the Whitehall II Study. *Psychosomatic Medicine 60*(3): 247–255.

Stansfeld SA, North FM, White I, Marmot MG (1995). Work characteristics and psychiatric disorder in civil servants in London. *Journal of Epidemiology & Community Health 49*(1): 48–53.

Stevenson B, Wolfers J (2008). Economic Growth and Subjective Well-Being: reassessing the Easterlin paradox. *Brookings Papers on Economic Activity 1.*

Suh E, Diener E, Oishi S, Triandis HC (1998). The shifting basis of life satisfaction judgements across cultures: emotions versus norms. *Journal of Personality and Social Psychology 74*(2): 482–493.

Wallace S, Nazroo J, Bécares L (2016). Cumulative effect of racial discrimination on the mental health of ethnic minorities in the United Kingdom. *American Journal of Public Health 106*(7): 1294–1300.

Wanderman A, Nation M (1998). Urban neighbourhoods and mental health: psychological contributions to understanding toxicity, resilience and intervention. *American Psychologist 53*(6): 647.

Ward K, England K (2007). Introduction: reading neoliberalization. In: England K, Ward K (eds). *Neoliberalization.* Hoboken, NJ: Blackwell (pp1–22).

Welzel C, Inglehart R (2010). Agency, values, and well-being: a human development model. *Social Indicators Research 97*(1): 43–63.

White MK (2000). *Reflections on Narrative Practice: essays and interviews.* Adelaide: Dulwich Centre Publications.

Wilkinson R, Pickett K (2010). *The Spirit Level: why greater equality makes societies stronger.* New York, NY: Bloomsbury.

Williams KD (2007). Ostracism. *Annual Review of Psychology 58*(1): 425–452.

Williams J, Keating F (2005). Social inequalities and mental health. In: Bell A, Lindley P (eds). *Beyond the Water Towers: the unfinished revolution in mental health services 1985–2005.* London: Sainsbury Centre for Mental Health (pp113–126).

Williams ED, Tillin T, Richards M, Tuson C, Chaturvedi N, Hughes AD, Stewart R (2015). Depressive symptoms are doubled in older British South Asian and Black Caribbean people compared with Europeans: associations with excess co-morbidity and socioeconomic disadvantage. *Psychological Medicine 45*(9): 1861–1871.

World Health Organization (2014). *Social Determinants of Mental Health.* Geneva: World Health Organization.

10

'We rebel because We misfit': anti-work politics and coalition work in the welfare action movement

Arianna Introna and Mirella Casagrande

Mirella Casagrande and Arianna Introna have been doing research together for eight years. Mirella is an independent researcher interested in Marxist and critical theory. Arianna has just submitted her PhD thesis, which brought together Scottish literature, disability studies and Marxist autonomist theory. She is passionate about and involved with welfare action and disability politics.

This chapter will consider the contribution that disability can make to anti-work politics, and about the connections that might be established between disabled people's and benefit claimants' solidarity groups. It develops what we might call an *autonomist disability perspective*, which brings together ideas from autonomist Marxism and disability studies to grasp and appreciate the value of the anti-productivist force of disability. Our reflections are underpinned by the assumption that there exists a fundamental overlap between capitalism and normalcy – the system that enforces 'normality by upholding some impossible standard to which all bodies must adhere' (Davis, 2002: 38).

What is notable is the extent to which current standards of normalcy seem to coalesce with ideas of the ideal employee. Consider Erich Fromm's still-relevant citation of the psychiatrist Edward Strecker in the 1950s, whose definition of maturity seems to encompass the same personal qualities one might expect to see in a typical job advertisement:

> I define maturity as the ability to stick to a job, the capacity to give more on any job than is asked for, reliability, persistence to carry out a plan regardless of the difficulties, the ability to work with other people under organisation and authority, the ability to make decisions, a will to life, flexibility, independence and tolerance. (Fromm, 1956: 73)

Rosemarie Garland-Thomson introduces the concept of the 'normate' – the imagined ideal figure, unmarked by the stigmatising symbols of disability. By way of their bodily configurations and cultural capital, the normate 'can step into a position of authority and wield the power it grants them' (Garland-Thomson, 1997: 8). The prestige of the normate, and the corresponding devaluation of disability, are inseparable from disability's marginal and resistant position with respect to waged work under capitalism. From our anti-capitalist perspective, the crucial question is: how can this marginality generate insights and potential for resistance that might be useful to working-class struggle, especially to today's welfare action movement? We will seek to answer this question by exploring the conflict that develops between, on the one hand, demands for productivity through waged work, and on the other, those non-standard embodiments that are impervious to these demands. What role can this conflict play in collective resistance under capitalism?

We will start by discussing the importance of coalition work in the welfare action movement and the related relevance of an anti-work politics, especially if sharpened by an awareness of the anti-productivist power of disabled bodies and minds. Moving on, we will consider how two strands of autonomist Marxism – Open Marxism and Italian post-operaism – have understood the social composition of anti-capitalist struggles and the possibility to unite people 'saying no, we are not willing to – or maybe we are just too stupid or backwards – to satisfy the demands of capital' (Holloway, 2015).

Coalition work and the contemporary welfare action movement

We are living through times where employment is increasingly precarious and exploitative, yet still remains morally and culturally central, and still remains the only way to survive. Discussing this conjuncture, David Frayne denounces as baffling 'the fact that the ethical status of work has still not been significantly destabilised by our disintegrating labour market' (Frayne, 2015: 6). The paradox identified by Frayne has also been unpacked by other theorists. Ivor Southwood has described how the desire for the end of work in times of crisis is inseparable from the continual search for a job, prompting 'contradictory but taken-for granted feelings – a fear of imminent destruction and at the same time a wish for this corrupted and imprisoning system to collapse' (Southwood, 2011: 3). Peter Fleming concurs by suggesting that the deconstruction of the work ethic needs to start from the awareness that 'the capitalist state is directly fostering conditions that make work a permanently present problem that merits our practical attention' (Fleming, 2015: 15). Once the socially and politically constructed nature of work and our failure to collectively organise around an anti-work politics are acknowledged, Frayne's call to 'challenge the work-centred nature of modern society' (Frayne, 2015: 5) becomes the starting point for both theory and practice. If, as Frayne argues, 'The question that hangs in the balance… is whether people's growing disenchantment with work can be harnessed and developed into a genuine political alternative' (Frayne, 2015: 1), mapping out the coalition work that can be done in the welfare action movement can provide a sense, through theory, of what it may be possible to materialise in action.

The work of Lynne Friedli and Robert Stearn has captured the importance of insights emerging from claimants' organising for the development of an anti-work politics. Under the pretext of tackling the alleged inadequacy of welfare claimants' 'employability' (Friedli & Stearn, 2013), the active labour market policies of the UK benefit system have attempted to force claimants to change their attitudes and beliefs about work, imposing an 'approved work personality' (Friedli, 2016). One of the novel things about the work of Friedli and Stearn, however, is that, as well as registering these policies as a form of social control, the authors recognise the extent to which these policies have catalysed collective action against the work ethic. One instance of this is the public reaction to workfare – the mandatory performance of unpaid labour in exchange for benefits – which 'has become an important site for satire on the fetishisation of paid work, [and] for struggle over definitions of a meaningful and productive life' (Friedli & Stearn, 2015). The image of a ball and chain, merged with the logos of key 'work providers' (who invariably state that their aim is to improve people's lives), has been a feature of banners displayed at protests against workfare organised by groups such as Boycott Workfare and disabled people's organisations and claimants' solidarity groups, such as the Edinburgh Coalition Against Poverty. This has helped popularise the association between workfare and modern-day slavery and legitimate the rejection of forced labour that workfare schemes embody. In order for collective action to graduate to counter power, however, we believe it is necessary to place the connections between disabled people's organisations and claimants' solidarity groups on firmer ground. Only in this way can more sustained and effective co-ordinated action be developed around a common anti-work focus.

Coalition work is fraught with difficulties. If 'even the smallest coalitions give expression to a diversity of beliefs, perspectives, and interests' (Long, 1997: 166), it is likely, as Aziz Choudry suggests, that 'tensions over meaning, frames, representation, and mandate... come to a head' (Choudry, 2007: 110). One particular point of friction exists around the demand for disabled people to be included more fully into the world of waged work. This demand originated within the social model of disability, which by the 1990s had become 'the central concept around which disabled people began to interpret their own experiences and organise their own political movement' (Oliver, 1996: 26). Indeed, the social model still informs the politics of most disability activists. The social model locates the roots of disabled people's oppression in social structures rather than in bodily and mental difference; its emancipatory power resides in the ways in which it approaches disability as a social and political category. 'Disabled' is treated as a verb – it is society that disables us, with its intolerances and exclusionary practices. The focus then becomes the removal of social barriers to disabled people's participation in society – and particularly employment – as equal members.

An autonomist disability perspective, by contrast, disallows the demand for inclusion and accommodation into waged work. It does so because the demand for access to work chimes dangerously with the Department for Work and Pensions' official rhetoric of helping (or, more accurately, forcing) disabled people back into employment – a rhetoric that positions participation in waged work as the superlative route to survival and fulfilment and the main way to make a contribution to society. Crucially, this rhetoric also deflects attention from what austerity measures designed to force claimants into work try to make illegible: the *impossibility* of making all activity produced through non-standard embodiments (physical, mental or cognitive) productive within the capitalist system of waged work. The rhythms of non-standard embodiments, intractable to management and modification, cannot be made to align with the rhythms and rigours of waged work under capitalist normalcy. Many of us who have non-normative bodies or minds cannot meet the demands of capital sufficiently enough, if at all, to allow employers to make a profit. Some disabled people cannot work. Some can, but only slowly, or with significant accommodations. In both cases, non-standard embodiments frustrate employers' demands for increased productivity; they fail the requirement to be constantly alert, available and on call to the demands of the production process.

The value of an autonomist disability perspective – drawing together insights from disability studies and autonomist thought – is that it allows us to zoom in on disability's anti-productivist potential. Such coalition work is essential because all of the working class under capitalism, including disabled people, increasingly face the daunting choice of either working, becoming destitute, or negotiating a cruel welfare system that has been reformed to force people to pursue waged work as the only means of survival.

Gosta Esping-Andersen argues that the welfare state potentially has a decommodifying function. If robust enough, it hypothetically allows people to 'maintain a livelihood without reliance on the market' (1990: 21), enabling them to survive without waged work and resourcing them with the time to pursue other activities. As the current situation in the UK shows, however, there is nothing inevitable about this potential for decommodification. Social assistance – as workfare and benefit cuts exemplify – can still maintain individual dependence on the market by forcing people to seek after waged work as a condition of their benefits. An autonomist critique of welfare capitalism reveals that this failure of the welfare state to fulfil a decommodifying function is *precisely the intention*; this failure is what renders today's welfare system a well-functioning part of the capitalist system. From an autonomist perspective, we see that the welfare state has been tasked with 'maintaining a useful working class... as a service to capital so that it can find the workers it needs even after it has discarded them' (Kittens, 2015).

In the contemporary context of welfare cuts, thinking about disability helps us see the structural intentionality that underpins the apparent failure of the welfare state: disabled people have become a prime target for cuts precisely because of the impossibility for many non-standard embodiments to meet contemporary demands for productivity and exploitation in waged work. Tellingly, this has not resulted in the stigmatisation of disabled people as 'non-productive' (which would have at least recognised the inability of many of us to work); rather, work capability assessments and cuts to support have functioned to artificially reduce the number of claimants deemed genuinely unable to sustain themselves as productive members of the labour force. The basis of the stigma is not that we are 'non-productive', but that we could be and should be productive, and have decided not to be.

In light of this, coalition work in the welfare action movement is necessary because of the vulnerability *we all share* under capitalism, whether as workers, benefit claimants or disabled people. Coalition work responds to the state's belief that as many of us as possible should be pushed into waged work. The rest of this chapter will explore how different strands of Marxist autonomist theory can foreground the ways in which disability, precisely through its incompatibility with waged work patterns, can sharpen the anti-work politics through which the compulsion to work can be challenged.

Disability and its problem with work

The problem with disability from the perspective of capitalism, and its power from an anti-capitalist viewpoint, resides in its problem with *work* – ie. in the extent to which disability conflicts with the goal of the capitalist mode of production, to increase private profits. It is for this reason that disability offers a particularly sharp focus through which to answer Chris Grover and Linda Piggott's call that we critically engage with the notion that people should be forced to participate in employment under threat of impoverishment (Grover & Piggott, 2015: 4).

Grover and Piggott's suggestion constitutes a departure from the traditional demand of the disabled people's movement, which, drawing on the social model of disability, has historically fought for the right of access to work, along with better accommodation within the workplace. From the perspective of the social model, 'capital accumulation [is] organised in such a way it [disables] people by excluding them from the activity – wage labour – through which people [are] expected to secure their income' (Hall & Wilton, 2015: 241). This view informed the Union of Physically Impaired Against Segregation (UPIAS) in 1976 when it demanded that, for working-age people:

> ... financial and other forms of help must above all be geared to the retention or achievement of integrated employment: dependence on the State must increasingly give way to the provision of help so that a living can be earned through employment.

Hence also the view of the scholar and disability rights activist Mike Oliver, who contends:

> To be constantly and consistently denied the opportunity to work, to
> make a material contribution to the well-being of society... is the root
> cause of us [disabled people] being labelled as 'other' or 'useless'.
> (Oliver, 1999)

Some disability theorists have taken a very different position and devoted consideration to how disabled people are incompatible with the demands and organisation of industrial capitalism. As Paul Abberley noted long ago, 'the abolition of an individual's disablement [central to the social model] is ultimately dependent upon and subordinate to the logic of productivity' (Abberley, 1987: 92). In the face of attempts to integrate disabled people into the world of work, it is clear that 'some will not be capable of producing goods or services of social value', he argues. For this reason, Abberley sees a need for an alternative vision that 'rejects work as crucially definitional of social membership' (Abberley, 1987: 92).

Within the field of disability studies, this alternative take on the relationship between work and disability has yielded several rhetorical benefits. First of all, questioning the demand for equality based on access to work has served as a way to avoid 'othering' those of us who are simply *unable* to work. For, as Grover and Piggott observe, 'the liberal acceptance of a right to work... means that those people who, for whatever reason, cannot do waged work are othered as being particularly problematic and burdensome'. However, if 'there was a recognised right not to work, the othering of workless disabled people would no longer be an issue' (Grover & Piggott, 2015: 251). A related benefit is that questioning the idea of work as definitional of social membership has allowed us to critically evaluate and make visible 'the value of disabled people's activities outside of paid work' (Roulstone, 2015: 269). In retrospect, we might want to question Mike Oliver's equation of social utility – 'material contribution to the well-being of society' – with *waged* work specifically, and instead draw attention to the importance of activities conducted outside the labour market, such as care work, community work, political work or artistic work and, indeed, the constant work of self-care that disability demands. Finally, this alternative approach also enables us to valorise disabled people's incompatibility with capitalism and waged work as something that reveals more general relations of oppression and exploitation.

Along these lines, Dan Goodley and colleagues have recently posited a privileged connection between disability and anti-work values under what they call 'neoliberal-ableism': namely, a historical epoch in which sustenance has become dependent on each person's individual ability to proactively secure their survival in response to austerity. On the one hand, 'we are all subjected to slow death, increased precarity and growing debility' (Goodley, Lawthom & Runswick-Cole, 2014: 980); on the other, we are 'expected to overcome economic downturn and respond to austerity' through identifying as workers and consumers, and through being energetically committed to hard work and getting ourselves 'back on our feet' in austere times – all of this under the over-arching assumption that 'work will set us free' (2014: 981). In opposition to this ideology, Goodley and colleagues argue that '[d]isability… offers opportunities for reconsidering our relationships with life, labour and slow death', and potential for 'a moment to intervene'. It prompts the questions 'Why work yourself to death? Why (just) work?... What do we gain when we fail to meet neoliberalism's normative labouring standards?' (2014: 981). In other words, the experience of disability under capitalism calls attention to the need for greater self-care in the face of those unhealthy work and life patterns that waged work and the benefit system alike have naturalised for *everybody*. It is this conflict between non-standard embodiments and the productive demands of employment that make disabled people so well placed to drive resistance to work and productivity and articulate the call for more humane social structures and relationships.

The insights of Goodley and colleagues are crucial for reflecting on the limitations of the social model of disability. Despite the emancipatory potential it still clearly retains, the co-optation of its rhetoric to justify the withdrawal of welfare support and enforce participation in employment means that the social model is not always helpful (on its own, at least) for understanding and resisting our oppression as disabled people under capitalism. Instead, our oppression has to be thought of as part of the wider conflict that constitutes the relations of production under capitalism. As Grover and Piggott suggest, the social model of disability pursues 'an activity – wage labour – that by its very nature is exploitative, to address the disadvantage of disabled people' (2015: 241). We suggest this is paradoxical.

A marriage of alternative perspectives, by contrast, allows us to grasp and valorise the impossibility of making productive for capital all activity provided through non-standard embodiments. A disability studies or politicised disability perspective enriches autonomist ideas by showing how capitalism and normalcy are intimately entwined through the prescription of standard patterns of waged work. In the other direction, an autonomist take on disability values it as a socio-political and cultural phenomenon that produces new subjects of struggle – subjects that are pregnant with an anti-productivist force because they slow down or fail to contribute to productivity.

This significance is overlooked by more orthodox Marxist scholarship, where it is the productivist force of the working-class that defines the co-ordinates within which subjects of struggle are visible to theorists and social movements. This oversight is one manifestation of the scenario drawn by Frances Fox Piven and Richard Cloward, who suggest that 'insofar as contemporary movements in industrial societies do not take the forms predicted by an analysis of nineteenth-century capitalism, the left has not tried to understand these movements, but rather has tended simply to disapprove of them'. It is always as if 'the wrong people have mobilized, for they are not truly the industrial proletariat. Or they have mobilized around the wrong organizational and political strategies' (Fox Piven & Cloward, 1979: x). To develop an autonomist disability perspective on coalition work and anti-work politics in the context of UK welfare action, there are insights to be gained from a less orthodox strand of Marxism – autonomist Marxism – which has perceived the potential value of anti-work politics, along with the struggles of those who practise it.

Lessons from autonomist Marxism

We suggest that two currents of autonomist Marxism – 'Open Marxism' and the tradition of 'post-operaism' that emerged in Italy in the 1960s – can provide useful insights into the anti-productivist force and anti-capitalist relevance of disability. We will illustrate this by focusing on contributions from John Holloway (Open Marxism) and Michael Hardt and Toni Negri (post-operaism). While the two traditions diverge in some significant ways, we think both approaches make a contribution to thinking through how disabled people's and claimants' struggles can be connected through a unified anti-work politics.

Writing about anti-capitalist struggle, John Holloway says of the options made available to disabled people by capitalism: 'We don't fit into any boxes, and we don't fit into any identities'. Hence, 'our politics, our anti-capitalism, is inevitably an anti-identitarian politics' (Holloway, 2016: 32). The composition of Holloway's 'we' is rooted in processes of co-operation that form between people who encounter capitalism through *misfitting* it: 'Humanity (in all its senses) jars increasingly with capitalism. It becomes harder and harder to fit as capital demands more and more' (Holloway, 2010: 9). For Holloway, it is important to 'understand the force of our misfitting' because, if we 'think the world from [the perspective of] our misfitting', we will be able to 'understand capitalism not as domination, but from the perspective of its crisis, its contradictions, its weaknesses' (Holloway, 2010: 9). We argue that a disability perspective is uniquely placed to speak about misfitting societal structures because, under the normalcy of capitalism, disability is an example *par excellence* of what *cannot fit in*. Speaking to this incompatibility between disabled bodies and the requirements of capitalism can also help to illuminate this impossibility of fitting in as the inevitable fate also of temporarily able-bodied people.

When Holloway suggests that 'We rebel because We misfit', his point is that the very fact of misfitting constitutes our dignity. We should be proud to be 'misfits because capitalism misfits us, because capitalism forces us into shapes in which we cannot fit. So We necessarily misfit' (Holloway, 2016: 13). For disabled people, this misfitting has a couple of specific forms. On the one hand it relates to the rigidity of working patterns under capitalism, where an increasing proportion of human activity is pushed into a commodity form, organised in hierarchical organisational structures and within pre-defined timetables. On the other hand, it relates to the productivist rationale of capitalism, which is governed by a 'constant drive to produce things more quickly'. For Holloway, the problem is that 'if capital is all the time saying to us faster, faster, faster, then it inevitably comes up against our insubordination, our nonsubordination, our incapacity to subordinate ourselves sufficiently' (Holloway, 2016: 57).

Holloway's point powerfully resonates with a passage from Marx on the subject of capital's disregard for the limitations of the human body: '[In] its were-wolf hunger for surplus-labour, capital oversteps not only the moral, but even the merely physical maximum bounds of the working-day' and 'usurps the time for growth, development, and healthy maintenance of the body'. This happens because 'it is the greatest possible daily expenditure of labour-power, no matter how diseased, compulsory, and painful it may be, which is to determine the limits of the labourers' period of repose' (Marx, 1867/1909). Both aspects of Holloway's understanding of misfitting under capitalism are amplified by disabled subjects, who can meet neither the inflexible nor the productivist demands of the capitalist labour process. In this way, disability might call greater attention to the more general unsustainability of a system under which it is 'the greatest possible daily expenditure of labour-power' that determines people's everyday routines and priorities.

In the same spirit as Holloway, post-operaists are also committed to understanding the changing social composition of working-class struggle and, through this, to contributing to the successful re-composition of a divided working class. Their central problematic focuses on how different struggles can be connected. Hardt and Negri's famous concept of 'the multitude', in particular, was formulated as a way of valorising the agents of anti-capitalist struggle beyond the factory walls. It is rooted in a broad conception of the proletariat as a 'category that includes all those whose labor is directly or indirectly exploited by and subjected to capitalist norms of production and reproduction' (Hardt & Negri, 2001: 52). This includes not only the exploited worker but also the precarious worker who moves between jobs, the unemployed person at the mercy of welfare reform, the student who prepares for a life of work, the domestic worker at home – indeed, anyone whose life and labour are shaped by the norms of production and social reproduction under capitalism. This notion of the multitude yields what Hardt and Negri define as 'the equal opportunity of resistance' (2004: 106), which includes all those who find themselves 'under the rule of capital and thus potentially as the class of those who refuse the rule of capital' (Hardt & Negri, 2004: 106). Crucially, the multitude also encompasses those disabled bodies that were previously excluded by more restrictive definitions of the working-class – a relevance that has been grasped by disability theorists David Mitchell and Sharon Snyder. As they point out:

> This definition of resistant subjects does not simply expand outward
> to include those who occupy 'nonproductive bodies', but rather takes
> its lead from those whose capacities make them 'unfit' for labor as the
> baseline of human value. (2015: 211)

Hardt and Negri would eventually call for an 'assembly of the multitude' in the service of anti-capitalist struggle: the assembly appears 'as a swarm, a multitude moving in coherent formation and carrying, implicitly, a threat' – namely, that of the 'power of coming together and acting politically in concert' (2017: xxi). The assembly of the multitude is imagined in terms of a 'social unionism' – an interweaving of trade unions and social movements, in which all parties stand to benefit from the alliance. Alliances with social movements renew the power of trade unions, and the organisational power of the trade unions enhances the effectiveness of the social movements (Hardt & Negri, 2017: 148). Disabled people's and claimants' solidarity groups, with their structures of solidarity, advocacy and organisation, can already be seen as a form of social unionism, and the idea of social unionism itself might allow us to reflect in more deliberate ways on how we can develop more effective coalition work. In this way, we might build a counter-power to capitalist exploitation that properly connects the struggles of the workplace, the job centre and the disability benefit assessment centre. Crucially, it is also the capacities of the multitude that have the potential to construct new and alternative social relations – relations within productive and socially reproductive work based on solidarity and co-operation, rather than the exploitation and competition on which the capitalist mode of production thrives (Hardt & Negri, 2017: 78).

For Holloway, the fundamental basis of such a coalition work is a shared quest to restore the dignity that has been lost under capitalism: if we are anti-capitalist it is because what 'we will not accept, at the end of the day, is the negation of our own dignity' (Holloway, 2016: 5). We can imagine the loss of dignity as disabled people, intractable to productivist imperatives, are forced to live up to impossible standards at work. We can imagine the loss of dignity as disabled people are forced to endure inhumane and arbitrary assessments for benefits (assessments that are themselves tasked with denying the non-productive nature of disabled bodies and minds). All of this unfolds to present a powerful exposure of the dehumanisation and loss of dignity to which *all* working-class people are subjected under capitalism.

Towards new coalitions

As we have explored, autonomist Marxism, including contributions from Holloway and Hardt and Negri, helps to illustrate the significance of disability as an important component of working-class struggle. Not only does it valorise the anti-productivist power of disability; it also supports the inclusion of disabled people into the anti-capitalist struggles from which they have previously been marginalised. Autonomist Marxism interprets the current crisis of capitalism as pregnant with potential for revolution and attributes a key role for disabled people within the struggle. For Holloway, the focus is on capitalism's savage exploitative drive and the refusal this is bound to incite. '[A] constant movement of faster, faster, faster and a constant extension of control over the whole of society, a constant tighter, tighter, tighter control', on the one hand, 'means a constant process of dehumanizing, of humiliating, of pushing us down onto our knees'. On the other hand, 'it also means a constant process of rebellion' (Holloway, 2016: 48). The result is an intensification of how, 'built into everyday experience, there is this kind of reluctance, a dragging of feet, a refusal... to accept that we are robots' (Holloway, 2016: 58). Faced with this situation, there are two possibilities: one possibility is to say, with Holloway (2016: 62): 'We are totally willing to co-operate... Please, capital, please come back, please exploit us more effectively, please, above all, give us jobs.' The other is to say: 'No, that's not what we want… We are the possibility of another way of living, of another form of social organization. Therefore we do not want domination to overcome its crisis; we do not want capital to overcome its crisis' (2016: 63).

Somewhat differently, although equally inclusive of disabled people as key agents of struggle, Hardt and Negri see the prospect of social unionism as offering the greatest hope. Hardt and Negri's theories suggest a form of social unionism based on the collective power of non-productive members of society. This entails the demise of the traditional form of strike in favour of what they call a social strike. As Hardt and Negri explain, the 'labor union since its inception has based its power on the threat of the organized refusal of work', but in this traditional frame, 'unemployed workers, unwaged domestic labor, the precarious, and the poor appear to be powerless; since withholding their labor does not directly threaten capitalist production and profit, the standard logic goes, they have no leverage' (Hardt & Negri, 2017: 150). Now, with the changed composition of the working class, a new form of unionism becomes necessary in which disabled people – through their very non-productivity – have a key role to play.

It is up to us to recognise our misfitting as a source of restored dignity and connect our struggles through a refusal of work – something we can perform collectively in the here and now. We must resist the enforcement of the work ethic and the activation policies tasked with instilling this ethic in benefit claimants. Claimants' solidarity groups offer one such example of how this resistance is being co-ordinated. The Edinburgh Coalition Against Poverty, for instance, has a decade-long history of providing advice, support and advocacy to claimants while encouraging them to join the group and help others. What brings together activists is not coalition work aimed at artificially connecting tightly-defined categories of oppression – for example, disabled people, individuals in poverty, or migrants – but a more inclusive resistance to the benefit system that all of these categories of people experience as necessary for dignity and survival. These same dynamics apply to the Action Against Austerity solidarity network (of which Edinburgh Coalition Against Poverty is a founding member), which is primarily held together by the exchange of information and expressions of solidarity between groups involved in welfare action. Disability issues and disabled activists have played a central role in both the Edinburgh Coalition Against Poverty and Action Against Austerity because of the ways in which disabled people bear the brunt of welfare state retrenchment and austerity.

New relationships have formed in a relatively spontaneous way, perhaps out of necessity rather than as a result of a more studied effort to achieve praxis and build protest around the anti-productivist force of disabled people. But we argue that a more studied effort could be very worthwhile. Holloway's call to contest the 'tendency to seek a positive understanding of struggle' (Holloway, 2011) must be balanced against the goal inspired by post-operaism to map out the social composition of the welfare action movement in order to connect different categories of claimants with one another and with the wider labour movement. The kind of social unionism envisaged by Hardt and Negri could help give 'the struggles of the poor, the precarious, and the unemployed a social reach and a continuity they would otherwise lack' (Hardt & Negri, 2017: 148). Indeed, while Holloway's call to take pride in and connect our misfitting is materialised by the mode of organising that prevails in contemporary welfare action (where energies and activist numbers are still quite limited), it is a coalition work aimed at bringing together *different* categories of oppression, so as to recompose a divided working class, that really holds the promise of advancing the next step in building an anti-work counter-power.

The recent organising of welfare action campaigns and protests has shown that this latter kind of coalition work is already germinating. For example, the Stop and Scrap Universal Credit action in the spring of 2018 saw Edinburgh Coalition Against Poverty respond to the call of Disabled People Against Cuts to produce leaflets warning that the introduction of Universal Credit would adversely impact multiple categories of claimants, not least because it would apply to a wider range of people and spur an intensified drive by job centres to instil the 'approved work personality'. Similarly, the Action Against Austerity network is now making a point of involving migrants' solidarity groups and disabled people's organisations, as well as establishing links with the traditional labour movement through a form of coalition work that speaks to the call for social unionism.

In conclusion, this chapter has attempted to show the usefulness of an autonomist disability perspective for developing models of coalition work in which disability's anti-productivist rationale provides a focal point for the connection of our struggles into a bigger and more unified anti-work politics. The way forward for welfare action might lie in a collective celebration and connecting-up of our mutual misfitting of capitalism, paired with a more organised form of coalition work in the shape of a social unionism that carefully examines and intervenes in the social composition of our struggles, so as to build a more powerful front of resistance. An autonomist disability perspective sees disability as central to both these forms of coalition building. We believe that disability is a privileged site for resistance to the productivist violence of capital that endangers the entirety of the working class, whether inside or outside the workplace.

References

Abberley P (1987). The concept of oppression and the development of a social theory of disability. *Disability, Handicap & Society 2*(1): 5–19.

Choudry A (2007). Transnational activist coalition politics and the de/colonization of pedagogies of mobilization: learning from anti-neoliberal indigenous movement articulations. *International Education 37*(1): 97–112.

Davis L (2002). *Bending Over Backwards: disability, dismodernism & other difficult positions.* New York, NY: New York University Press.

Esping-Andersen G (1990). *The Three Worlds of Welfare Capitalism.* Cambridge: Polity Press.

Fleming P (2015). *The Mythology of Work: how capitalism persist despite itself.* London: Pluto Press.

Fox Piven F, Cloward RA (1979). *Poor People's Movements: why they succeed, how they fail.* New York, NY: Vintage Books.

Frayne, D (2015). *The Refusal of Work.* London: Zed Books.

Friedli L (2016). Psycho-resistance: solidarity in the struggle against psychological coercion. [Online.] *Base 1*: 26–27. www.basepublication.org/?p=139 (accessed 14 January 2019).

Friedli L, Stearn R (2015). Positive affect as coercive strategy: conditionality, activation and the role of psychology in UK government workfare programmes. [Online.] *Critical Medical Humanities 14*(1). http://dx.doi.org/10.1136/medhum-2014-010622 (accessed 14 January 2019).

Friedli L, Stearn R (2013). *Whistle while you work (for nothing): positive affect as coercive strategy – the case of workfare.* [Blog.] Centre for Medical Humanities; 10 December. http://centreformedicalhumanities.org/whistle-while-you-work-for-nothing-positive-affect-as-coercive-strategy-the-case-of-workfare/ (accessed 14 January 2019).

Fromm, E. (1956) *The Sane Society.* London: Routledge.

Garland-Thomson R (1997). *Extraordinary Bodies: figuring physical disability in American culture and literature.* New York, NY: Columbia University Press.

Goodley D, Lawthom R, Runswick-Cole K (2014). Dis/ability and austerity: beyond work and slow death. *Disability & Society 29*(6): 980-984.

Grover C, Piggot L (2015). Disabled people, work and welfare. In: Grover C, Piggott L (eds). *Disabled People, Work and Welfare: is employment really the answer?* Bristol: Policy Press (pp1–24).

Hall E, Wilton (2015). Thinking differently about 'work' and social inclusion for disabled people. In: Grover C, Piggott L (eds). *Disabled People, Work and Welfare: is employment really the answer?* Bristol: Policy Press (pp219–238).

Hardt M, Negri A (2017). *Assembly.* Oxford: Oxford University Press.

Hardt M, Negri A (2004). *Multitude: war and democracy in the age of empire.* London: Penguin.

Hardt M, Negri A (2001). *Empire.* Cambridge, MA: Harvard University Press.

Holloway J (2016). *In, Against and Beyond Capitalism: the San Francisco lectures.* Oakland, CA: PM Press.

Holloway J (2015). *Greece: hope drowns in the reality of a dying world. Or does it?* [Video.] YouTube; 11 September. www.youtube.com/watch?v=k3qc7LrqOs0&feature=youtu.be (accessed 14 January 2019).

Holloway J (2011). *Going in the wrong direction. Or, Mephistopheles: not Saint Francis of Assisi.* [Blog.] John Holloway. www.johnholloway.com.mx/2011 /07/30/going-in-the-wrong-direction/ (accessed 14 January 2019).

Holloway J (2010). *Crack Capitalism.* New York, NY: Pluto Press.

Kittens (2015). *What is Wrong with Free Money?* [Blog.] Antinational; 28 July. https://antinational.org/en/what-wrong-free-money/ (accessed 14 January 2019).

Long D (1997). The precarious pursuit of justice: counter hegemony in the Lubicon First Nation Coalition. In: Carroll WK (ed) (2nd ed). *Organizing Dissent: contemporary social movements in theory and practice.* Toronto: Garamond (pp151–170).

Marx K (1867/1909) *Capital: a critique of political economy. Vol 1: The process of capitalist production.* Chicago, IL: Charles H Kerr & Co.

Mitchell DT, Snyder SL (2015). *The Biopolitics of Disability: neoliberalism, ablenationalism, and peripheral embodiment.* Ann Arbor, MI: The University of Michigan Press.

Oliver M (1999). *Disabled people and the inclusive society: or the times they really are changing.* [Blog.] Independent Living Institute; 27 April. www.independentliving.org/docs4/oliver.html (accessed 15 January 2019).

Oliver M (1996). A sociology of disability or a disablist sociology? In: Barton L (ed). *Disability and Society: emerging issues and insights.* Harlow: Longman (pp18–42).

Roulstone A (2015). Disability, work and welfare: the disappearance of the polymorphic productive landscape. In: Grover C, Piggott L (eds). *Disabled People, Work and Welfare: is employment really the answer?* Bristol: Policy Press (pp257–276).

Southwood I (2011). *Non-Stop Inertia.* Alresford: Zero Books.

Union of the Physically Impaired Against Segregation (1976). *Fundamental Principles of Disability.* London: UPIAS.

11

Unrecovery

Recovery in the Bin

Recovery in the Bin is a user-led group for mental health survivors and supporters who are fed up with the way co-opted 'recovery' is being used to discipline and control those who are trying to find a place in the world, to live as they wish, trying to deal with the mental distress they encounter on a daily basis. We believe in human rights and seek to place mental health within the context of social justice and class struggle. We are unaffiliated with any mental health organisation and would like to keep it that way. A summary of our key principles can be found at https://recoveryinthebin.org/ritbkeyprinciples

---

Recovery in the Bin (RITB) is a group of people made up of mental health service survivors and our allies. We are people who have serious concerns about the concept of Recovery in the current political and economic climate that services and policy operate in.

We will first introduce RITB and explain why we formed and why we are so critical of Recovery. We'll then outline our concept of Unrecovery and share our Unrecovery Star and Unrecovery Guide. We see Unrecovery as a concept that gives us space to psychologically and politically resist the co-opted Recovery agenda in UK mental health and welfare reform.

How this chapter was written

The admins of the RITB Facebook group shared the request from David Frayne to write for this book. We invited members to tell us what Unrecovery meant to them. We also used quotes from posts on the RITB website and Facebook, which were also based on discussions in the group. One of the admins took responsibility for gathering the comments, writing the background and structuring the chapter, with support from other admins.

We wanted to capture some of the richness of the discussions in our group and show the collective building of ideas, but at the same time we wanted to preserve the anonymity of members. So, no names are given – every paragraph with a dash before it is from an individual but, collected together, they give a sense of larger discussions.

What was interesting as we collated the discussions was the variety of voices that emerged – the academic, the provocative, the personal, the political, the funny, the surreal, the despairing. Each person added to the conversation and this is what makes RITB a unique place to theorise from our experiences and take this theory back into our lives and thinking.

So, what's Recovery in the first place?

Recovery is one of those words that sounds great – who doesn't want to recover from a serious mental health problem? Why does this group want to put Recovery in the bin? But, like many ideas that become part of the mainstream, things are a bit more complicated.

The idea of Recovery arose among people in the US who had been written off by psychiatry – people like Pat Deegan, who had been told aged 16 that she was schizophrenic and that her life from there on would all be hospital and medication:

> ... many of us who have been psychiatrically labelled have received
> powerful messages from professionals who in effect tell us that by virtue
> of our diagnosis the question of our being has already been answered
> and our futures are already sealed. (Deegan, 1996)

This powerful message of defiance rapidly spread throughout the English-speaking world. It came to the UK in the early 2000s and, despite resistance from some mental health professionals, it was soon taken up by policy-makers and services.[1] A typical definition, from the Scottish Recovery Network, states:

> Recovery is being able to live a meaningful and satisfying life, as defined
> by each person, in the presence or absence of symptoms. It is about having

---

1. https://recoveryinthebin.org/2017/06/25/the-mainstreaming-of-recovery

control over and input into your own life. Each individual's recovery, like his or her experience of mental health problems or illness, is a unique and deeply personal process. (Scottish Recovery Network, undated)

At the same time, the wider political context was changing, and progressive concepts such as Recovery, independent living and other disabled people's ideas were seized on to support an altogether different agenda. When something so quickly appeals to the mainstream, it is worth being concerned! Neoliberalism, first under New Labour (1997–2010), then under the Coalition government (2010–15) and the current Conservative government, was redefining the relationship between the state, the economy and society by 'reforming' public services and the UK welfare system (Beresford, 2016).

As part of this, Recovery has been reframed and co-opted to support the drive to reduce people's 'dependency' on benefits and to promote paid employment as the most significant factor contributing to positive mental health. Some advocates of Recovery (in its co-opted form) have even claimed that benefits and mental health services hinder recovery (for example, O'Hara, 2010).

So, what seemed to be a challenge and an alternative to mainstream mental health services soon became something that put the responsibility onto the 'mentally ill person' to 'recover' in ways that fitted the demands of neoliberalism.[2] At the same time, this kind of recovery denies the effects of austerity on the 'mentally ill person', which causes more problems. Services now focus on independence for people with mental health problems, which in practice means focusing on short-term interventions, outcomes determined by services and policy, and discharge as soon as possible. Alongside this, the punitive benefits system focuses on getting people off disability benefits regardless of the cost to the disabled person (Butler & Pring, 2016). They call this welfare reform, we call it democide.

People in RITB have said:

– I used to have security, the system was so much fairer and easier to negotiate and with support. Now, it feels like they have a list and when your time is up, they will get you and they will crush you to death whilst hoping you will jump before you're pushed.

– Does anyone else feel this constant guilt for being on benefits? However

2. https://recoveryinthebin.org/ritbkeyprinciples

much I understand where the guilt comes from (outside ideology) it never goes away.

– Yes, constant.

– Yes, all the time and deep shame, like I no longer qualify as human in others' eyes.

There are more humanistic ways of understanding mental distress and responding to people in distress, but they are harder to access and practice in a punitive system designed around discharging people in the name of making them more independent, without giving us the support we need.

– Everything about benefits is so counterproductive to being as well as you can be, as and when you can.

– They have taken the concept of independent living to mean self-sufficient living – which is total bullshit. Independent living means living your life and getting the support you need to live it, including financial help.

What is Recovery in the Bin?

RITB was started in 2014 by English survivor activists who were concerned by the rise of this corrupted form of recovery in mental health services and policy. They stated:

> We believe that this rise is a symptom of neoliberalism and that a meaningful 'recovery' is impossible for many of us because of the intolerable social and economic conditions, such as poor housing, poverty, stigma, racism, sexism, unreasonable work expectations, and countless other barriers.
>
> The underfunding and under resourcing of mental health services means that service users are under pressure to conform to a narrow idea of recovery.
>
> The changes to the social security system promote the ideal of work being good for everyone's health while undermining any real hope of a good life, which is what recovery is supposed to be about.[3]

---

3. https://recoveryinthebin.org

Recovery in the Bin argues for a robust 'social model of madness and distress', from the left of politics, placing mental health within the context of the wider class struggle. We know from both experience and evidence that capitalism and social inequality can be bad for your mental health!

What is unusual about RITB is that it is one of the few mental health groups (another is the Mental Health Resistance Network) that came from the Left and centres on an analysis of the state of mental health services and policy in the context of capitalism. It has since developed into a Facebook group of more than 500 people, primarily from England, Scotland and Wales, as well as some in the US, Australia, the Netherlands and elsewhere. Three quarters of the membership were actively commenting, posting and reacting in December 2017 (when this chapter was written) and there was an average of seven posts a day in that period. RITB is also on Twitter (@RITB_), where it engages with a wider range of people about issues to do with austerity, power and mental health. The RITB website publishes posts based on discussions on the Facebook group and guest blogs on similar issues.

So, what is Unrecovery?

Unrecovery is a concept developed by the early members of the RITB group as a way of articulating the complexity of our concerns around how recovery has been co-opted (Recovery in the Bin, 2017). We have found that, by actively engaging with the idea of Unrecovery, we are better able to psychologically resist the dominant neoliberal discourses around mental health, recovery and employment. This chapter is our account of how we created the concept of Unrecovery, what it means to us and how it has affected us in our lives.

Unrecovery is a position of resistance and opposition towards the imposition and authority of Recovery-based ideology prevalent in mental health. We consider 'unrecovered' to be as valid and legitimate as 'recovered'. This doesn't mean we want to stay 'unwell' or 'ill' (whatever that means), but that we reject this new neoliberal intrusion on the word 'recovery' that has been redefined and taken over by marketisation, and certain languages, techniques and outcomes.

From a discussion:

– Some may feel the language of 'Unrecovery' is a backwards and regressive step, but we believe the word 'recovery' has been co-opted from its more radical roots. We consider that the language of 'recovery' is no longer a helpful word to describe the outcomes that MH services now expect of us.

– Unrecovery is a conversation with the original ethos of survivor activism that affected recovery before it was co-opted under a neoliberal ideology.

– Against the appropriation of our language and selling back to us by those with power…

– Appropriation of the word recovery?

– Yes, I think so and the sanitising and repackaging of it.

– Recovery WAS a rebellion.

– Yes, it promised so much. I really believed in its potential to make great changes. But bit by bit…

So how did we get to Unrecovery?

A discussion with the RITB admins:

HH: My hazy memory thinks it emerged just before doing the principles. Reclaiming 'Recovery' was the passion.

JM: Unrecovery changed it from reclaiming to an entirely different position. It all happened very naturally during open discussions.

HH: But it may have been spoken, not long after we started?

JM: Yes.

AK: I remember Unrecovery involving jokes about unbirthday… it was mentioned as simply a term to explain why we disagreed with both individualised entrepreneurial recovery regimes and state-sanctioned, coerced recovery (or that the 'choice' was one or the other)… As most of us had been involved in recovery for at least a decade, if not two, before austerity came along, we all seemed to accept that at least some people were able to recover, we just accepted:

a) it wasn't always possible

b) it was contingent on circumstances

c) it didn't mean [a binary between] permanent recovery or failure

d) that to deny this was punitive.

So, we came up with a term that was NOT anti-recovery. And Unrecovery just sort of came up. I think I play with the Lewis Carroll nonsense and

Freudian unpleasure around the term more than most, but that developed out of those early conversations and wasn't part of them early on.

One of the RITB founders, AK, explains the thinking behind Unrecovery further:

At its simplest, Unrecovery is a form of techniques and practices undertaken when someone is unable to recover. At a more complex level, it is a collection of autodidactical techniques and practices outside the remit of services. These range from artistic practices, solidaristic practices, critical practices and resistance practices. It also involves activism and critical engagement. It includes support with DWP forms (advocacy) to campaigning and academic endeavours. It also involves just surviving, mutual support and sheer bloody mindedness.

It is not anti-recovery but it does recognise that recovery is not always possible, whether due to more severe intractable trauma or insecure housing and/or finances; whether it is due to inner city pressure or, for some, capitalism itself.

Many of these practices may indeed in the long-term lead to recovery, but it is not assumed that it is the inevitable consequence and there is no sense of failure if the individual does not do so. It respects the trauma model, communication model, social model and [the] left-wing version of the ideological model.

For some, psychotherapy is a reasonable practice; for others, it isn't. Others are broadly supportive of the embodied model. For others, importantly, there are practices [that] ostensibly [have] nothing to do with mental health at all (and that can't be coded, exploited and turned into narrow techniques and protocol).

It has affinities with the 'refusal of work' movement (that work – including unpaid productive activity, child care and emotional labour – should be pleasurable and creative, and not a conformist duty to unsustainable capitalist profit as a normalised activity).

It is particularly critical of coercive mental health governmentality. It is especially critical of austerity and service cuts to both therapy and social support, as well as to cuts to benefits – it does not consider benefits to be financially sufficient to cultivate dependency – and, in active opposition to such right-wing views, sees social security as an active resource and human right for those struggling with ongoing mental distress (hence [its] role in welfare advocacy) and is broadly anti-capitalist. As such, it is a class-based practice of everyday life rather than a model guided by outcome measures.

Hearing again from RITB members on social media, to find out how they perceive Unrecovery:

– I don't have reset to a previous 'healthy state' and I see recovery in general health terms, ie. I recovered from my cold or from an operation. Recovery regarding my 'mental health', marbles, madness, distress, psychosocial, existential, spiritual state of being isn't open to being recovered, simply because the concept doesn't mean anything to me. It's like a word from a foreign language to me that has no direct translation into English. It's also a political position for me in that I am consciously objecting to the defined positions of recovery being imposed directly and indirectly on us via mainstream and alternative.

– Unrecovery for me is about not having to comply with conventional/other people's/society's/[the] government's/the DWP's ideas of what being 'mentally well' is. It is about fighting having those ideas imposed on me/us and finding ways to survive in spite of all of them and, ideally, ways to live my own life my own way. It is also about rejecting mainstream mental health services and all of the vacuous, lip-service campaigns and bringing to light the harm they can and do do to too many of us on a daily basis and trying to find better ways to have our needs met in a genuinely (not seen to be) personalised, joined-up way on an ongoing, not *ad hoc*, basis and in crisis.

– Not having to live up to anyone else's ideas of recovery, particularly since this has been appropriated by government/mental health services for the main purpose of discouraging dependency and service use for those who may have long term or 'complex' difficulties. Unrecovery is an alternative to recovery being pushed our way as the best and only position. The recognition of Unrecovery then helps me to feel less of a recovery failure and to evaluate my life as having some worth. I think that Unrecovery can still be valid for those who do work, as we may not have gained the level of career that society expects or we may need time off sick or feel like we are just about surviving/not always 'enjoying' our work. I feel like I have to work a lot harder than others in the workplace since I am also dealing with the background challenges and personal history of involvement with services (particularly pathologisation). It feels like being a disaster survivor often but having to shut up about it. I don't get the Time to Change [a national anti-stigma campaign funded by the mental health charities Rethink and Mind] campaigns and how we are meant to speak out when the reality is there is little support or empathy available. Honesty around Unrecovery could mean we could accept ourselves and others more as human beings rather than 'outcomes.'

– Unrecovery is a concept essential to the liberation of mental patients. The distinction between movements that are recovery-based (most) and those that are liberation-based has become confused, to the detriment of everyone involved or impacted. People who are in distress are often pushed into various kinds of recovery schema, essentially offering that they can exchange an unacceptable way of being for an acceptable one. Recovery is prescriptive and value-based. Unrecovery is the flip side that offers to value folks who find non-prescriptive ways of reducing their distress, or who may never find a way to reduce it. A true life, lived in liberation, is not available to the mental patient without the option of Unrecovery.

– Recovery used to mean carving out a life worth living with empowerment and as much peace as was possible with your mental distress. Now that is the meaning of Unrecovery for me. I am seeking Unrecovery through applying therapeutic concepts I find useful and through actively striving for social justice through protest and online actions to achieve a calmer state of mind, fighting against what makes me sick – austerity and oppression of sick and disabled people. I work independently of charities, recovery colleges and CMHTs [community mental health teams] to deal with my childhood trauma through support for organisations that help with childhood emotional abuse and personally through therapy through FPN [Free Psychotherapy Network]. Unrecovery is truly the social model of mental distress and physical disability.

– By trying very hard to remain outside the mental health system and finding solidarity and support from other like-minded survivors. The end goal is demanding real social justice through activism and protest.

– I still descend to the depths regularly; I still have crazy anxiety issues; I still have obsessive rituals that take up most of my waking hours BUT, discovering Unrecovery and the sense of solidarity with others who relate to not wanting to/not being able to work with mainstream mental health services and then the consequences of that with agencies, such as additional DWP fear; not wanting to/not being able to comply with so many things society tries to dictate as to how we should live and where we fit it, and feeds [to] us as normal and acceptable – and so much more – has given me the greatest feeling of identity and sense of being supported I have known in 20-odd years.

– When I hear the word 'recovered' I picture myself living quietly in a wasteland beyond the pale of settlement, maybe in a cave: reading, writing, sniffing glue. The machine, however – that is, the mass institution of normalcy inside that pale of settlement – has heard I'm there and doesn't like it one bit. It can't stand the idea of anyone sitting around doing nothing – which is obviously what I must be doing if I don't have an owner, a boss – and it's sent out its recovery vehicles to reclaim me, to put right this huge injustice of me not working for them. Bigass JCBs with razor-sharp teeth. But I like it here; it's quiet, there's little pressure, there are far fewer idiots. The obvious thing for me to do is to destroy the recovery vehicles – they're violating my sovereignty. It looks like there's a war on now, but they started it. I was born into a world where everything is owned by somebody else, and as such I don't think a base level of support from the machine, so that I can just live my life on my own terms, is unreasonable, but I've been battered by its propaganda so long and hard, I can no longer remember whether this is a selfish attitude or not.

To summarise, members of RITB see Unrecovery as a profound way of understanding our current situations and of being able to exercise some agency in a structurally unjust world in terms of political activity and looking after ourselves individually and collectively. Unrecovery is a way of reintroducing the social and political causes of distress back into the picture. It critiques the normative ideas of illness, deviance and so on by scrutinising the idea of working as a 'healthy' thing to do, for instance, and seeing the damaging impact of employment on us. Unrecovery can help us resist these ideas.

– [Unrecovery helps us resist] the corrosive nature of neoliberal framework we live in, which can get right into the fabric of our experiences.

– Just saying that the DWP are causing us 'stress' doesn't even begin to cover it and people can't understand why people are killing themselves over the 'DWP experience'.

– Saw the phrase 'capitalism's temporal bullying' yesterday – the idea that capitalism changes the way we experience time... makes us feel guilty for being too slow, lazy, not getting enough done etc.

– I am currently in work, so relatively 'safe', but do worry about the what ifs. I've lost three good jobs because of my mental health, which was really traumatic each time, but applying for benefits was relatively straightforward and the money came through within a couple of weeks. With recent welfare 'reform', I feel I've lost my safety net.

– That's part of why they are doing this. They don't want people to have a safety net. That way we are more compliant workers willing to put up with worse and worse conditions. And those who can afford it will get private insurance. I am in work too and I worry about what will happen should I lose it – whether because of my health or because of losing funding for my post. Insecurity and precarity are the tactics.

Long-time activist and service-user led researcher, Diana Rose (2014) argues:[4]

> We have to tackle head on the fact that our society is intolerant of difference. And people labelled mad are the most frightening group of the different because they threaten to expose the insanity that lies beneath the surface of all.

And how to do this?

> I suggest we be upsetting, that we use humour and that service users should take the lead in this rather than follow in the wake of recovery workers.

Unrecovery is part of this 'upsetting' of normative, individualistic ideas of recovery. And just as we are not against people being well, we are not against

---

4. https://recoveryinthebin.org/2017/06/25/the-mainstreaming-of-recovery

the idea of self-care. However, we are against the accepted ideas of what wellbeing and self-care look like. From what people have already said, it is clear we value the connection and solidarity in the group. Having a space with one another to understand our experiences and therefore feel less alone and less crazy is self-care of a kind that challenges the dominant and prescriptive ideas from services.

For many of us, the main reason we keep on going is not to 'give the bastards the satisfaction of seeing me die'.

Paid employment and recovery

Central to the neoliberal idea of recovery is paid employment. Never mind the high unemployment rate and the reluctance of employers to take on people like us, who they consider to be risky. Never mind that the main cause of people being off work sick is stress. Paid work is considered central to our recovery and we must be made employable.

Members talked about the current situation:

– I think a huge problem is the amount of unpaid labour in paid work. Seeing frontline workers (charity, support) doing extra hours as meetings are out of service times, deliveries, answering emails, taking emergency phone calls. Also, in academia I think the whole system is broken: again, so much unpaid labour, emails, meetings etc. And the fact that you almost do internships until you are established, with nothing but precarity and all the admin put on early career, then expectation to publish, build CV, organise events. I'm not an academic but have seen how tough it can be and [it] pushes forward the narrative of resilience.

– In terms of unpaid labour, it's a problem because it's an expectation, but unwritten and it exploits vulnerability/precarity. In my mind, it abuses a trust here, almost making unpaid labour your choice. So, if [you have] any illness, this is also your choice. I guess from how I'm thinking about it, it requires such a huge paradigm shift that acknowledges our health first. But that ain't economic?

– The hostile culture of the workplace where, if people don't become submissive worker bees, [if] they don't leave their personal identity at the door and suppress whatever makes getting through the day difficult, then they're considered useless. Most people have a lot to offer others, but anybody who falls short of the unreasonable expectations of the vast majority of workplaces [is] just written off. I think this needs to change.

– The best employment I've had has been when my managers have also experienced mental health distress and therefore get it. So, things like 'reasonable adjustments' have simply just been done and not been a big deal.

– My tuppence worth! Even though I enjoy my current job a lot, it is still part of a system where most of the adult population have to sell our labour for income. Those of us who can't are given very low incomes, which are increasingly difficult to live on, and with increased conditionality and both formal and informal demands to become more 'employable' in an economy where such jobs as exist are increasingly precarious and bad for our physical and mental health. Back in the days of full employment and decent benefits, it was still not a great system for most. There is no golden age to hark back to – just one that was for a few decades a bit better than what we've had recently. All the reasonable adjustments and mental health awareness won't really compensate for the way employment is. Whether in benefits or in paid work, the system makes us sick and blames us for it.

– Work has always been meaningful and something that I benefit from therapeutically. BUT it has to be the right environment etc – I've left jobs before if they've not been helpful mentally and am v lucky with my current job, given the reasonable adjustments I get. Not all people get this or do not feel able to ask for this. I think part-time work – even if it's a couple of hours a week – can be beneficial for people if it's the right work, but our welfare system does not support this stepwise approach to enabling people to dip their toes in the water for however long – increase gradually and decrease flexibly... I feel myself losing other aspects of me and my life to work – which I'm coming to resent. I fear we are moving backwards to the Victorian era when people worked 12-hour days, 6/7 days a week. I think this will have massive health implications and our life expectancy will stabilise or fall. People are becoming robots in the workplace and it's sad.

– I think you sum up my thinking perfectly – work can be really fulfilling if done in a way that takes workers' needs into account more.

– Yes, the right work for the person can be very therapeutic. For me, it gives me a sense of self-esteem etc and independence and gives me social connections… Equally, these things could be achieved via other means, but for me I get it from work.

But can the system take workers' needs into account?

– I wouldn't do other activities that damaged my health (hobbies, seeing people, whatever), so why is work any different?

– Work and money are the mass religion of our times. If you were able to ask someone from two or three hundred years ago whether they could imagine a life without God, they'd likely say, no, of course not, are you mad? Transpose that to modern times and ask, 'Can you imagine a life without work and money?' – you'd get the same response. Likewise, people seem able to imagine a world post-civilisation, but not a post-capitalist one. With close to full automation coming, and with first-world technology and abundance, there's plenty of scope for those who are unable (or unwilling, for whatever reason) to work not to have to do so. But the billionaires seem unlikely to let go of any sizable chunk of their enormous slice of the pie. So, the real problem isn't work and money in and of itself, it's inequality. Selling yourself, in whatever capacity, to another human being, amounts to prostitution. The current orthodoxy that therein lies the only dignity is illogical at best, and the very definition of madness.

– Part of what made me realise I'm anarchacommunisty is the fear and anger I feel around the compulsion to sell labour power to meet basic needs – tough anyway, for all the reasons you mention, but also the internalisation of this dominant culture, the logics of capitalism if you like. So, it makes me desperately sad that so many people seem just fine with their precious life and energies used up and structuring their entire being in the service of a system that keeps people busy doing rubbish things in order to perpetuate itself, the mechanics of which necessitate the oppression and poverty of billions, the most vulnerable people in the world being the ones who are most shat upon. (So far so standard anti-capitalism.)

– But there is clearly a lot of socially necessary activity that needs doing: teaching each other, taking care of each other, maintaining our shelter, feeding ourselves, keeping our water supply clean, dealing with the bodily waste we produce etc. I think the fundamental approach to how to organise this should begin locally, within communities, self-organising, which of course means people need the time and energy to do it, and also an understanding of how to have basic conversations (speaking and working *with* each other without reproducing oppressive social relations), and then networking with each other across larger geographical areas to meet needs. It would mean all of us having a working knowledge of basic sanitation, how to grow food, basic medical knowledges etc. I think every single one of us is not just prevented from enjoying our lives fully by the time that capitalism takes up, but also held back from what our minds can do, how much we can all learn and do together. So much that disables people would no longer exist, and when those logics are gone then there's no question of how to 'do' care with people who have more physical needs/adaptations, for example, because we just do, we've got the time, and it would be unthinkable to disable someone by *not* mutually providing for each other.

– And doing this all strikes me as a massive struggle in our current context but also (to tempt the naturalistic fallacy) the most natural way for us to be with each other. It's a huge cultural shift but also really, really simple. So yes, I'm obviously utopian!

– Ok, so if we are talking about a complete political, societal, economic, cultural change, then no, I would prefer to not have to work in a capitalist neoliberal system. I like the idea expressed above of working as a community to meet the community's needs etc. I was just thinking about the current situation but if I look beyond it etc, then I think things could be a lot different, more humane and community focused.

– You are born into a world that, unless you are the wealthy minority, you are forced to exchange labour for the means to not die. This is upsetting. Especially as:

1. not everyone is subject to this (ie. the wealthy)
2. you have no choice but to conform or face poverty, poor quality of life and early death

3. 'good work' is generally in the gift of patronage and is apportioned through influence and other corrupt filters.

So, the delightful neutral language of technocrats when talking about work is dishonest. It pretends work is not an imposition by the powerful upon the powerless. So, it is normalisation of oppression. Now, once we have that caveat out of the way, we can talk about work honestly. So, first point of discussion: I want to be Queen, why can't I be? If they answer that honestly, they might get a hint that maybe we are not entering into this arena as equal players. And that is the elephant in the room.

– I have always considered my madness as a logical response to a damaged system. Not working is a political act, overthrow the capitalist system through non-compliance.

– Employment just for its own sake strikes me as absurd, really. I read somewhere recently that the ideal age to retire from having to work is 40 years... Oh dear! :)

Most of us recognise that paid employment is difficult for many of us, that it is precarious and stressful and that it can be damaging. Some of us see this as part and parcel of capitalism and we try to imagine a better way of organising what needs to be done in a just way. It's just hard to think about, given the current orthodoxy that work is good for our health and social inclusion.

The Unrecovery Star

– The Unrecovery Star is a game changer for me.

So, what's the Unrecovery Star? Maybe first we need to talk about the Recovery Star. This is an outcomes measure used in mental health services to assess service users' progress on 10 predetermined goals: living skills, relationships, work, identity and self-esteem, managing mental health, physical health and self-care, social networks, addictive behaviour, responsibilities, and trust and hope.[5] We think that such assessment tools

---

5. https://mentalhealthpartnerships.com/resource/recovery-star

are focused on very individualist and normative ideas of what matters to people. It is a blunt and unhelpful, narrowing way of judging how someone should be expected to 'recover'.

In response, we came up with our own tool, which we called the Unrecovery Star. The Unrecovery Star was developed directly from open discussions in the RITB Facebook group. This is what it looks like:

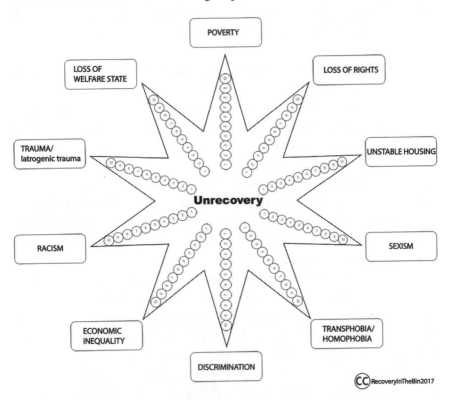

The Unrecovery Star can be described as a 'social justice tool', which highlights not only the reasons why we go mad but also what can hinder our 'recovery' and maintain our distress. We really mean it when we say some of us will never feel 'recovered', due to the social and economic conditions we experience, because these conditions frame everything. Therefore, the Unrecovery Star is political as well as personal – two things that are intrinsically linked for many of us. It challenges the individualism inherent in the Recovery Star and emphasises collective action and social justice as necessary to work with mental health survivors.

Producing the Unrecovery Star started as more of a way to undermine the Recovery Star – a thought experiment, a bit of fun. But we actually found it a helpful tool to outline the impacts on us of politics and discrimination of all kinds. People on the RITB Facebook group describe how showing the Unrecovery Star to their community psychiatric nurse or support worker can open up more meaningful discussions. Survivors can take mental health professionals to task by asking what they will do as an intervention in the 'therapeutic relationship' about the issues that the 'Unrecovery Star' raises. In other words, we can use this 'social justice tool' as a means of advocacy to try to address any unmet needs: ie. needs for housing, welfare (both in and out of work), advocacy and professional reports.

As survivors and allies, we can also use the Unrecovery Star as a means to campaign for greater social equality and protest against psychiatry and psycho-compulsion, which dominate mental health treatment and welfare in the UK. We need social and political solutions for social problems, which the Unrecovery Star simply and clearly identifies.

The Unrecovery Star clarifies that humans are social beings and that the determinants of distress are to be found in families, communities, wider society and social policies. The value of the Unrecovery Star is that it demonstrates that we need to not just pay attention to distressed people but to deal with the problems that surround us in communities and wider society – that mental health is a profoundly political issue.

Examples of this work are seen in Psychologists for Social Change, Walk the Talk, Mental Health Resistance Network, films such as *Psychocompulsion and Workfare*,[6] the work of Lynne Friedli and Robert Stearn (2015), and resources written by RITB.[7] The Unrecovery Star is also being used as a teaching tool to highlight social inequalities that are still prominent in society and help students make the links to the causes of mental distress. Because the Unrecovery Star makes clear that people's problems are not merely individual problems rooted in something wrong with them, it counters much of the teaching in professional courses that focuses on faulty brains, genetic abnormality or faulty personality.

Jonathan Gadsby, blogging on the Critical Mental Health Nurses website, describes Unrecovery as:

> ... a term which [RITB] define in a number of precise ways. It is a
> project which continues to evolve. Their attack is a political one: far
> from opening the frames of reference from narrow medical illness

---

6. https://vimeo.com/157125824

7. https://recoveryinthebin.org/2016/04/23/yippee

to more holistic personal wellbeing, the Recovery Star continues an onslaught of neoliberalism in mental health, in which people are to be made individually responsible for difficulties which would be better thought of as originating in society. Through this lens, the holism of the Recovery Star becomes a complete co-option of a person with a set of ideas that appear to be liberating but in fact absolve the powerful from the need to acknowledge and address inequalities of all kinds. For example, widening the conversation to include work and financial skills might seem welcome because loss of role, loss of meaningful activity and financial worries are very significant drivers of distress. However, in so doing, we may be failing to notice with the service user that they live in an unjust society in which finding one's way and having access to decent housing, meaningful roles, security, having protected rights and simply being allowed to be different seem to be increasingly the domain of the privileged. Being valued in society may be based on assumptions which many nurses may readily agree are insane. Nurses who unquestioningly agree with the Recovery Star that mental health is synonymous with self-reliance are perhaps the perfect agents of a State which would like its population to internalise and individualise their distress, to look to themselves for solutions and to suppose that the reason some people have yachts and others have bailiffs is because some people have more personal skills: far from a balanced perspective. (Gadsby, 2015)

Unrecovery 'model'

We've been developing an Unrecovery Guide, based on a table of mental health models (Fulford & Woodbridge, 2004).[8] We see it as a participatory tool for our own use that can also be used by services/professionals/others to reflect on ways current practice is being implemented. It is tentative and certainly not something to be used in services.

---

8. https://recoveryinthebin.org/2018/01/14/some-models-of-mental-health

Unrecovery Guide		
What is the nature of mental distress?		
1	Diagnosis/ description	• Mental distress and human suffering are a reality. • Mental 'illness' is constructed within political, social, economic, historical, cultural and racial contexts.
2	Interpretation of behaviour ('symptoms')	• Driven by intolerable social pressures and inequality. • Degree of distress may not be visible in behaviour, leading to misinterpretation by 'treatment' providers.
3	Labels (that might be applied)	• 'Unrecovered' is a political self-definition. • Medical labels control individuals' access to support eg. welfare benefits/treatment programmes. • Labels hold a particular understanding of mental distress that an individual may or may not choose to apply to themselves.
4	Aetiology (the cause)	• Addressing social issues is the priority. • Political and socio-economic factors and multiple forms of adversity, including racism, contribute to and maintain distress. • Open-minded about aetiology.
What should be done about it?		
5	Treatment	• Political/social changes to reduce marginal status/social stresses and increase access to whatever tools people want to use to manage any remaining distress. Pragmatic – if an individual finds psychiatric drugs helpful, use them. Must recognise power dynamics in interventions eg. diagnosis/formulation. • Opposed to treatment techniques that stifle dissent.
6	Function of the hospital	• Ideally provides protection and support to people experiencing extreme mental distress. • In practice may be a source of further adversity and harm (iatrogenic).
7	Hospital and community	• 'Recovery' ideology reduces community support and masks coercion. • Recovery colleges are a means of promoting this ideology. • Community care and non-medicalised alternatives should be available to those who wish to use them.

8	Prognosis (the outcome)	• People may or may not experience recovery (clinical or personal). • People who do not recover can experience a reasonable quality of life through ongoing support and/or changes at social/political level. • 'Recovery' ideology is driven by neoliberal politics and imposes outcomes (political targets) that do not reflect the reality of mental distress.

How should the people involved behave towards each other?

9	Rights of the patient	• To apply to themselves the political self-definition 'unrecovered', particularly in social/political contrast to 'recovered'. • To develop their own theory of their experiences. • To be free to dissent. • To co-produce their own care if they wish. • Autonomy/self-determination through personal and collective struggle. • Human rights/social justice.
10	Rights of society	• To engage in dialogue with those seeking fundamental change.
11	Duties of the patient	• To engage politically as far as they are able in order to promote social change. To resist models of distress and policy decisions that reduce the social and political down to the individual.
12	Duties of society	• To guard against coercing people to 'Recover'. • To acknowledge the role of ideology in creating adverse environments that increase mental distress. • To reduce adversity. • To recognise a wide range of 'survivor narratives'.

Many critics of psychiatry are focused on removing diagnostic labels, but at the moment these medical labels control people's access to support, such as treatment and welfare benefits. Critics argue, for instance, that the Department for Work and Pensions does not require a diagnosis because the forms are about symptoms and how they affect a person's functioning. We know, however, that in practice, without a diagnosis, an application for disability benefits goes nowhere. We are therefore somewhat critical of the movement to remove diagnostic labelling.

This does not mean we all believe diagnoses are valid or helpful. Nor does it mean we agree generally with psychiatry. Above all, we are pragmatic about using diagnostic categories, recognising that we need them in order to access the benefits and support that keep us alive in the current political and economic context. Until there is a significant change to the welfare system in the UK and elsewhere, fighting to get rid of diagnosis is to deny many of us of the material conditions for anything approaching a decent life.

What next?

It's hard to know – even during the time of writing this chapter, the situation for most of us has become even bleaker. The brown envelopes are arriving on more doormats and our energies are constantly being sapped by the anxiety and precariousness these envelopes bring. We are determined to carry on and not give up.

Dedicated to Robert Dellar[9]

Robert was one of the founders of Recovery in the Bin in 2014. He was a long-standing mental health activist and founder of Mad Pride and Mental Health Resistance Network. He was a talented writer and musician and a good friend to many of us individually. We remember him for his kindness, his intelligence and his deep commitment to justice. We miss him greatly.

References

Beresford P (2016). *All Our Welfare: towards participatory social policy*. Bristol: Policy Press.

Butler P, Pring J (2016). Suicides of benefit claimants reveal DWP flaws, says inquiry. *The Guardian*; 13 May. www.theguardian.com/society/2016/may/13/suicides-of-benefit-claimants-reveal-dwp-flaws-says-inquiry (accessed 27 December 2018).

9. http://mentalhealthresistance.org/2017/01/obituary-robert-dellar

Deegan P (1996). *Recovery and the Conspiracy of Hope*. Paper presented at 'There's a Person in Here': the Sixth Annual Mental Health Services Conference of Australia and New Zealand. Brisbane, Australia, 16 September. www.patdeegan.com/pat-deegan/lectures/conspiracy-of-hope (accessed 27 December 2018).

Friedli L, Stearn R (2015). Positive affect as coercive strategy: conditionality, activation and the role of psychology in UK government workfare programmes. [Online.] *Medical Humanities; 41*(1). http://dx.doi.org/10.1136/medhum-2014-010622 (accessed 4 March 2019).

Fulford B, Woodbridge K (2004). *Whose Values? A workbook for values-based practice in mental health care*. London: Sainsbury Centre for Mental Health.

Gadsby, J (2015). *The Recovery Star meets the Unrecovery Star*. [Blog.] Critical Mental Health Nurses' Network; 19 October. https://criticalmhnursing.org/2015/10/19/the-recovery-star-meets-the-Unrecovery-star (accessed 27 December 2018).

O'Hara M (2010). The trouble with mental health treatment. [Online.] *The Guardian*; 25 August. www.theguardian.com/society/2010/aug/25/mental-health-treatment-rachel-perkins-mind (accessed 27 December 2018).

Recovery in the Bin (2017). *Unrecovery*. [Blog.] Recovery in the Bin; 8 August. https://recoveryinthebin.org/2017/08/08/Unrecovery (accessed 19 January 2019).

Rose D (2014). The mainstreaming of recovery. *Journal of Mental Health* 23(5): 217–218.

Scottish Recovery Network (undated). *What is recovery?* [Online.] Scottish Recovery Network. http://scottishrecovery.net/what-is-recovery (accessed 19 January 2019).

Name index

Subject index

The Industrialisation of Care: counselling, psychotherapy and the impact of IAPT

Edited by Catherine Jackson and Rosemary Rizq

PCCS Books (2019)
ISBN 978 1 910919 45 3

Since 2008, the government's Improving Access to Psychological Therapies (IAPT) programme has been rolled out across England and Wales. In the 10 years of its existence it has transformed primary care mental health services and changed the landscape of counselling and psychotherapy across the UK. While IAPT services provide therapy to thousands of people experiencing depression and anxiety, they also absorb millions of pounds in government funding. This has resulted in wholesale cuts to numerous voluntary sector and GP-attached counselling services run by qualified and experienced counsellors and psychotherapists. Current plans to expand the reach of IAPT to 25% of need (NHS Five-Year Forward Plan) rely on an economic model of treatment that has more in common with the principles of Henry Ford than with those of either Rogers or Freud.

This book, with chapters written by experienced therapists, psychiatrists and academics, unravels and exposes the neoliberal roots from which the IAPT programme sprang.

Together, contributors question whether and to what extent the IAPT 'factory' system of care, driven by psychiatric diagnosis, fast through-put and quick-win 'outcomes', can really provide a solution to Britain's growing mental health crisis.

Buy at www.pccs-books.co.uk for discounted prices and free postage & packing.

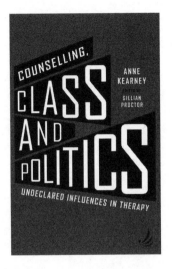

Counselling, Class and Politics: undeclared influences in therapy (2nd edition)

Anne Kearney

Edited by Gillian Proctor

PCCS Books (2018)
ISBN 978 1 910919 36 1

First published in 1996, Anne Kearney's ground-breaking book on class in counselling and its invisibility within the training curriculum and the counselling relationship is reissued here with new commentaries from practitioners, clients and educationalists writing today.

Anne died before she could start work on a planned revision of her text. But how much has really changed? Her motivation, back in 1996, 'to persuade readers to the view that politics and political ideas matter in counselling' is just as powerful today. So too is her driving belief that counselling training, regulation and awareness in general too often fail to acknowledge the political environment that practitioners and their clients inhabit and their influence on the counselling relationship. Anne's book, accessible, unashamedly unapologetic and searching in the questions it asks of readers, is still a vibrant, challenging text for any student, practitioner or trainer today.

'I have frequently heard class dismissed as no longer important... I find class as relevant today as I did in the 1990s. This new edition of Anne Kearney's book has a major contribution to make to the debate.'
Liz Ballinger, counselling MA programme director, University of Manchester